Tumbler, engraved with a representation of the Great Seal of the United States. Signed on the reverse: "New Bremen Glassmanufactory / 1792." H. 20.9 cm; D. rim 14.9 cm. Collection of Mr. and Mrs. George M. Kaufman, Norfolk, Va. Currently on loan to the Chrysler Museum, Norfolk, Va.

JOHN FREDERICK AMELUNG

JOHN FREDERICK AMELUNG
Early American Glassmaker

DWIGHT P. LANMON
Director, The Corning Museum of Glass

ARLENE PALMER SCHWIND
Consultant; former Associate Curator,
The Henry Francis du Pont Winterthur Museum

IVOR NOËL HUME
Chief Archaeologist, Colonial Williamsburg

ROBERT H. BRILL
Research Scientist, The Corning Museum of Glass

VICTOR F. HANSON
Formerly Scientific Coordinator, The Henry Francis du Pont Winterthur Museum

CORNING
The Corning Museum of Glass Press
LONDON AND TORONTO
Associated University Presses

Associated University Presses
440 Forsgate Drive
Cranbury, NJ 08512

Associated University Presses
25 Sicilian Avenue
London WC1A 2QH, England

Associated University Presses
P.O. Box 488, Port Credit
Mississauga, Ontario
Canada L5G 4M2

The paper used in this publication meets the requirements
of the American National Standard for Permanence of Paper
for Printed Library Materials Z39.48-1984.

Library of Congress Cataloging-in-Publication Data

John Frederick Amelung, early American glassmaker.

  Revised version of the 1976 issue of the Journal of
glass studies, issued by the Corning Museum of Glass.
  Bibliography: p.
  1. Amelung, John Frederick, 1741 or 2-1798.
  2. Glassware—United States—History—18th century.
  3. Glass manufacture—United States.   I. Lanmon,
Dwight P.   II. Corning Museum of Glass.
  NK5198.A44A4   1990   748.2913   86-72706
  ISBN 0-87290-075-4 (alk. paper)

PRINTED IN THE UNITED STATES OF AMERICA

Errata

Tables 1 and 2 were omitted from the article by Dr. V. F. Hanson (pages 225–28). These are printed below:

TABLE 1
ANALYSES OF SIGNED OR DOCUMENTED AMELUNG GLASSES

Date	Object		K_2O	CaO	TiO_2	MnO	Fe_2O_3	Rb_2O	SrO	Y_2O_5	ZrO_2	PbO	As_2O_5	Sb_2O_5	BaO
1788	"Bremen"	foot	13.6	7.6	0	.24	.57	.010	.016	.0039	.013	.14	0	.13	.039
		goblet	10.5	8.9	0	.41	.15	.010	.012	.0058	.009	.17	0	.14	.038
1788	"Ghequiere"	tumbler	15.9	8.9	.028	.21	.10	.012	.019	.008	.008	.32	.052	.091	.058
		cover	15.9	9.0	.029	.25	.19	.014	.021	.010	.009	.38	.053	.098	.046
1788	"Tobias & Angel"	tumbler	16.1	9.2	.012	.50	.23	.010	.015	.0034	.008	.11	0	.082	.044
		cover	16.5	8.9	.015	.48	.22	.010	.015	.016	.008	.61	0	.086	.067
		finial	14.2	8.1	.012	.48	.25	.010	.012	.016	.008	.64	0	.056	.039
1789	"Boston"	tumbler	14.8	11.4	.006	.55	.15	.010	.018	.0056	.009	.22	0	.17	.026
1791	"Mifflin"	goblet	17.1	10.5	0	.75	.17	.015	.016	.0005	.013	.003	0	.13	.047
1791	"Guest"	tumbler	17.7	10.2	.031	.59	.11	.015	.020	.0004	.007	0	.003	.15	.075
		cover	17.9	10.5	.029	.05	.08	.014	.021	.001	.007	.025	.005	.53	.033
1792	"Great Seal"	tumbler	17.2	10.3	.015	.38	.25	.010	.015	.001	.008	.008	0	.12	.055
1792	"Repold-Amelung"	goblet	17.2	11.2	.002	.54	.12	.014	.016	.0008	.008	0	0	.14	.017
		foot	10.0	6.4	0	.64	.03	.007	.014	0	.002	0	0	.10	.012
ca. 1972	"J. Amelung"	goblet	17.0	10.5	.038	.17	.08	.022	.025	.001	.009	0	.001	.20	.022
		foot	12.9	7.9	.013	0	0	.012	.014	0	.002	0	.002	.18	.02
1792	"Mauerhoff"	goblet	16.9	9.8	0	1.15	.24	.005	.010	.0018	.008	.044	0	.14	.066
		foot	12.9	7.0	0	.69	.10	.003	.004	0	.002	.026	0	.15	.072
	MEAN VALUE		15.2	9.2	.013	.45	.17	.011	.016	.0044	.008	.15	.006	.15	.043

TABLE 2
ANALYSES OF LAUENSTEIN GLASSES

CMG. No.	K_2O	CaO	TiO_2	MnO	Fe_2O_3	Rb_2O	SrO	Y_2O_3	ZrO_2	PbO	As_2O_5	Sb_2O_5	BaO
64.3.94	10.5	6.8	0	.20	.13	.040	.053	.004	.010	.060	.007	0	.006
61.3.126	15.9	8.3	0	.05	.02	.022	.005	.0009	.001	0	.001	.003	.029
50.3.44	12.1	6.2	0	.12	.09	.030	.020	.002	.004	0	.001	.001	.005
61.3.134	15.2	8.7	0	.32	.08	.020	.013	.006	.008	.25	.012	.004	.04
61.3.131	12.6	6.7	0	.16	.18	.034	.026	.002	.005	.003	.002	0	.009
61.3.126	14.4	7.6	0	.54	.21	.035	.011	.003	.006	.012	.002	.002	.029
64.3.93	6.3	4.9	0	.06	.07	.020	.023	.012	.004	.027	.002	0	.01
MEAN VALUE	12.4	7.0	0	.21	.11	.029	.022	.004	.005	.05	.004	.001	.018

Material appearing on page 235 has been repeated on pages 242 and 243.

CONTENTS

PREFACE

When The Corning Museum of Glass chose John Frederick Amelung and his glass as the focus of its 1976 Bicentennial exhibition, it was with the idea that a little-known glassmaker of the young republic be given the recognition he deserved.

An exhibition, unhappily, is but a temporary form of recognition; thus The Corning Museum of Glass devoted the 1976 issue of its *Journal of Glass Studies* to the one topic of John Frederick Amelung, a signal honor never awarded any other glassmaker by the *Journal*. Copies of the 1976 *Journal* were soon depleted, and it became obvious that Amelung's endeavors were worthy of publication in a separate, updated volume.

Since the publication of the 1976 *Journal*, three hitherto unknown but firmly identifiable works by Amelung have come to light: the "Federal" tumbler, an amethyst bowl cover, and a sugar bowl. These are included in this revised version of the original publication.

FOREWORD

ALTHOUGH AMERICA BECAME a politically free and independent nation in 1783, the economy of the new republic remained firmly bound to Europe. The American colonies had existed for the benefit of the British Crown, providing raw materials for manufactories and markets for finished products. Colonial manufactures had no place in this system, yet from the beginning of settlement Americans had some interest—if only minimal success—in fashioning goods of various kinds. In the 1760s, when anti-British sentiment was growing, American manufacturing activities multiplied. Numerous groups professed a desire to promote the domestic arts, and consumers were urged to support local industry.

The encouragement of American manufactures became a recurring theme in the immediate post-war period. As George Washington explained to Thomas Jefferson, "A desire of encouraging whatever is useful and economical seems now generally to prevail."[1] In 1790 Congress asked Alexander Hamilton, Secretary of the Treasury, to outline a plan for "the promotion of such manufactures as will tend to render the United States independent of other nations for essential, particularly military, supplies."[2]

If this climate seemed ripe for a positive commitment to the advancement of American manufactures, the situation was, in fact, more propitious in appearance than in reality. Phineas Bond, British Consul at Philadelphia, recognized that the hopes of "lovers of American manufactures" were somewhat premature. He correctly assessed the situation in his report of November 10, 1789: "America must for a long time my Lord be under the necessity of purchasing and importing vast quantities of British or other European manufactures. . . . Manufactures w^h require art, labor, and expence to any great extent of either, may be attempted but they will often fail for want of capitals. . . ."[3]

Nevertheless, the view of America as a land of unlimited opportunity persisted and permeated Europe. American merchants traveled throughout Europe seeking both buyers for agriculture commodities and merchants who would supply the United States with manufactured goods. At the same time, European merchants came to America to offer their services as commission agents. Trained craftsmen and manufacturers of the Old World were drawn to the New by the promise of abundant raw materials, unrestricted manufacturing opportunities, and an eager market.

Extraordinary among the many talented emigrés who could not resist the attractions of the new republic was Johann Friedrich Amelung (1741–1798). He established a glasshouse in Maryland one year after the Treaty of Paris (Fig. 1). Over the next ten years he invested more money in glassmaking than had anyone in America before him; indeed, few manufacturers of any kind matched his total investment until the nineteenth century. Although Amelung produced the most ambitious and impressive table glass made here in the eighteenth century, his glass making venture ended in bankruptcy.

Interest in his New Bremen factory has grown continuously over the past fifty years. After the

7

FIG. 1. Tentative reconstruction of the Amelung glasshouse excavated in 1962–1963.

discovery of a signed glass in 1928, ten additional glasses, either signed or made for the
personal use of the family, have been found.
Nearly fifty engraved pieces are now associated
with the factory, and more are certain to follow.

The first exhibition that dealt extensively with
the products of the Amelung factory was held at
The Maryland Historical Society in 1952. In the
years following that pioneering exhibition more
has been learned about the factory, its products,
and its owners.

The Corning Museum of Glass has long had
an active interest in the Amelung factory. In
1962 and 1963 the Museum, with the Smithsonian Institution, conducted an excavation of one
of the glasshouses under the inspired direction
of Mr. Ivor Noël Hume, Chief Archaeologist of
The Colonial Williamsburg Foundation. The
Museum has also scientifically analyzed fragments from the factory site and sponsored research into the history of Amelung's enterprise.

In 1976, a special exhibition of the known
glass objects by Amelung was brought together
in Corning, and the first edition of this publication was issued.

This study reflects the generous assistance of
many individuals and institutions who have
given of their time and resources. It is a pleasant
duty to acknowledge their contributions.

The Museum is especially indebted to The
Henry Francis du Pont Winterthur Museum for
permitting several members of its staff to under-
take extensive programs of research and analysis which are reported here. It is with sadness
that we note the death, in 1982, of one of the key
members of this team, Dr. Victor F. Hanson. The
research for this publication and for the exhibition was also supported by grants from the National Endowment for the Arts.

The historical research was made enjoyable by
the enthusiastic and efficient staff of the Maryland Hall of Records at Annapolis. Thanks are

also due to Mrs. Paul Amelung, Fairfield, Connecticut; the Maryland Historical Society, Baltimore; and the Museum of Early Southern Decorative Arts, Winston-Salem, North Carolina, for sharing the results of their own research on John Frederick Amelung. Dr. Erich Mäder, Grünenplan, Germany, has also shared his research on the Grünenplan factory. Mr. Paul N. Perrot, formerly Director of The Corning Museum of Glass, now Director of the Virginia Museum of Fine Arts, Richmond, Virginia, and Mr. Kenneth M. Wilson, formerly Chief Curator and Assistant Director at Corning, and formerly Director of Collections and Preservation at Greenfield Village and the Henry Ford Museum, Dearborn, Michigan, initiated many of the studies which are reported here; they have also given freely of their knowledge and insights. The photographs in the Catalogue are by Mr. Raymond F. Errett of The Corning Museum of Glass and Mr. George J. Fistrovich of The Henry Francis du Pont Winterthur Museum. To the countless other people who gave us assistance and counsel we are equally grateful.

The Museum is also grateful to those individuals and institutions who lent their glasses for analysis at Winterthur and for the 1976 exhibition at Corning: The Baltimore Museum of Art, Mrs. Graham John Barbey, Mr. James C. Brand, the Connecticut Historical Society, Miss Josephine Etchison, Greenfield Village and the Henry Ford Museum, the Germanisches Nationalmuseum Nürnberg, Mr. and Mrs. Albert J. Henry, The Maryland Historical Society, Senator Charles McC. Mathias, The Metropolitan Museum of Art, the Museum of Fine Arts (Boston), the Museum für Kunst und Gewerbe Hamburg, the New Hampshire Historical Society, The Newark Museum, the New Orleans Museum of Art, Quincy Historical Society, Mrs. August J. Raggi, Mr. and Mrs. Lewis Rumford III, the Smithsonian Institution, Staatliche Kunstsammlung Kassel, Mr. Jerome Strauss, The Toledo Museum of Art, Mrs. Ruth Troiani, The Wachovia Historical Society, Miss Elizabeth Morris Wistar, the Yale University Art Gallery (Garvan Collection), and two anonymous lenders; also to the Charleston Library Society for lending their copy of Amelung's *Remarks on Manufactures*.

The Museum also acknowledges the many people and institutions who helped in the excavation and interpretation of the Amelung factory site. We are especially grateful to Colonial Williamsburg for permitting Mr. Ivor Noël Hume to direct the excavation. His acknowledgements follow.

DWIGHT P. LANMON
ARLENE PALMER SCHWIND

I AM SURE that I speak for both The Corning Museum of Glass and the Smithsonian Institution when I express the deepest gratitude to Professor and the late Mrs. William R. Quynn of "Amelung House," and to Mr. Charles Smith, the late Mr. Vernon Yingling, and Mr. and Mrs. Exel Yingling for permission to pass across and excavate on their various properties. To Mrs. Quynn I was particularly indebted for much valuable information over and above that already published in her important paper "Johann Friedrich Amelung at New Bremen."

As director of the excavation I am indebted to Mr. Paul N. Perrot and his colleagues from The Corning Museum of Glass, as well as to Mr. Malcolm Watkins and the Smithsonian Institution's Division of Cultural History for the provision of field personnel; also to Colonial Williamsburg Inc., for providing the services of Mrs. Noël Hume. I also remember with gratitude the hard work contributed by Mrs. Joanne Perrot, Mr. Kenneth Wilson, then head curator at Old Sturbridge Village; Mr. Cary Carson, then fellow of the Henry Francis du Pont Winterthur Museum; Mr. Stuart Feld, then curatorial assistant, The Metropolitan Museum of Art; Mr. Frederick Wilding-White; and Mr. and Mrs. T. Latimer Ford of the Maryland Archaeological Society. I recall, too, the willing volunteers from The Henry Francis du Pont Winterthur Museum under their equally willing director, Mr. Charles Montgomery, now curator, Garvan and related collections of American Art, Yale University Gallery.

Offers of counsel and assistance came from many much-appreciated quarters from Frederick to Park Mills. I was particularly grateful to Mr. John S. Patton and Mr. Calvin S. Bartgis of the C & P Telephone Company, and to the company itself, for placing one of its "cherry pickers" at our disposal for photographic purposes. Equally valuable were the services of Mr. Thomas B. McNeill and the able staff of his surveying company of Chillum, Maryland.

Photography in the field was executed by Mr. Raymond Errett of The Corning Museum of

Glass and most of the artifacts were photographed by Mr. G. E. Rossner of Colonial Williamsburg. I am much indebted, too, to Mr. Richard Stinely of Colonial Williamsburg for the final drawing of the tentative reconstruction which serves as the first figure for this publication. The master plan of the excavation and the sections were drawn by Mrs. Frances Mitchell.

I would like also to express my appreciation for the many valuable criticisms, suggestions, and sources of information provided by Miss Helen McKearin; Mr. Robert Charleston, formerly Keeper of the Department of Ceramics at the Victoria and Albert Museum, London; Mr. Kenneth Wilson, formerly Director of Collections and Preservation, Greenfield Village and Henry Ford Museum; Mr. John N. Pearce, State Historic Preservation Officer, The Maryland Historical Trust; Dr. Grace L. Tracey of Hampstead, Maryland; Mrs. Ralph B. Hunt of Alexandria, Virginia; and Mrs. Harriet N. Milford of Baltimore, Maryland. Mr. Robert Elder of the Smithsonian Institution also provided helpful advice as well as practical assistance during parts of the 1962 excavations.

In conclusion I wish to acknowledge the support of both the Frederick and the Maryland Historical Societies and, most valuable of all, the active encouragement of Senator, then Congressman, Charles McC. Mathias Jr., of the Sixth District of Maryland.

IVOR NOËL HUME

JOHN FREDERICK AMELUNG
AND THE
NEW BREMEN GLASSMANUFACTORY
Dwight P. Lanmon, Arlene Palmer Schwind

I. THE BACKGROUND OF
GLASSMAKING IN AMERICA

THE HISTORY OF GLASSMAKING in English America began 176 years before the time of Amelung when a glasshouse was erected at Jamestown, Virginia, in 1608, a little over a year after the first settlers arrived. Jamestown was initially conceived as a profit-making venture for its London backers and a glasshouse was considered a top priority. Its purpose was to supply some of England's needs for glass and to help alleviate her dependence on foreign products. Although changes in eating habits and social customs during Tudor times had increased consumer interest in articles made of glass, glass-making did not thrive in the mother country in the early 1600's. Glassmakers were discouraged and, eventually, prohibited from burning wood fuel in their furnaces, while the technology of coal-fired ovens was in embryonic stages of development. Consequently, glasswares made in Venice and other Continental cities enjoyed a virtual monopoly of the English market. Because a striking feature of the New World was its endless forests, it is hardly surprising that the Virginia Company envisioned a flourishing glass industry that might turn this resource into the profits it sought.

The story of American glassmaking could have been very short because the first Jamestown effort and the succeeding attempt of 1620 were spectacular failures. Some glass was made there—a "tryal of glasse" was actually sent overseas—but intensive research and archaeological investigation of the site has failed to determine exactly the quality or quantity of production.[4] The glass furnaces operated only in-termittently as the settlement struggled to survive in the face of poor management, debilitating sickness, starvation, and hostile Indians. The glassblowers learned that the technological problems inherent in their craft were exacerbated in a wilderness setting and, finally, in 1624 the project was completely abandoned.

Colonists in Salem, New York, and Philadelphia, probably unaware of the Virginia fiasco, also built glasshouses during the seventeenth century. Their intention, as far as is known, was not to send glasswares to England but to meet the American settler's growing demands for glass, especially bottles and window panes. Of the craftsmen, operations, and products of these short-lived manufactories almost nothing can be said. Only in the eighteenth century, with the successful enterprise of Caspar Wistar, was glassmaking assured of a future in America.[5]

In 1717 Wistar emigrated from Germany to Pennsylvania where he learned the trade of brass button-making. Recognizing the possibilities for advancement in the expanding town of Philadelphia, he opened a store and sold general merchandise. By 1730 he had become a prominent figure in the Quaker-dominated mercantile community. His surviving correspondence proves that he maintained business connections in Germany. His correspondents probably informed him of the declining state of the glass industry in the homeland and asked him to gauge the encouragement a transplanted German glassworks might expect in America. As someone who would be sympathetic to the problems of his countrymen, and as a German who had successfully made the transition from the Old World to the New, Wistar was a logical sponsor for such an undertaking. Four glassblowers duly arrived in Philadelphia in September 1738 and as co-partners with Wistar began to construct a glasshouse at Alloway in nearby Salem County, New Jersey. Thus began the German domination of the glass industry that was to continue in America until the nineteenth century. Certainly the forest glasshouse traditions of Wistar's workers were readily adapted to the American environment. Moreover, the immigrants' creations were sure to strike a familiar chord with the many Germans who had settled in the mid-Atlantic colonies.

Actual production commenced in the fall of 1739; glassblowing would continue, apparently uninterrupted, until the Revolutionary War—a length of time that is remarkable in the history of American glassmaking. After Caspar Wistar died in 1752, his son, Richard Wistar, managed the business which retained some of the artisans as part-owners until 1767. Unlike the later Amelung adventure, the Wistarburgh works was conceived and maintained on a realistically limited scale, one suited to the utilitarian needs of a fast-growing colonial population that was attuned to quality imported goods.

Newspaper advertisements and other records show that the Wistars offered bottles in various shapes from half-pint to gallon capacities. Their extant ledger proves that bottlemaking was a major facet of production. In one eight-month period of operation, for example, the Germans are credited with having blown £292.2.11 worth of bottles, possibly as many as 17,000.[6] The only bottle presently attributed to Wistarburgh descended in the Wistar family and is believed to have belonged to Richard Wistar himself. Of a clear green, good-quality material, the bottle features a seal with the initials RW. It is, at the present time, the only seal bottle that can be assigned to an eighteenth-century American glasshouse.[7] Distinct in its style and finishing treatment from imported bottles of the period, the Wistar bottle relates to bottle fragments found at the factory site and is chemically comparable to other green glasswares of Wistar origin.

The window panes made at the Salem County factory were fashioned by the cylinder method, a typically, but not exclusively, Germanic pro-

cess. Governor William Franklin described the Wistar product as "very coarse Green Glass for Windows, used only in some of the Houses of the poorer Sort of People."[8] His opinion, although the proper political one, is somewhat supported by a pale green, bubbly window pane from the Quaker meeting house in Salem that is almost certainly from the Wistars' factory. Unlike other American glass manufacturers of the eighteenth century, the Wistars recognized that popular prejudice in favor of British goods would be difficult to sway, no matter how refined the American offering. Realizing the limitations of their own products, they imported and sold English glass, chiefly Bristol crown glass. Richard Wistar remarked in 1760 that without the English window glass, "I Shall Not be able to serve half My Customers."[9]

In spite of their emphasis on bottles and window panes, the artisans at the South Jersey works created tablewares of both "common" [green] and "white" [colorless] glass for limited commercial consumption.[10] Among the common wares that can be firmly attributed to the factory are five covered bowls (Fig. 2). Besides documenting the use of part-size molds of sixteen and twenty vertical ribs, the bowls illustrate, in their finials and handles, some of the Germanic decorative motifs brought to America.

FIG. 2. Covered bowl, green glass, attributed to the Wistarburgh Glassworks, Salem County, New Jersey, ca. 1739–1777. Published by permission of The Newark Museum, Newark, N.J.; photo: Winterthur Museum.

A recently discovered group of blue and colorless table forms that can be attributed to Wistarburgh has altered our concept of eighteenth-century American glass significantly. Two blue-tinted tapersticks have descended in the Wistar family; one was recorded in the mid-nineteenth century as an example of Wistar-made glass (Fig. 3). Of distinctive construction suggesting Germanic influence, they reveal an effort in Salem County to experiment with colored glass. Stylistically and chemically similar is a colorless full-size candlestick in the Winterthur collection that was found some years ago in South Jersey. A blue sweetmeat basket or cream bucket has been assigned to the factory because it has the same history of ownership as one of the candlesticks and was recorded about 1840 as being of Wistar manufacture. A colorless basket with identical bird finial is also believed to be a Wistarburgh product. The baskets and candlesticks have very similar chemical compositions and contain about seventeen percent lead. This amount, considerably less than the thirty percent associated with deliberate lead glass production of the English industry, suggests that the cullet used to improve the batch was most likely English.

The Wistars' efforts to compete with the tremendous variety of imported table glass were

Fig. 3. Taperstick, blue-tinted glass, attributed to the Wistarburgh Glassworks, Salem County, New Jersey, ca. 1739–1777. Published by permission of The Henry Francis du Pont Winterthur Museum; photo: Winterthur Museum.

paltry compared to the ambitions of Henry William Stiegel. Stiegel had opened a modest glasshouse in 1763 near his Elizabeth iron furnace in Lancaster County, Pennsylvania. Production focused on the usual bottles and window panes. At his second factory, however, erected two years later in Manheim, Stiegel added some tablewares to his line. At his third glasshouse, also in Manheim, the manufacture of fine quality table glass became Stiegel's prime concern.

During the 1760's, the demand for articles made of glass was tremendous. Americans owned glasses for every imaginable kind of beverage, from posset to punch. Their tables were set with glass bowls, cruets, and milk pots. Their cellars were stocked with dozens of glass bottles. Even their persons were adorned with glass buttons and necklaces. These needs were met chiefly by British factories; enough English glass was exported to the colonies to lead Charles Townshend to include glass among the taxable commodities in his revenue-raising plan of 1767. Colonial glassmakers were quick to turn the tax to their own advantage and urge their countrymen to "buy American."[11] Sensitive to the changing environment, Stiegel expanded his facilities so that he might cater to the anticipated increase in demand for domestic glass.

Although there is considerable written documentation concerning Stiegel's eleven-year adventure in glassmaking, no objects have been assigned with any degree of certainty to any of his glasshouses. Because he employed blowers of both English and German experience—some of the latter hired away from Wistarburgh—a variety of technical and decorative influences can be expected in his wares. According to the surviving factory records, the blowers at Manheim fashioned a wide variety of forms from decanters to mustard pots and from syllabub glasses to cans. In addition to plain glasses, Stiegel offered glasses ornamented with engraved, enameled, and molded designs.

Because Stiegel advertised his wares as being of "flint" glass, students of early American glass have assumed this meant a substance made with lead oxide in the manner of English production. In the seventeenth century the term "flint" was correctly applied to glass using a silica derived from flintstones rather than sand or quartz. By the eighteenth century "flint" also became a synonym for quality. If Stiegel did indeed develop a lead glass technology—and he presumably observed English glassmaking practices when recruiting workmen abroad—it may well be impossible to distinguish Pennsylvania glass from the quantities of low-grade English glasswares exported to America during that period. The American Philosophical Society judged specimens of Manheim glass to be "equal in beauty and quality to the generality of Flint Glass, imported from England." Governor Penn of Pennsylvania had expressed less enthusiasm for Stiegel's glass some four years before, noting it was of "very ordinary Quality."[12]

Such contemporary opinions of the merits of American glass must be read with caution, however, colored as they were by political considerations. As Richard Wistar observed in 1760, "it was not for the Honour of England to Suffer Manufactories in the Colonies."[13] After 1760 America's industrial development was deliberately understated in the light of tightening controls over colonial activity. Thus Benjamin Franklin, an early patron of Wistarburgh, instructed his son William, Governor of New Jersey, to report in 1768 that Wistar made only "coarse window-glass and bottles." Franklin, like Penn, dismissed the influence of Stiegel and Wistar, claiming they satisfied only a limited local market. Yet Wistarburgh's scientific glasswares, used in electrical experiments, were sent from Boston to Charleston and window glass was sold in New York.[14] Newspaper evidence proves that Stiegel established retail outlets for his glass throughout the colonies far beyond the "Villages and Farmers in the adjacent Inland Country" reported by Penn.

Stiegel, however, grossly misjudged the potential market for his American glass. Just as Amelung would do twenty years later, Stiegel had erected his flint glass works at Manheim "at immense expense."[15] His labor force was huge, his warehouses became filled with unsold glass. In 1771 Pennsylvania's Provincial Council granted Stiegel £150 as token encouragement, but that did not retard the impending failure. Stiegel resorted to a lottery but failed to earn the amount of money necessary to keep the works operating. Glassmaking finally ceased in 1774 and the proprietor was briefly held in debtors' prison.

The declining condition of Stiegel's business did not deter Messrs. Tower and Leacock of Philadelphia from establishing a "white glass" factory in the Kensington section of Philadelphia. No doubt propelled by the belief that Americans were ready to patronize local manufactures, the proprietors nevertheless were required to look overseas—to England, ironically—for able craftsmen.[16] The business changed hands several times and operated intermittently during the war years. A wide range of glasswares was blown, evidently of competent quality. While other manufacturers endeavored to keep the success of their achievements a secret from officials in the mother country, some examples of Kensington glass were proudly sent to England:

As I Conclude thou may have heard of our new Glass houses erected here for making Window Glass—Decanters—& Glasses of all Sorts I thought it might be agreeable to thee to see a Specimen of the Sort—I have now Sent in a small Box half a dozen Wine Glasses—The Box is directed for thee at Joseph Frys wine Street Bristol— . . . It may not be improper to Inform thee That these are of the first trial of ye Glass house in this City—It is a New One setup & built within these 6 Months and Just begins to Work— . . . and We have some Glass Cutters lately Come over who cut Words—Grapes Coats of Arms or any Device that may be desired— This They do at less than I think is given in Bristol—Glasses cut at 14d stg p Doz.n and Decanters with Grape Vines at 3½d apce stg & So in pportion—Our Window Glass I am told but I have not Seen any of it Yet, exceeds yr Bristol Glass, but not the London Crown and They say They Can and Will Sell it Cheaper yn what is imported from Bristol can be bought at—These Glasses now sent I bot 2/—p Dozen lower than what is imported are sold for—[17]

In the meantime, Richard Wistar continued to supply Philadelphians with bottles, window glass, and common tablewares. More conservative than Stiegel, Wistar had not rushed to expand his works in the wake of the Townshend Acts, although in 1768 he did arrange for a family of German glassblowers to emigrate. If Wistar's extensive personal expenditures in the late 1760's and early 1770's are any indication, the glass business was prospering. In spite of his appeals to the public to support American glass, Wistar may well have continued to import and sell British glass. Production at Wistarburgh slowed in the early war years and ceased by 1778.

As a result of the demise of the Manheim and Alloway factories, a number of skilled glass craftsmen were unemployed. While some of those who had blown glass at Manheim may have joined the staff of the Kensington factory, or even Wistarburgh, others drifted farther afield.

Among these were Martin Eberhardt, Conrad

Foltz, Balthaser Kramer and his brothers George, Martin, and Adam. They had all arrived from Rotterdam on the Britannia, September 18, 1773.[18] By October 25 Balthaser and Martin Kramer, and a Conrad Waltz—"blower, shearer and window glass"—were on Stiegel's payroll. Within a year the Manheim factory closed and the three moved some forty miles south to Frederick County, Maryland. Together they built Maryland's first glassworks and commenced production before the end of the Revolutionary War. Proof of the existence of this factory occurs in the will of Conrad Foltz, written on July 20, 1784 and registered on October 26.

Whereas I am now Carrying on a Glass Factory, in Company with Balser Cramer Georg Cramer and Martin Everhart. It is my Desire and I do Order (that if in Case my Executors hereinafter named can Settle with my Creditors and is Agreeable to the parties concerned) that the Works be Carried on and Continued in such a manner as they think Fit Otherwise that my Executors are Hereby Impowered and Directed to sell the Works Together with the Land and Utensils thereunto belonging. . . .[19]

The executors saw fit to sell the works to John Frederick Amelung.

II. AMELUNG IN EUROPE

JOHANN FRIEDRICH AMELUNG (anglicized to John Frederick when he came to America) was born on June 26, 1741, the third child of farming parents in Hettlingen, Germany, near Hannover.[20] His brother, Anton Christian Friedrich, six years his senior, was a glass manufacturer, but the precise origin of his interest in glass has not been traced. After distinguished service in the Seven Years' War, Anton married the daughter of the musician and organist of the Hannoverian court. Eight years later, in 1773, he leased the Duke of Brunswick's mirror factory at Grünenplan, a town in the hilly area of Alfeld, south of Hannover.

John Frederick Amelung had married Magdalena Carolina Lucia von Leseburg and taken over the management of an important farm at Rodewald near Bremen. When his brother leased Grünenplan, John Frederick joined him, supposedly serving as technical director of the works. What background, if any, the younger Amelung brought to Grünenplan is not known. Nevertheless, his years at Grünenplan and what he learned there about the management of a glassworks strongly influenced his American experience.

Glass had been made at Grünenplan from the fourteenth century.[21] As was typical of such industrial villages, the workers' dwellings conveniently clustered around the factory buildings. As the works expanded, new housing pushed the village limits outward at the expense of farming and grazing land. Eventually fewer houses could be built and existing structures became overcrowded. Housing problems made it difficult to attract new workmen to the factory and

hindered the growth of the works. This pattern of unregulated building was unchecked until 1750 when an ambitious plan was adopted to organize the direction of expansion (Fig. 4). A new village site was selected to the northeast and laid out in a rectangular grid plan (Fig. 5). A school (#32), a church (A), and a parsonage (#10) were to be in the center of the village and each home was allocated a garden plot.

Although the glassworks would remain the principal employer of the residents, the administrators hoped that their liberal benefits would attract a broader range of settlers. In fact, they envisioned an integrated, self-sufficient, industrial community—an idea that was remarkably advanced for its time.

Under the new program, workers were expected to build their own houses and were given the right to cut the necessary wood from the Ducal forests. Constructed according to a uniform plan, each house was to shelter two families (Fig. 6). The builder retained ownership of the entire house but was required to rent the second half. The families shared a kitchen but each had a private bedroom, living room, and attic. By 1755 twenty-four houses had been built.

Although the village prospered for a time, the factory was inefficiently managed and did not thrive. The Seven Years' War disrupted trade and only aggravated the factory's internal problems. By 1768 there was an enormous stock of unsold glass; the factory lease was finally terminated and administrative control was resumed by the Duke of Brunswick, Karl I. In spite of his efforts to enlarge and modernize the works,

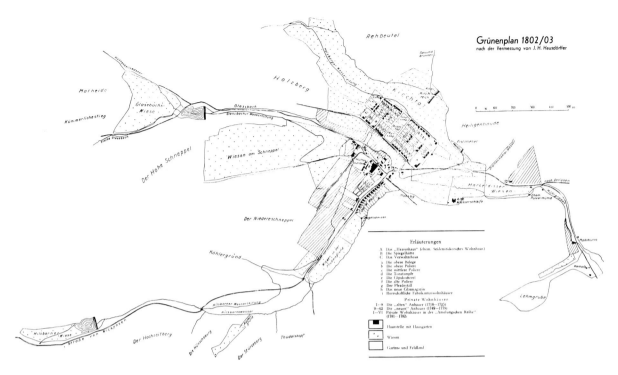

FIG. 4. Map of the area of Grünenplan. From Eberhard Tacke, *Bilder aus der Geschichte der Gemeinde Grünenplan. . . . ,* Grünenplan, 1949.

FIG. 5. Plan of the village of Grünenplan. From Eberhard Tacke, *Bilder aus der Geschichte der Gemeinde Grünenplan. . . . ,* Grünenplan, 1949.

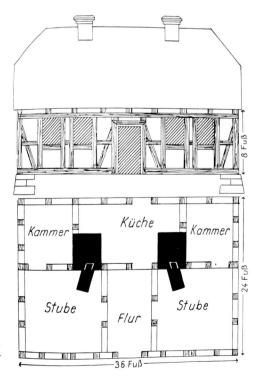

FIG. 6. Plan and elevation of a two-family dwelling. From Eberhard Tacke, *Bilder aus der Geschichte der Gemeinde Grünenplan. . . . ,* Grünenplan, 1949.

Grünenplan still did not become a profitable undertaking. Concessions to the workers, such as free wood for building and grazing privileges, were gradually reduced or completely eliminated, resulting in considerable labor unrest.

In 1773 Crown Prince Karl Wilhelm Ferdinand took over the administration of his father's government which, like the glassworks, was nearly bankrupt. Effective November 1 of that year he leased the factory at Grünenplan to Anton C. F. Amelung, John Frederick's older brother. The situation could only be described as challenging: the works was 6,000 Thalers in debt, there was 9,000 Thalers worth of unsold stock, and the village was overcrowded. Although the government assumed the debt, Anton Amelung was required to make a 5,000-Thaler security deposit. Moreover, he had to absorb all the unsold stock over a nine-year period, but this requirement was deferred for three years. His annual rent was 650 Thalers for the first six years of his eighteen-year lease, 750 Thalers for the next six years, and 850 Thalers for the last.

When Amelung assumed control, Grünenplan produced both mirror and window glass, but he felt the venture might be profitable if attention were focused exclusively on the manufacture of looking glasses. He hired skilled artisans from elsewhere in Germany who were able to fashion the very large mirror plates that were in great demand. The largest plate made there by 1774 was six and one-half feet long and just over two feet wide—an extraordinary accomplishment because it was blown. To produce large mirror plates by blowing was a difficult process; to fabricate unblemished plates by this method was virtually impossible. Until about 1770 mirrors of excellent quality had been cast at Grünenplan; in 1777 Amelung decided to resume production using this technique. The Duke's administrative board agreed to pay the 1,000-Thaler cost of the iron plate needed for the bed of the casting table, and it was delivered five years later.

Amelung initiated various other improvements, the cost of which was absorbed by him. The Board did lend him 3,000 Thalers so he could expand and modernize the facilities for polishing mirror plates, but the interest on the loan of 100 Thalers per year, in addition to the 200-Thaler tax on the casting table, only increased his annual expenditures.

In order to offer looking glasses of the finest

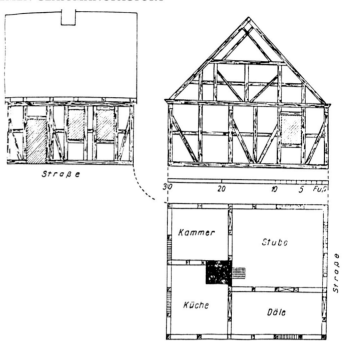

Fig. 7. Plan and elevation of a one-family dwelling. From Eberhard Tacke, *Bilder aus der Geschichte der Gemeinde Grünenplan. . . .* , Grünenplan, 1949.

quality, Amelung realized he would have to attract new and better-trained craftsmen. They would, of course, require housing; in 1780, however, when the factory employed 800 people, the village had only sixty-two dwellings. With the building privileges so reduced, there was little incentive for the workmen to build, and only ten new houses had been constructed between 1773 and 1780. Amelung's solution was to erect the necessary structures himself and to sell them to his laborers on an installment basis. The original tract was nearly filled, so he asked that meadow land to the southwest of the glasshouse be designated for single-family dwellings (Fig. 7). Because he personally underwrote the cost, he requested the Board to grant him the customary 20-Thaler subsidy to offset his expenses. Finally, after two houses had been completed and five others were under construction, Amelung was given a mere 12-Thaler rebate on the wood tax for each house. Bitterly disappointed, Amelung nevertheless continued to provide dwellings for his employees at his own expense.

By 1783, cast mirrors of good quality—and fifty percent larger than those made in France—were manufactured at Grünenplan. Amelung's most important market, Russia, was dwindling because of import duties and war; Holland was at least temporarily cut off because of international disputes. The cost of raw materials rose dramatically at this time: potash, a basic material of his glass and one which for some reason he did not manufacture himself, increased by over fifty percent, adding 2,000 Thalers to his annual production expenses. No wonder Amelung found himself in financial difficulty by 1783. The Board continued to be grossly unsupportive and repeatedly refused Amelung's requests for help, despite an official report that emphasized the importance of the glassworks to the economy of Brunswick. According to the report, "Eine Spiegelhütte ist eine so ausgebreitete wichtige Fabrik, als wohl wenige zu finden sein werden. Sie ist die Zierde Eines Staate, sie setzt das Holz in Wert, sie veredelt Naturprodukte als Sand und Kalk, die sonst ungenutzt vergraben bleiben würden, sie zieht viel fremdes Gelt ins Land, sie bevölkert Oerter, die ausserden unbewohnbar sein würden, sie beschäftigt viel und noch mehr Menschen als ein Eisenhütte." ("A mirror plant is such a uniquely important factory, as not many others could be. It is a prize of a state, it makes wood profitable, it uses natural materials such as sand and lime, which would otherwise not even be dug out. It brings in foreign currency, it develops areas which would remain desolate. It provides work for more people than an iron plant.")[22]

At a time when Anton's fortunes were in serious decline, probably after the Board refused his offer to purchase the factory outright, John Frederick decided to leave his brother and to establish a glassworks in America. With technical and managerial training from his eleven years at Grünenplan he must have felt he could manage a glasshouse and an industrial village better than the Duke's Board. It was almost certainly with an idealistic spirit that Amelung, as had glassmakers before him, sought financial backing for a glassmaking village in America. Presumably, all would share in the profits, but Amelung, alone, would manage the enterprise.

In his pamphlet, *Remarks on Manufactures, Principally on the New Established Glass-House, Near Frederick-town in the State of Maryland,* he implies that the plan to form the glass company was his.* If the idea of his own glass factory in America was not first implanted in Amelung's mind by Benjamin Crockett, a Baltimore mer-

chant whom he met in Bremen either in 1784 or, more likely, 1783, Crockett at least influenced his choice of Maryland as the location for the glasshouse. Initial funding came from the Bremen merchants, Hermann Heymann, Heinrich Talla, and the brothers von Lengerke.[23]

With "flattering expectations" and £10,000 capital, he hired workmen, bought equipment for "three different Glass Ovens," hired the ship *Fame* for their transport, and settled his personal affairs. In 1784 he sold his wife's mortgaged farm at Rodewald, allegedly to satisfy his creditors. His wife agreed to the sale of her property, as did her sister, Wilhelmina Griepenkerl, with the proviso that the money, about $2,500, be reinvested in land in America.[24]

He secured glassblowers from Bohemia, Thuringia, "and other parts of Germany"—undoubtedly some were from Grünenplan. All went according to plan until the severe winter of 1783/1784 made travel difficult. Some workers nearly died from starvation on their way to Bremen, while others were delayed because the rivers on which they were to be transported were frozen.

There were, according to Amelung, political efforts to disrupt his scheme: ". . . some English Merchants, and sea Captains, who were at that time in Bremen, wrote to England about it, and this jealous Nation, who look on the glass trade as an important one, desired the Government of Hannover, to do all that was in their power to frustrate a plan which they feared, would be to their loss, and greatly to the benefit of this country [America].—Brunswick, Hess, and other neighbouring Princes of the Roman Empire, were called upon to join for that purpose—now all possible obstacles were partly by intrigue, partly by force and despotic behaviour thrown in my way—the workmen I had engaged were detained, and nothing left untried to oppose me."

The emigration of Germans had not been prohibited previously, but in response to the complaints against Amelung, the city of Hannover declared it illegal to advertise for immigrants.[25] Fearing that he might be stopped, Amelung hastily departed Germany in May or early June, 1784, with his family (wife, son, and three daughters, his wife's unmarried sister, his own younger sister) and as many of the workers as were ready to leave. There were sixty-nine people in all, including Amelung. He later learned that his fears were well-founded: the English

---

*Amelung's *Remarks* are published in their entirety in Appendix 2. Material from the *Remarks* cited in the text has not been footnoted.

had planned to capture his ship in the Channel, but because of an extraordinarily quick passage, the vessel and its passengers escaped. The rest of his voyage was not so speedy: sixteen weeks elapsed before he arrived in Baltimore on August 31, 1784. An "agent" he had left behind followed him, arriving in Baltimore on November 22 with fourteen additional workers.

When he arrived in Baltimore, he had letters of introduction to several wealthy and influential men: General Thomas Mifflin, President of Congress; Thomas Johnson, the first Governor of Maryland and a member of Congress; Charles Carroll of Carrollton, the wealthiest man in Maryland and a Signer of the Declaration of Independence; William Paca, Governor of Maryland, also a Signer; "and a great number to the first mercantile houses. . . ". The letters were written by the most prominent Americans then in Europe: Benjamin Franklin, John Adams, and the American Consul in Paris, Thomas Barclay. Amelung felt confident that the letters "will prove that I had the character of a worthy and honest man in Germany, and kept the same until I left it."

III. THE NEW BREMEN GLASSMANUFACTORY

THE AVAILABILITY of an established glassworks in Frederick County, Maryland, must have been a strong inducement for Amelung to settle in that area. Benjamin Crockett, the man who influenced Amelung to settle there, had undoubtedly undertaken a site search for Amelung's glasshouse even before Amelung left Germany. When Amelung arrived, he was immediately in touch with Crockett's firm, as well as with the Frederick-Town merchant, Abraham Faw. He also may have sought the advice of Thomas Johnson and Charles Carroll of Carrollton, to whom he had letters of introduction. From these men Amelung must have learned about Foltz's glasshouse and that it soon might be for sale. Faw, Johnson, and Carroll all had extensive land holdings nearby.

Situated in the western part of the state, Frederick County had all the features a glassmaker required: plenty of trees that could be burned for fuel and for potash, good sand, and easy access to navigable water for the transport of raw materials and finished goods. Because the area was heavily populated with German immigrants, Amelung could expect considerable sympathy and support for his project. The rapidly expanding town of Baltimore, forty miles to the east, promised a lively market for American glass; there, a number of merchants and businessmen of German extraction were working to strengthen the economy of the republic and to support manufacturing ventures of many kinds.

A little over a month after Foltz's death, on November 30, 1784, Amelung purchased the glassworks property from the executors of the estate. He paid £1,000 for the tracts "Tobacco Hook" and "I don't care what" and an additional £1,000 for "Gantt's Garden." At the same time he also bought "Adam's Bones" from Abraham Faw for £700.[26] To judge from their radically different costs per acre, it is probable that the glasshouse was located either on "Tobacco Hook" (71 acres) or "I don't care what" (51¼ acres), and that "Gantt's Garden" (1577¾ acres) was valued for its timber. "Adam's Bones" (194 acres) probably had houses, gardens and orchards. Oddly enough, in Amelung's description of his land, published in his *Remarks*, he neglects to mention Foltz's glasshouse: ". . .I have purchased an advantageously situated tract of land on Patowmack [River], not far from Monocasey [River], of two thousand one hundred acres. . . ." Amelung's land was actually located on either side of the Monocacy, not on the Potomac. In 1787, when the pamphlet was published, his land holdings amounted to 2,016 acres.

That Amelung was quick to adapt Foltz's facilities—and absorb his labor force—is clearly seen in his first newspaper advertisement. Writing only two and one-half months after purchasing the property, Amelung announced that "Window-Glasses of two sorts, as also green and white hollow ware, are actually prepared."[27]

Little is known about the Foltz-Kramer-Eberhardt factory beyond the fact that it existed. Presumably, it was neither large nor complex, even though the British Consul, in 1789, claimed it had been founded "at a vast expence."[28] When Amelung bought the land on which Foltz's glasshouse must have been located he paid only £500 more than Foltz had four years earlier. If the difference in buying and selling price did equal the value of all improvements, the factory was small. There could not have been many potential buyers, however, so Amelung may have acquired the plant for less than had been invested in it. It is unwise to try to determine real estate values in this period, because currency fluctuated widely during the Revolution and post-Revolutionary years.

Bottles and window glass, as well as some tablewares, probably in the "Stiegel" style, must have been blown by Foltz, Eberhardt, and the Kramers. From Amelung's early newspaper notices it is obvious that he intended to expand their production and operate a "compleat" glass manufactory, that "will consist in making all kinds of glass-Wares, viz. Window-Glass, from the lowest to the finest sorts, white and green Bottles, Wines and other Drinking-Glasses, as also Optical Glasses, and Looking-Glasses, finished compleat."[29]

The archaeological evidence from a later Amelung factory site (Amelung operated four separate glasshouses, as will be shown later) suggests that the bottles were of a transparent green glass. They were blown in oval, bulbous forms, had indented bases, and had tapering necks with trailed, rounded rims. Such bottles were easily made and required no molds for their forming. The materials used to make the glass did not have to be especially pure, for neither their color nor clarity was critical. What did matter were their cost and durability. The archaeological evidence also suggests that Amelung, and perhaps Foltz, did not produce the heavy-walled, cylindrical bottles which were commonly used to store beer and wine. These were usually of dark green or amber, almost "black" glass and were made to be binned on their sides. The absence of such bottles from Amelung's or other American glassworks is supported by a Philadelphian's comment in 1789: "No factory is more wanted . . . than a capital glass manufactory for bottles similar to those of Bristol, in Great Britain. Considerable orders for Philadelphia beer and porter are now in the city, some of which cannot be executed for want of proper bottles."[30]

Window glass was more difficult to manufacture than bottles because of the purity of substance that was required. Bottles could be dark green, but window panes could have only a faint green tint. Amelung's remark that he of-

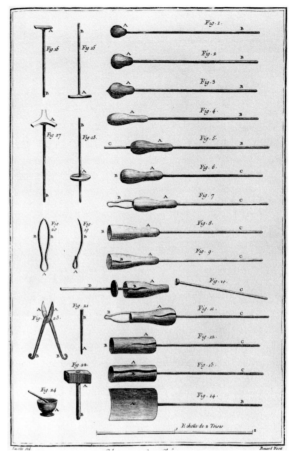

FIG. 8. Steps in blowing "cylinder" window glass. From Denis Diderot, et al. *Encyclopédie ou dictionnaire raisonné des sciences, des arts et des metiers.* (ed. 1772)

fered "Window-Glasses of two sorts" may mean that he produced two grades of quality.[31] Contemporary opinion of Amelung's window glass varies widely and was rarely unbiased. Phineas Bond dismissed it as being "thick, irregular and dim." The following year a Southerner expressed a more patriotic view: "The window glass manufactured in Maryland is equal to the best of that imported from Europe. It is hoped all young ladies and gentlemen of the beau monde will give the preference in future, to American reflections."[32]

On the other hand, Amelung's "two sorts" suggests perhaps that both "cylinder" and "crown" glass were blown at New Bremen. In the first process, the traditional German method, a long hollow cylinder was blown, the ends removed, and the cylinder slit lengthwise (Fig. 8). It then opened out or flattened in a special oven. Window panes of better quality were fashioned by the crown technique, where

Fig. 9. Carrying a "crown" of glass on a pontil rod. From Denis Diderot, et al.

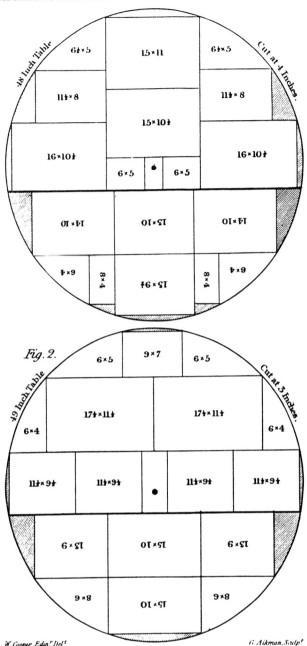

Fig. 10. "Crowns" of glass marked for cutting into window panes. From William Cooper, *The Crown Glass Cutter and Glazier's Manual*, Edinburgh, 1835.

a crown-shaped bubble of glass was attached to a pontil rod. When the crown was spun, centrifugal force caused it to open into a flat circular sheet (Fig. 9).

The surface of cylinder glass was likely to be less regular than that of crown glass, since the latter did not come into contact with another surface while it was hot enough to be deformed. Because of the pontil scar ("bull's eye") left in the center, the entire crown was not usable. The size of the panes was, therefore, limited by the diameter of the disk a man could hold—about four to five feet, maximum (Fig. 10). Cylinder sheets, on the other hand, had no pontil marks and could be used in their entirety. The range of window pane sizes which Amelung advertised was from four by eight inches by ten by twelve inches and could have been made either by the "cylinder" or "crown" methods.

Amelung's implication, in his February 1785 advertisement, that colorless hollow wares were already being made in Frederick County by Foltz, ties Amelung firmly to the tableglass tradition of earlier eighteenth-century American factories, specifically that of Henry William Stiegel. Although the Kramers and Foltz worked at Manheim for only a short time, it is very possible that they obtained some of Stiegel's pattern molds—articles that would have been expensive to have made—and used them in Maryland. This might explain the fact that several "diamond-daisy" pattern-molded flasks, hitherto thought only to have been made at Stiegel's works, have strong chemical resemblances to glass known to have been made at New Bremen.

The 1783 household inventory of Capt. Jacob Good is replete with interesting hollow glass

forms, from glass cups and saucers to quart mugs. Since "Balser Cromer" was one of the creditors of his estate, some of those glasses might have been blown at his factory.[33]

Whatever Foltz's products were, his factory was clearly an important stage in Amelung's industrial development, even though Amelung never mentions it in his wide-ranging account of the founding of the factory. The main purpose of the *Remarks* was, it seems, to impress politicians with the scale of his enterprise and its importance to the national economy. Amelung obviously wanted total credit for establishing glassmaking in Maryland. Could this omission mean that Amelung razed Foltz's factory as soon as he completed a new one? Or did he, literally, bury it with additions and modifications? Perhaps it was simply not politically expedient to remind others that he was the second manufacturer to attempt glassmaking on the site. Whatever his intention, Amelung did succeed in pushing his predecessors into obscurity. Only two eighteenth-century accounts of the Foltz enterprise have been found, and no twentieth-century author has previously published knowledge of its existence.

Although the operation of his factory may have been uppermost in his mind, Amelung's concern for providing housing for his workmen and their families must have been almost as pressing. By the end of 1784, Amelung had brought from Germany at least eighty-two people who were dependent on him. There may have been a few houses on the land he bought, but there could not have been enough to answer his extensive needs. Adequate housing may have been available in nearby Frederick-Town, but if his workers had to live there and commute to the factory, construction of new facilities would have been hampered, especially during the winter. His only alternative was to build houses and to build them quickly: by 1787 Amelung had erected "dwelling houses for one hundred and thirty-five now living souls." Unlike

the practice at Grünenplan, the houses were built at Amelung's own expense and he retained their ownership. Of one and two stories,[34] they were probably similar in plan to those built at Grünenplan (Figs. 6 and 7) and were intended for single families. Local building practices were certainly influential, but since Frederick County had a large German population, the Grünenplan style may have been familiar already.

The records of the subdivision of the property in 1795 indicate that the houses were apparently not concentrated in a single location but were scattered over the Amelung properties. This lack of centralized dwelling area is confirmed by the only known land plat of part of the property, a document which dates from the nineteenth century.

Amelung's own house was built near the brow of a hill on "Adam's Bones" (Fig. 11). It still survives and is an imposing two-story brick structure. With elaborate architectural details on both the interior and exterior, the house attests to its builder's affluence—or pretensions. A dated brick in one of the chimneys may be evidence that the building was finished in 1789, yet it seems unlikely that Amelung would have waited four years to complete his own dwelling. Originally there were a detached kitchen, springhouse, and stables, but these no longer stand.[35]

Amelung not only provided housing for his employees but was determined to offer educational opportunities to their children. His arrangements were detailed in his *Remarks:*

Persuaded that no greater happiness can be for the succeeding generations than to give them a good education in their younger years, and impress religion and morals early in their breasts; for this purpose, I have (directly after my settlement here) established a German School. The master,[36] a worthy man, is fully aquainted with this duty, and has a yearly salary from me, a commodious house, in which every Sunday divine service is kept, a garden, some land, and free fire wood. The inhabitants, who send their children to this school, pay a trifle to him.

I am now establishing an English School, for which purpose I have built a house on my land, and as I advance, I intend to put the same upon such a footing, that children may get a complete education in the same, as in English, German, and French Languages, writing, ciphering, music, to play on the harp, harpsichord, flute, and violin; I have the masters for this purpose already here, and will contribute all that is in my power to make the

FIG. 11. The house of John Frederick Amelung, ca. 1789. Photo: Raymond F. Errett.

charges easy, and will pay attention to the education and morals of these children, who will be sent to this school.[36]

On August 12, 1785 Amelung petitioned to have his three contiguous tracts of land, "Gantt's Garden, "Tobacco Hook," and "I don't care what," resurveyed and combined into a single tract which he intended to name "New Bremen" to honor the city of his backers. When the tracts were surveyed Amelung learned that instead of 1,700 acres he held clear title to only 1,498 acres. However, he was able to acquire 324 acres of adjacent "vacant" land for £7.10.0: six acres were cleared, there were an old log house, 2,000 old fence rails, and fifteen peach and cherry trees left by an earlier owner. The resurvey of Amelung's tract, now of 1,822 acres, was completed on April 26, 1786. The land was officially patented "New Breman" [sic] on December 18, 1787.[37] Henceforth, the land was referred to as "New Bremen" and the factory became the "New Bremen Glassmanufactory" (See Chart 1 and Fig. 12).

Legally, only Gantt's Garden," "I don't care

what" and "Tobacco Hook" were included in the "New Bremen" tract, but Amelung appearently used that name to describe all that he owned. The name "New Bremen Glassmanufactory" certainly encompassed more than just the facility on "New Bremen" proper.

Amelung indicated in his *Remarks* that he had built at least one new "oven" (by which he presumably meant a melting furnace) and that a second one was to be completed in 1786. He did not specify where those "ovens" were. They may have been additions to Foltz's factory or, more likely, they may have been constructed on "Adam's Bones," purchased by Amelung in 1784 at the same time he acquired Foltz's land.

The "Adam's Bones" factory was excavated by the Corning-Smithsonian-Williamsburg team in 1962 and 1963. The foundations uncovered regrettably do not answer the question of when it was first built. The evidence, discussed in detail in a later section by Ivor Noël Hume, indicates that the structure had been at least partially rebuilt once and that after it was destroyed by fire it was not rebuilt or converted to another use. Whether the factory had been built in one or

CHART 1

	"Gantt's Garden"	"Tobacco Hook"	"I don't care what"	"Adam's Bones"	"Resurvey on right & good reason" (560 acres)	"Resurvey on right & good reason" (378 acres)
1780	Conrad Foltz (for wood)	Conrad Foltz (for glass- or house?)←	Conrad Foltz (for glass- →house?)			
1784	J. F. Amelung (for wood)	J. F. Amelung (for glass- or house?)←	J. F. Amelung (for glass- →house?)	J. F. Amelung (builds glass-house)		
1787	combined to form:	"New Bremen" (1822 acres)				
ca. 1788–1789 (?)					J. F. Amelung (wood)	J. F. Amelung (wood)
1790				Glasshouse burns; new glasshouse built	(builds glass-house)	
1793	Sold to Labes (as partner)			Sold to Labes (as partner)		Formal transfer to J. F. Amelung— Sold to Labes (as partner)
1795	Advertised for sale			Advertised for sale	Formally transferred to J. F. Amelung— to J. F. M. Amelung	Advertised for sale
1797	Bankrupt, deeded to trustee			to trustee		to trustee
1798	Auction, in tracts			Auction		Auction

two stages is not clear. Since the "Adam's Bones" glasshouse had two melting furnaces, one may conclude that Amelung's comments concerning his construction before 1786 refer to this glasshouse.

There is, however, some evidence that the "Adam's Bones" glasshouse may not have been built until after 1788 or 1789. Sometime in those years Amelung bought 560 acres of a tract called "Resurvey on right and good reason," with funds received from the sale of his wife's and her sister's land in Germany. In 1801 Amelung's son, Frederick Magnus claimed that his father had purchased the land for its timber, which was ". . . cut and employed for the use of the glass Manufactory, which at the time of the said purchase was carried on upon an adjacent Tract called New Bremen. . . ."[38] This suggests that Amelung's only glasshouse before 1790 was located on "New Bremen." It is more reasonable to assume, however, that there was a factory on "Adam's Bones" and that the wood from "Resurvey on right and good reason" was not for the "New Bremen" facility. Foltz's factory on "New Bremen" was already adequately supplied with wood from "Gantt's Garden," so there would have been no reason to buy more wooded land if that were Amelung's only factory; if there were a factory on "Adam's Bones," it would not have had *direct* access to the tract of wooded land on "New Bremen" because it did not connect with any of the boundaries of that tract. "Resurvey on right and good reason" was adjacent to "Adam's Bones," and was not "adjacent" to any of "New Bremen." Thus, it seems more likely that "Resurvey on right and good reason" was acquired at about the same time the "Adam's Bones" factory was under construction. That Amelung's son referred to it as the factory on "New Bremen" is another indication that his father called his entire enterprise "New Bremen."

Although Amelung assumed rights to the 560-acre part of "Resurvey on right and good reason" by 1788 or 1789, it was not officially conveyed to him until 1795. The delay in transfer was apparently due to the fact that Amelung paid for the land in installments and that he made the final payment about March 25, 1795.[39] Amelung acquired an additional 378 acres of "Resurvey on right and good reason" in 1793, but the transfer of this parcel, like the other, was probably also arranged in 1788 or 1789.

Amelung's hand-written notes in his *Remarks,* added in June 1790, imply that these tracts were intended to supply more than just fuel: "I have also purchased one Thousand Acres of Land more and erected another new Glass House on that Spot. . . ."[40] There can be no doubt that this "new Glass House" was erected—at the expense of Amelung's son[41]—on the "Resurvey of right and good reason." The 938 acres of "Resurvey on right and good reason" was the only land Amelung bought after his initial purchase of "Adam's Bones" and the tracts which became "New Bremen." There was definitely a glasshouse on that land by the time Amelung died.

By the beginning of 1790, after being in America for just over five years, Amelung could look upon his achievements with considerable pride: he had acquired a fledgling factory and had transformed it into an extensive industry; if the former Foltz factory was still in operation, he had two glasshouses in production and a third about to be completed; he had built an industrial "village" which housed between 400 and 500 people;[42] his total investment had reached £22,000, with additional funds coming from his wife, her sister, his son, the State of Maryland, and probably some American investors. He claimed that the value of his enterprise, as gauged by the number of workers and the factories' productivity, had increased at three times the rate of investment.[43] Most satisfying of all was achievement of a national reputation as a result of his efforts.

In 1788 the French traveler, J. P. Brissot de Warville, knew the factory; he noted in his travel diary: "In the United States, the prodigious consumption of glasses, bottles and window glass is increasing the number of glassmanufactories. It is said that the one on the Patowmac [sic] now employs more than 500 persons."[44] The following year George Washington wrote about the business to Thomas Jefferson, then U.S. Minister to France: "Several capitol artists, in different branches, have lately arrived in this Country. A factory of Glass is established, upon a large scale on Monocasy, near Frederick-Town in Maryld. I am informed it will this year produce Glass of various kinds, nearly to the amount of three thousand pounds value."[45]

In 1787 he claimed that he had brought the factory "to a tolerable degree of perfection," but by 1790 he could only note that his glass was: "coming to Perfection from degree to degree almost every Month, owing to the Experience I have acquired since these 6 Years Past which

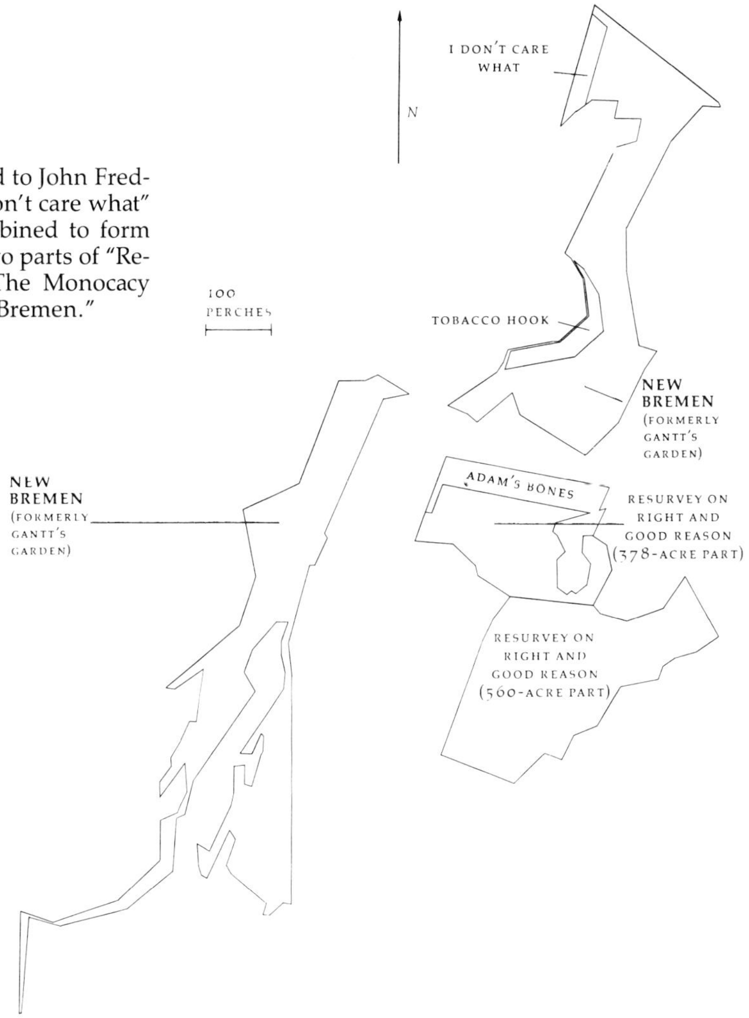

FIG. 12. Plot of properties that belonged to John Frederick Amelung: "Gantt's Garden," "I don't care what" and "Tobacco Hook" which were combined to form "New Bremen"; "Adam's Bones" and two parts of "Resurvey on right and good reason." The Monocacy River separates the two parts of "New Bremen."

I DON'T CARE
WHAT

N

100
PERCHES

TOBACCO HOOK

NEW
BREMEN
(FORMERLY
GANTT'S
GARDEN)

NEW
BREMEN
(FORMERLY
GANTT'S
GARDEN)

ADAM'S BONES

RESURVEY ON
RIGHT AND
GOOD REASON
(378-ACRE PART)

RESURVEY ON
RIGHT AND
GOOD REASON
(560-ACRE PART)

enabled me to be better acquainted with the Materials here consequently making a better use of it, then [sic] in the beginning & therefore do not in the least doubt, if a Moderate Assistance should [be] given me, the Glass made here, will Exceed the imported in a short Time."[46]

The operation of Amelung's factories apparently was plagued with difficulties. Amelung may have had trouble securing suitable raw materials for his glass as well as clay needed for crucibles in which the glass was clay melted (presumably, "Fullers earth, which will stand the fire," which he sought in 1787, was used in making crucibles). Like most glassmakers, he may have had problems with his furnaces.

One reference has come to light concerning the source of Amelung's potash. In June 1790 William Henderson of Green Castle, Pennsylvania, sent a sample of his pearlash to a Philadelphia firm. He claimed that "Mr. Emelong who owns the Glass house in Maryland says it is the best he has seen in America, and has purchased a Considerable Quantity from me" [William Henderson to Andrew Clow & Co., June 25, 1790; Claude W. Unger Collection, Historical Society of Pennsylvania].

While the range of glasswares listed in Amelung's first advertisement was rather limited, by the end of 1786 many more forms were available: "Gallon bottles, half do. [ditto], quart do. pint do. and pocket do. assorted in hogsheads and tierces, from £7-7s. to £3-7s. the cask; window glass, 8 by 10, and 7 by 9, in boxes, glass tumblers, from a pint to half a gill, in barrels, assorted."[47] In 1789 an even more extensive and detailed list of products was published: ". . . He makes Window-Glass transparent and substantial, equal to the London Crown, an inferior Quality equal to the Bristol Crown; all Kinds of Flint-Glass, such as Decanters, and Wine

Glasses, Tumblers of all Sizes, and any other Sort of Table Glass.—He also cuts Devices, Cyphers, Coats of Arms, or any other Fancy Figures on Glass, and in a short Time hopes to be able to furnish Looking-Glasses of all Sizes."[48] It is important to note that although Amelung stated that he made "Flint-Glass," there is no evidence that he made "lead glass," the usually accepted definition of the term. The potash-lead composition was an English innovation of the late seventeenth century; although imitated on the Continent, most German glass was made with potash and lime. By "flint" Amelung meant only that he was making a good quality, colorless glass. Also, in spite of his stated intentions to the contrary and his Grünenplan experience, there is no proof that Amelung ever made mirror plate or optical glass in America.

Amelung frequently invited potential buyers to compare his glass with the imported product in both price and quality. In his *Remarks* in 1787 he noted: "The goodness of the glass is such that the gentlemen in Baltimore, Frederick, and Elizabeth-town, to whom I have sold my glass are contented; by inquiry it will be found, that my glass is cheaper, and of a better quality, than a great deal of what is imported."

Perhaps his most effective strategy designed to stimulate political and mercantile interest in his factory was a series of splendid glasses presented to influential politicians and merchants. Elaborately engraved goblets and tumblers were made over a period of at least five years, from 1788 to 1792. It is probable that all were gifts and, just in case the recipient's memory was short, all were fully signed.

To date, seven glasses inscribed with the full name of the factory, and sometimes its location, are known. (See Catalogue.) In four cases the recipients have been identified: one politician, two merchants, and one glass manufacturer. Two glasses may have been made for Amelung's European investors or merchants. The original owner of the most resplendently nationalistic piece of all, the tumbler engraved with the Great Seal of the United States, is also unknown.

Amelung presented, in person, a pair of goblets to General George Washington in 1789. An eyewitness account of the presentation was published in several American newspapers:

I am just returned from Mount-Vernon, where I was present at a scene which made every patriotic pulse vibrate with the most pleasurable sensation. This, Sir, was a tribute of a new citizen of the United States, to their illustrious President.

Mr. John F. Amelung, a native of Germany, and an artist of considerable eminence migrated to this country with a large family and extensive fortune; having contemplated the soil, commerce, &c. he selected with great prudence a central situation, for the establishment of a manufactory of the first magnitude and importance, in which he has succeeded beyond all hopes and expectations; through his vast exertions he is now enabled to supply the United States, with every species of GLASS, the quality of which is equal if not superior to that imported, while he actually undersells all foreign traders in that article in our own markets.

To the testimony of the ablest connoisseurs and characters of trade and respectability, it only remained for Mr. Amelung, to court the patronage of the great Patriot, and I had the good fortune to have been present at an offering to his Excellency of two capacious goblets of double flint glass, exhibiting the General's coat of arms, &c.[49]

Unfortunately, these goblets apparently have not survived. In form, they must have been related to the goblets shown in the Catalogue.

Amelung's gesture was not in vain: four months after his visit to Mount Vernon, President Washington approved a ten percent duty on glass imports. Governor Thomas Mifflin of Pennsylvania, also the recipient of a Maryland-blown goblet (Cat. #7), was apparently not as obliging. When the presidential mansion was being built in Philadelphia, Mifflin asked the Proprietors of the Boston Crown Glass manufactory to supply the glass needed for the dome.[50] There is no record that he asked Amelung.

The published account of Amelung's visit with Washington is the only known reference to Amelung's presentation glasswares. He must certainly have made other goblets if their purpose was a form of advertising. There were numerous other politicians and merchants who would have been logical "targets": John Adams, Thomas Jefferson, and Alexander Hamilton, among others. The presentations would have been accompanied by conversations like those he had with Washington, which "naturally embraced and discussed our manufacturing interests. . . ."

From the beginning, Amelung's glasswares were distributed to retail merchants in several cities. In 1785 he had agents in New York, Philadelphia, Baltimore, and Frederick-Town. While he may have succeeded in attracting some new merchants to sell his products, his sales soon lagged behind his production. By 1790, when cash was in short supply and trade was generally depressed, Amelung had "upwards of four thousand pounds worth of Glass of all kinds on hand, as well as nearly the same sum in outstanding debts. . . ."[51]

Although he said that he was not personally in debt in 1790, he sought state and national assistance at least as early as 1787 when he published his *Remarks on Manufactures*. Amelung apparently felt that the future of manufactures in America had been exaggerated, at his expense, by Crockett and the others who initially encouraged him. From his experience, the United States government was "unaccustomed to grant particular privileges, to any citizens" and "no man who has had sense and fortune enough to make any progress in Manufactures, got any public preference and encouragement whatsoever." He argued that no nation could flourish without manufacturers, dramatically contrasting those European states which had assisted manufactories and those which had not. The examples were obviously intended to spark official interest in manufacturing in general, in the "New Bremen Glassmanufactory" in particular, and to offer guidelines for official support.

Amelung's plan was comprehensive; he proposed that manufacturers be exempt from taxes, that their employees be excused from military service and civil arrest (the employer was to be held accountable), and that loans of at least one-half the value of the manufactory be made, to be interest-free for a period of five years or more. In return, the public interest could be secured by the formation of a board of supervisors who would oversee the manufacturers. After the production was perfected, and a market secured in America, the money customarily sent to Europe for those products would be retained in America; as soon as export became possible, the balance of trade would be favorably shifted. Income for the state could be derived from duties on types of imported goods which were made here; at the same time, such tariffs would benefit manufacturers by making imported goods more expensive. The manufacturer, he emphasized, contributed to the well-being of the nation by utilizing its abundant raw materials and by increasing the population of trained workmen who had to be brought from Europe. In this program Amelung anticipated Alexander Hamilton's recommendations for government

patronage of manufacturers detailed in his 1791 Report to Congress on manufactures. In fact, Hamilton and his assistant, Tench Coxe, must have been aware of, if not influenced by, the Maryland glassmaker.

Amelung's first known request for governmental aid was successful; in 1788 he received a loan of £1,000 from the State of Maryland which was tax-free for five years. It was secured for Amelung through the efforts of Thomas Johnson, Benjamin Ogle, and George Schnertzel. The bond was still unpaid in 1792 when it was replaced by one secured by George Schnertzel and James Labes. In the end, George Schnertzel repaid the loan.[52]

During this period the number of employees at New Bremen had increased significantly. The initial group of sixty-eight, who had accompanied Amelung in his hasty departure from Germany in 1784, had swelled to 135 by 1787. There was a dramatic increase to 342 employees in 1788, and by 1790 "between four and five hundred people" were employed.[53] Even if Amelung had slightly overstated these figures for effect, his venture was of obvious economic significance to America.

The glassworks may have been damaged in the flood of the Monocacy on October 11, 1786, when the river rose ten feet. In mid-April 1790, a strong wind collapsed four houses at the Manufactory and destroyed several nearby mills; it also may have damaged the glasshouses.[54] Three weeks later, one of his factories and a warehouse were consumed by fire.[55] Which glasshouse burned was not noted, but according to tradition, it was the one *below* the house—the one excavated by the Corning-Smithsonian-Williamsburg team. On the day after the fire someone scratched the poignant inscription, "Denken an den 7ten May 1790" ("Thinking on the 7th of May 1790") on a second floor window pane which faced the factory site (Fig. 13).

Undaunted by the tragedy, Amelung immediately began to rebuild the factory. On May 19th a new "superstructure" was nearly completed. The factory excavated in 1962–1963, discussed later in this study, showed no evidence of rebuilding after it was destroyed by fire. However, a factory in roughly the same area was in existence in the nineteenth century. The excavated factory was most likely the one burned on May 6, 1790. The new factory building was not built on its foundations but was constructed nearby.

In the wake of his tragedy, Amelung expected

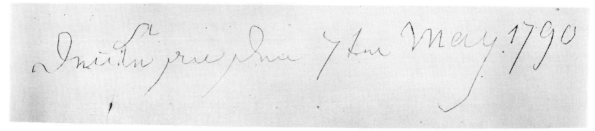

FIG. 13. Scratched inscription on a window pane removed from a second-floor window in the Amelung house. Marshall Lingan Etchison collection; published by permission of Miss Josephine Etchison. Photo: George J. Fistrovich.

not only sympathy but also tangible support. Nineteen days after the fire, he petitioned the United States Senate for ". . . the Aid of the Government of the United States in this most important Undertaking, either by granting him a loan of Money, upon the most undoubted and unequivocal Security, or by such other means, as Congress in their Wisdom may see fit." He claimed that his funds were nearly exhausted, that efforts were being made in England to assure his failure and that ". . . some additional Works ought still to be erected to compleat [sic] the original design. . . ."

A careful consideration of the petition ensued. The Congressmen assessed Amelung's abilities and explored the principles under which the government might make such a grant or loan. A decision against the petition was finally made on June 3 on the basis of an undeniable flaw in Amelung's proposal: William Laughton Smith of South Carolina argued that if the factory were on the verge of collapse after £20,000 had been invested, what could Amelung offer that was "the most undoubted and unequivocal Security?"[56]

Undeterred by the decision, Amelung sent a second petition to Congress on June 29, probably accompanied by copies of his *Remarks* which he had updated by hand. Far from a plaintive plea for money to save his factory from the reversals he cited in his first petition, Amelung's unusual proposal outlined an ambitious plan to erect glasshouses in Virginia and the Carolinas, the better to supply the South with glass. He wrote, "The Advantages. . . . [are] very obvious, as the Number of Inhabitants in a few Years would amount to upwards of five Hundred. The Neighboring lands would increase to more than double their value. Such a Number of People living together on a small spott would be a greater Barrier against the Invasion of the Indians than scattered Plantations,

whom they would be able to protect."

For his Maryland undertaking he solicited a grant to rebuild the burned glasshouse and to pay the transportation costs of German workers who were expected in Baltimore soon. In order to begin his southern expansion, he requested only a grant of land. Finally, to lessen foreign competition, he asked "that the Honourable Houses will please to raise the Duty on imported Glass, which in the beginning will not only increase the Revenue of the united States, but at the same Time enable him to execute his Plan with more ease and certainty."[57]

The differences between this second petition and the first are intriguing. He hoped that his proposals would be granted not out of sympathy but out of respect for his achievements and the enormous financial contributions he had already made to the well-being of the United States. Instead of emphasizing that many workers depended upon him for their existence and that the factory was on the verge of collapse, he announced a rather amazing scheme to extend the industry to the frontiers. Amelung did not want a monopoly, however, and reiterated his offer to share his hard-won expertise with any glasshouse in the United States.

This second petition must have been drafted after Amelung learned that the first had been defeated. Strangely, the proposals he made do not refute the arguments which led to the defeat of the first. The new petition not only avoided them, it almost taunted William Laughton Smith of South Carolina, who had raised the most damaging argument against the first petition. If Amelung's second petition were granted, Smith's state would have gained the most.

Amelung's efforts were again in vain; the second petition was tabled. One suggestion, however, was adopted. The duty on imported glass that had been ten percent from August 1, 1789 was raised to twelve and one-half percent on

Sugar bowl with swan finial. Attributed to the New Bremen Glassmanufactory, ca. 1785–95. OH. 21.2 cm. Collection of the Henry Francis du Pont Winterthur Museum, Winterthur, Del.

The "C. G." sugar bowl, engraved with the inscription "To Ms. C. G. / In Washington Cty" within a wreath with flowers, including a floral spray on the cover. Attributed to the New Bremen Glassmanufactory, ca. 1785–95. OH. 20.4 cm. Collection of the Henry Francis du Pont Winterthur Museum, Winterthur, Del.

Amethyst glass cream jug with engraved star and wreath. Attributed to the New Bremen Glassmanufactory, ca. 1785–95. H. 12.0 cm. Collection of the Henry Francis du Pont Winterthur Museum, Winterthur, Del.

Pocket bottle molded in a "checkered diamond" pattern. Possibly made at the New Bremen Glassmanufactory, ca. 1785–95. H. 15.6 cm. Collection of the Corning Museum of Glass.

Blue glass salt (?) dish molded in a "checkered diamond" pattern. Possibly made at the New Bremen Glassmanufactory, ca. 1785–95. H. 7.1 cm. Collection of the Corning Museum of Glass.

December 31, 1790. It was maintained at that level until May 2, 1792, when it was increased to sixteen and one-fourth percent (if the cargo was carried by foreign ships; if carried by American ships the rate was fifteen percent). On June 7, 1794, the tariff was again increased, to twenty-one and three-fourths percent and twenty-per-cent, respectively. That rate prevailed through the end of the century.

Amelung's failure to get aid from the government must have been a severe disappointment. One might assume that he would have turned to the public to attract new customers, but he did not; newspaper advertisements of his products do not appear as frequently. He continued to make presentation glasses for influential Americans: in 1791, a goblet for General Thomas Mifflin on the occasion of his inauguration as Governor of Pennsylvania, and a covered tumbler made for the Philadelphia merchant, John Guest. Both are decorated with the Arms of Pennsylvania. The tumbler, with the Arms of the United States, was made in 1792, as was the goblet for "G. F. Mauerhoff," who is unidentified as yet and who may have been European.

In June 1793, Amelung concluded his purchase of 378 acres of "Resurvey on right and good reason" from the Frederick merchant, Abraham Faw. The land connected the previously isolated "Adam's Bones" and the 560-acre part of "Resurvey on right and good reason" which he had agreed to purchase in 1788 or 1789. On July 1, 1793, with debts increasing rapidly, Amelung acquired a partner, the Baltimore merchant, James Labes. Amelung sold Labes three of his four properties: "New Bremen" and "Adam's Bones" for £12,000, and the 378-acre part of "Resurvey on right and good reason" for £264/12/-.

It was obvious that Amelung's finances had begun to deteriorate before the fire. By 1789 Abraham Faw, acting as Amelung's agent and purchasing goods for him in Philadelphia, was to be paid in glass. When the bills of several merchants were not paid, Faw was sued in 1793 and lost the judgment. By 1794, Amelung's debts to four Philadelphia merchants, through Faw, were over £800. On January 17, 1794, James Labes mortgaged the properties "New Bremen" and "Adam's Bones" to Abraham Usher, a Baltimore merchant, for £1,000 to satisfy another of the firm's debts. This transaction was quickly followed by a second mortgage on the properties "New Bremen," "Adam's Bones" and the 378-acre part of "Resurvey on right and good

reason" to Abraham Faw, in consideration of the Amelung and Labes debt with him and an additional payment of £750.[58]

According to the family archives, Amelung suffered a stroke in 1794 and was at least partially paralyzed until his death.[59] It is probable that he had little to do with the operation of the factory after 1794. His son John Frederick Magnus Amelung, who had served as the company bookkeeper for several years, must have assumed a more active role.[60]

Probably because of Amelung's illness and mounting debts, the factory was advertised for sale on March 23, 1795:

A BARGAIN! A BARGAIN!

The Subscribers Offer for Sale,
The New-Bremen GLASS WORKS, and 2,000 acres of LAND, about nine miles from Frederick-town, within forty miles of the Federal city, and not more than six miles to the river Patowmac. There are on the premises, 30 one and two story Dwelling Houses; two Glass Houses, two Flattening Houses; Warehouses and Stables; the necessary Buildings for boiling potash; in short, all the Buildings that are wanted to carry on the manufactory of blowing Glass, on a large and extensive plan. Thre are only two small FARMS cleared on the Land, the remainder is all in woods. The Land is mostly of a kind and good quality. There is a valuable MILL SEAT, about two hundred yards from the Works, on Bennett's-creek, on a large and never-failing stream. As every person inclining to purchase will wish to see the premises, we think it unnecessary to give a more minute description. For terms apply to Mr. Abraham Usher, of Baltimore, or to Amelung & Labes, living on the premises.[61]

It is not known if anyone was interested enough to examine the property. In any event, it remained unsold.

On March 25, 1795, two days after the first public notice of Amelung's and Labes' decision to sell the glassworks, Thomas Jefferson officially transferred the 560-acre part of "Resurvey on right and good reason" to Amelung. As mentioned before, it was alleged that Amelung was unable to pay for the property and that his son finally paid the amount due in that year. The glasshouse, built on that property about 1790, was also paid for by Frederick. Not surprisingly, Amelung transferred the property to his son on March 27, 1795 in "Consideration of natural Love and Affection" and 5 shillings.[62]

The transfer does raise a perplexing question.

In the March 23 advertisement two glasshouses were mentioned. In the bankruptcy papers filed by Labes in 1796, on the other hand, only one glasshouse was listed among the firm's assets.[63] Thus, it seems evident that Amelung had two operating glasshouses in 1795: one was the factory on "Adam's Bones" which had replaced the one which burned in May 1790; the second was on "Resurvey on right and good reason," which Amelung did not mortgage to James Labes but transferred to John Frederick Magnus, his son, in 1795. The Foltz factory must have ceased operations some time before. If that is correct, we are left with the uncomfortable but inescapable conclusion that there was no "New Bremen Glassmanufactory" located on the tract of "New Bremen" in 1795. When or why the Foltz glasshouse was closed is not known.

On May 23, 1795, Labes was forced again to mortgage his properties, "New Bremen" and "Resurvey on right and good reason" (the 378-acre part), to three Baltimore merchants for an unpaid debt of £487.

On May 23, 1796, James Labes and the firm of Amelung and Labes petitioned the State to be judged insolvent debtors. Labes listed as assets: "All that Tract of Land Resurveyed Called New Breman [sic]. Situate in Frederick County State of Maryland. Containing 2000 Acres more or less with About 40 Dwelling Houses. Glass & Flattening House. Stables & Other Improvements thereon made." plus other credits of personal notes and unsold stock in the hands of dealers in George Town and Alexandria. The total value of these assets is not given. (It is especially unfortunate that the glasshouse and associated buildings were not appraised.) The debts of the firm amounted to £12,419.3.11 and were listed in detail.[64]

On January 2, 1797, the courts named Samuel Moale trustee on behalf of the creditors of James Labes and John Frederick Amelung. On January 11, both Labes and Amelung deeded "all and every household goods and furniture effects and chattles debts and sum and sums of money belonging to and due and owing . . . and also all other property real personal and mixed of what kind nature or quality soever excepting the wearing apparel. . . ." The trustee divided "New Bremen" into thirteen lots, ranging from nine acres to 156-½ acres in size. They, together with the tracts "Adam's Bones," part of "Resurvey on the Hope" and a part of "Resurvey on right and good reason" were sold by auction on December 10, 1798.[65]

John Frederick Amelung did not witness the final disintegration of his dreams. On April 21, 1797, Amelung's nephew, Heinrich, wrote to his sister: "Gesund sind wir Alle, es scheint auch, als wenn der gute Oncle Amelung sich wieder erholte, denn seit einiger Zeit Fängt er doch an, im Hof an seinen Krücken zu spazieren." ("We are all in good health, and it seems as if even our good uncle Amelung is making progress, since he has started to walk again, and goes up and down his garden on a pair of crutches.") On August 30, 1798, Amelung wrote to the nephew from "New Bremen": "Meine Augen sind so schwach, dass ich kaum unterscheiden kann, was ich geschrieben,— . . . Empfiehl mich deiner lieben Mutter . . . meinem Bruder sage ewig Lebewohl von mir, bald, ja bald sehen wir uns wieder, dort wieder, wo kein Trenner sein wird. Bald, bald, —lebe wohl. . . Dein dich liebender Onkel Joh. Fr. Amelung." ("My eyes are so weak that I can scarcely read my own handwriting . . . Love to your dear mother . . . say good-by to my brothers. We shall soon meet again where there is no parting. Be well . . . Your loving uncle Joh. Fr. Amelung.").[66]

John Frederick Amelung died on November 21, 1798, at the house of his son-in-law, Peter Volkman, in Baltimore. His obituary concluded: "The many amiable qualities of this truly worthy man, will ever endeare his memory to his family, and many friends."[67]

IV. THE AMELUNG POSTSCRIPT

THE CLOSING of John Frederick Amelung's New Bremen Glassmanufactory did not signal the end of glassmaking in Maryland, or even in Frederick County. Before 1800 Frederick Magnus Amelung, Adam Kohlenberg, and George Christian Gabler blew glass at the works Amelung had built on the "Resurvey of right and good reason." Amelung's "Old Glass-Works" located on "Adam's Bones" eventually housed the Fleecy Dale Wool-Factory (Noël Hume Section, Fig. 1).[68]

The glassmaking effort of Amelung, Kohlenberg, and Gabler must have occurred in one of the two glasshouses mentioned in the January 20, 1798, issue of *The Key,* and one of the three works listed in 1798 assessment. In 1799 Frederick Amelung transferred the property to Gabler and Kohlenberg for a sale price of 725 boxes of window glass, worth approximately £4,000.[69] From the Varlé map (Fig. 14) it is clear that Kohlenberg was still making glass in the "New Glass Works" in 1808. In the inventory of Kohlenberg's estate, taken in 1813, appraisers evaluated a "Set of Glasswork Tools old & much worn" at $34.10. Although Kohlenberg produced window glass, some of the "plain glass decanters," "old tumblers," bowls, and cream jugs noted in his inventory may have been of his own creation.[70]

Other glasshouses in operation after 1795 were those of Maryland's first governor, Thomas Johnson. By 1793 he had erected a glasshouse, a saw mill, a tan yard, and a grist mill on Tuscarora Creek, three and one-half miles north of Frederick-Town. Another glasshouse was situated on a 1,700-acre tract five miles southeast of Frederick on Bush Creek (Fig. 14). The latter factory, known as the Etna Glass-House, had commenced production sometime in 1792. By February 1793 Johnson was able to offer "a good many Snuff and common Bottles." The "Two large flatting houses and flatting ovens" mentioned later proved that window panes were also blown. Although Johnson had hoped to sell his glasshouses in 1793, he still owned one in 1798 on Tasker's Chance, presumably the Etna works, and his brother Baker and his son Thomas owned the other, on Hatherly's Adventure. The latter was "out of repair" at that time, while the Etna was said to be "in a thriving state."[71] By 1808 both were called "old" glassworks (Fig. 14).

Where Thomas Johnson originally found his workmen is not known, but in 1793 he employed a "full set of good hands . . . who are very Comfortably settled, and like the place." Certainly after New Bremen closed, some workmen turned to Johnson for employment. Others went west to work at Albert Gallatin's New Geneva factory and other factories in the Pittsburgh area. If any glassworkers remained "in the neighbourhood of the old glass works or elsewhere," they were invited in 1814 to consider employment at a glasshouse to be constructed in Cumberland County in the far western part of Maryland. Few were interested, apparently, for the enterprise did not get underway until 1817; the proprietors recalled that they had had "great difficulty . . . procuring hands that were competent to carry on the business." By 1820 all glassmaking in Frederick County had ceased.[72]

FIG. 14. Section of "A Map of Frederick and Washington Counties, State of Maryland" by Charles Varlé, 1808. Courtesy Enoch Pratt Free Library, Baltimore.

Perhaps the most significant outgrowth of the New Bremen enterprise was the glasshouse erected in Baltimore by Frederick Magnus Amelung. The younger Amelung's financial situation was very complicated and has not yet been unraveled. Considering his father's failure, however, his fortune could not have been great. Indeed, Frederick Amelung was himself declared a bankrupt in 1804 and the Frederick County property offered for sale.[73] Although he continued to manufacture glass on a limited scale at New Bremen after 1795, the idea of starting yet another *new* glassworks must have seemed an impossible dream. A financially sound and interested father-in-law, however, enabled Frederick to continue the Amelung glassmaking traditions in Baltimore.

At that time, at the very end of the eighteenth century, Baltimore was a flourishing town with an atmosphere that was encouraging to new business. Although planned in 1729, the town on the Patapsco River, some forty miles east of Frederick, had a minor, if not insignificant, role in the life of Lord Baltimore's province. Annapolis was without question the social, political, economic, and cultural center of Maryland. Only after the Revolutionary War was the geographical potential of Baltimore realized and exploited. With an excellent harbor, its commanding position on the Chesapeake Bay, and easy access to the expanding farming areas to the west, Baltimore began to attract many businessmen. A visitor to the city in the 1780's remarked that "Philadelphia excepted, there are nowhere in the country so many merchants gathered together and ready to take up what is offered."[74] The opportunity for investment in the original Amelung enterprise was but one of the offerings, and Baltimore's merchants, from Benjamin Crockett to Charles Ghequiere, were eager to become involved. The European wars of the 1790s served as a great boon to Baltimore's economy. The increased foreign demand for American wheat aligned the considerable wheat trade of Baltimore's markets with the important shipbuilding industry that had developed on the coastal area. Baltimore shipowners profited as well from the opportunity for the re-export and carrying trade which resulted from the hostilities overseas. The expansion of the city was phenomenal at the end of the eighteenth century. Between 1790 and 1800 the population doubled, to 26,000.

As we shall show, Baltimore provided an ea-ger market for the products of both American and European glasshouses. Yet no glassworks was established within the city until 1800, when Frederick Amelung opened his factory on the south side of the Basin, at the foot of Federal Hill. The undertaking was modest in comparison with the sprawling town of New Bremen, as seen in the view of the factory included in a painting of Francis Guy in 1804 (Fig. 15). In spite of the small scope of the business, Amelung proposed on July 1, 1800, to make "all kinds of Glass Ware and Bottles."[75]

The factory apparently prospered, but Alexander Furnival, Amelung's financial backer, decided to withdraw his support within two years. When he advertised his holdings were available in August 1802, Furnival assured the public that no problems with the glassmaking had forced his action. On the contrary, he wrote that "all the difficulties connected with a new establishment of this nature, as finding out the proper clay for pots and furnaces, good sand, and other materials necessary for different kinds of glass and preparing the proper mixture of these materials . . . . having been overcome by the proprietors . . . . no expence from disappointment of that nature can occur."[76] This was no doubt due to the experience gained in Frederick County.

A Baltimore merchant of German birth named Philip R. J. Friese assumed control of the F. M. Amelung and Company Glassworks and retained Amelung as superintendent. A surviving ledger from this early period of Friese's proprietorship documents the raw materials, production, and sales of the firm, and proves that Amelung remained in Baltimore until September, 1806.[77] He then acceded to offers from Colonel James O'Hara, a glass manufacturer in Pittsburgh, and worked there for several years. In 1811 Amelung journeyed to South Jersey to investigate possibilities for glassmaking in that area, but he died before committing himself to another manufactory.[78]

Even after Amelung left Baltimore, the glassworks at Federal Hill remained something of an extension of the old Frederick works. Glassblowers who are known to have worked at New Bremen appear in the city directories of Baltimore as employees of "the glass house."

Of the actual glass made in this early period of the Baltimore industry very little is known. Window glass and bottles certainly constituted the bulk of production. Window panes were of suf-

FIG. 15. "Baltimore: the basin and Federal Hill from the brickyard," showing the glasshouse of F. M. Amelung and Co. in the center; by Francis Guy, oil on canvas, 1804. Courtesy The Peale Museum, Baltimore, Maryland.

ficient quality to be used in Robert Cary Long's masterpiece, the Union Bank, completed in 1807.[79] Quart, pint, pocket, and snuff bottles of both green and "black" glass are advertised by the works. By the late 1820's the Baltimore firm became an important producer of pictorial flasks.

The quantity of table glass that was imported into America's coastal cities, particularly Baltimore, hinders the identification of locally-blown hollow forms.[80] It is nevertheless tempting to suspect that the Baltimore glasshouse made some table glass related in style and quality to the New Bremen products. A "general assortment of hollow white glass" was advertised, and at least two independent glass cutters and engravers had shops in the city in the beginning years of the nineteenth century.[81] A group of early nineteenth-century lead and non-lead tablewares, many of them finely cut and engraved, have been found in the Baltimore area. None, however, are documented. One glass which may be a Baltimore piece is the wineglass shown in Figure 16. This non-lead object had been attributed to the New Bremen Glassmanufactory, yet it differs significantly in

FIG. 16. Wineglass engraved with an American flag and inscribed "Fair won, dearly belov'd," possibly Baltimore Glass Manufactory, ca. 1814.

chemical composition from the documented Amelung wares. Moreover, its engraved design featuring the American flag and the inscription, "Fair won, dealy belov'd," is best interpreted in a War of 1812 context, even though its form was quite out of fashion by that time. A major engagement between the British and Americans took place at Baltimore's Fort McHenry in September, 1814. When Francis Scott Key saw the American flag was still flying, he knew the battle was "fair won" and was moved to compose the "Star Spangled Banner."

V. CATALOGUE

TODAY AMELUNG'S FAME rests chiefly upon his elaborately engraved wares—the most ambitious and accomplished decorated glass made in America during the eighteenth century. They may have been of minor commercial importance in the factory's scheme of production, but their promotional value was, presumably, great. Their cost was considerable. Amelung advertised that: "glass may be had, cut with *letters, cyphers, crests, flowers,* or *devices,* agreeable to the fancy of the purchasers, from 4d. . . . to 40 a piece, besides the price of the glass."[82] His signed glasses may have been meant as advertisements to attract the attention and support of influential merchants and politicians in America and Europe. Some of the most ornate were made for friends or family, perhaps to commemorate special occasions.

Until the "Bremen" goblet was discovered in 1928 in Bremen, Germany, Amelung's contributions to the development of American glass were largely unrecognized. But when the Metropolitan Museum of Art acquired that goblet, Amelung's accomplishments attracted considerable interest. A few engraved, attributed specimens had been known before, but none were so successfully conceived and executed and none were signed.

The identity of Amelung's engraver is not known, and there is certainly no evidence that it was Amelung himself. In style, the engraver's hand is Germanic, and it is not inconceivable that he was hired away from one of the important German or Bohemian centers by Amelung, perhaps from Kassel, not far from Grünenplan,

where related engraving was done. By comparing the decoration on these glasses with that on European glass, it is evident that Amelung's engraver was well-trained and talented, though he was by no means among the most skilled Continental engravers. His compositions are frequently complex, sophisticated, and entailed the use of a number of different wheels. His depictions are, however, frequently amateurish, especially his portrayals of animals.

One must not assume that Amelung's engraver worked only at New Bremen. Indeed, he must have trained (and worked) elsewhere; if he outlived the New Bremen factory, he must have continued to engrave for others after it closed. There were many independent engravers in America engraving glassware and cutting inscriptions and other devices on stone seals. One engraver, probably not Amelung's engraver, claimed to be the first in Baltimore: "Engraving, Seal-Cutting, on Glass or Stones. Devices, Cyphers, or coats of arms elegantly cut or engraved on Glass or Stone, in a superior style, by ROBERT BURFORD, No. 10, Marsh Market. He respectfully requests citizens who may feel an inclination to encourage the first essay of this ingeinious [sic] art in this city, to call as above, and view the specimens of his abilities."[83]

The engraving on Amelung glass, is to a certain extent, repetitive. The same, or similar, flowers, birds, and scrolls are used again and again. The similarity of details on signed glasses dated between 1788 and 1792 suggests that only one "hand" was involved, even though the quality of the engraving improves considerably.

40

Glasses dated 1791 and 1792 display a new excellence, perhaps indicating a different engraver was engaged. Even so, the engraved pieces

Fig. 17. Page from *Round Hand* by George Bickham, London, n.d. Published by permission of Winterthur Museum Libaries; photo: Dwight P. Lanmon.

dated 1788 and 1789 exhibit a continuity of style with those of later date.

It is this continuity which provokes the attributions of unsigned glasses to New Bremen. Specific flowers and leaves have been noted in publications as Amelung "characteristics," but many similar ones are to be found on Continental glasses also.

The most distinctive feature of engraved Amelung glasses seems to be their inscriptions. Nearly every glass assigned to New Bremen is lettered, some with just the initials of the original owner, but many with lengthy texts. On those with longer inscriptions, the letters' close similarity is proof that the engraver was able to repeat details.

The style of lettering used on Amelung's glasses, known as "Round Hand," was used frequently in English-speaking areas during the eighteenth century. The fact that a glass has an inscription engraved in "Round Hand," how-

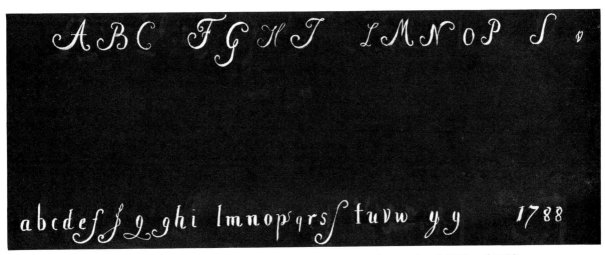

Fig. 18a. Letters engraved on documented Amelung glasses, dated 1788 and 1789.

Fig. 18b. Letters engraved on documented Amelung glasses, dated 1791 and 1792.

ever, does not mean that it was done in New Bremen. Students were taught how to write from copy books, such as that illustrated in Fig. 17. A comparison of the "Round Hand" alphabet in this book, with that assembled from a number of documented Amelung glasses (Fig. 18a, b), demonstrates how closely the artisan followed the prevailing style. He may well have used just a copy book as a guide.

The Amelung alphabets shown here are from *documented* specimens and are divided into two groups: the first is taken from four pieces dated 1788 and 1789; the second is from four dated 1791 and 1792. The specific letters illustrated are "typical" examples, although in a few cases letters occur only once. When more than one distinct form of a letter is known, both are shown.

The most obvious difference between the two alphabets is that the "later" letters are more free and their curves more fluid. Occasionally in the 1788 and 1789 glasses the letters are intricately curved: for example, the lower-case "g" and the upper-case "H" (Fig. 18a), but the curves are generally "choppy." In general, extra curves are avoided.

This is not true of glasses dated 1791 and 1792: for example, the lower-case "d" and the upper-case "A" of Fig. 18b. There the tight, thin curves are still composed of short, straight incisions, but they demonstrate control and have a less ragged outline. A few other specific differences should be noted (see below).

Similar technical development is seen in the ways in which numerals were formed. The "1788," from the Bremen goblet, and the "1792," from the Great Seal of the U.S. tumbler, illustrate the differences. On the first, the "8" is formed by "brushing" the glass against the engraving wheel, so that the number is only "abraded," not incised. The numbers in the later date are clearly incised.

In the catalogue of signed and attributed, dated and undated, Amelung glasses that follows, similarities of engraving are noted. The objects listed are the most significant of identified Amelung products. The forms do no represent the wide range suggested by fragments found at the factory site, but it has not always been possible to differentiate between cullet from outside sources and factory waste. Attributing surviving glasses which have no documented association with the factory or no identifiable decoration is equally difficult. Chemical analysis may, some day, facilitate the attribution of many more glasses to the factory.

There is one particular group of glasses that has been associated with New Bremen but evidence now suggests they were not made there. Many taper-form decanters, square-footed wineglasses, tumblers, and other table forms had been found in Maryland and attributed to the factory. They often have polished bases, cut flutes, faceted necks or stems, engraved stars, garlands of flowers, and Masonic emblems, in the neoclassical style. The specific *motifs* are not in the New Bremen vocabulary of ornament; indeed, they share no characteristics with documented Amelung glasses beyond the fact that

Letter	1788–1789	1791–1792
e	The letter is formed by two broad, vertical bars connected with thin, usually parallel slices; the curved tail is made up of short slices.	The left side is a broad line, but the loop and tail are thin.
f	Two styles are used, one elaborately curved.	No more elaborate, but they are "lighter."
g	Two styles are used.	Occurs only once; graceful.
ſ	Generally smooth and languid, frequently ending in curls at top and/or bottom; sometimes looped at top and bottom.	Smooth curves looped at top and bottom.
y	Two styles used.	Both styles continued to be used, but the curves are generally more accomplished.
A	The letter occurs only three times; the one shown is the most curvilinear.	Occurs only once, but is dramatically different from the earlier group.
M	Fluid, but the curls are tight.	Similar, but more free.

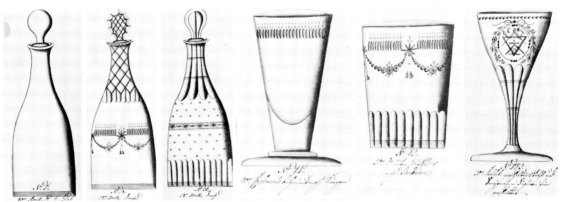

FIG. 19. Six illustrations from the *Gardiner's Island Glass Catalogues*. Published by permission of the Winterthur Museum Libraries. Photo: the author. (a) "Decanter [entirely plain, with polished stopper]," ½ pint. (b) "Decanter [cut base, scaly neck and engraved garlands]," one pint. (c) "Decanter [cut base, scalloped and grooved neck, delicate festoons and small stars]," one pint. (d) "Conical tumbler, with engraved festoons." (e) "[Beerglass], scalloped at the base and engraved garlands." (f) "Cup, grooved stem and engraved Freemason symbols."

they are of non-lead glass. Two illustrated catalogues in the library of the Henry Francis du Pont Winterthur Museum prove that *exactly* the same sorts of glasses were made in Bohemia.

The catalogues, dating from the early nineteenth century, belonged to John Gardiner of Gardiner's Island, New York. They contain colored drawings of glass table and ornamental wares, as well as lighting fixtures which could be ordered from Bohemia. Included are decanters ranging in size from one-half pint to quart, in addition to matching tumblers, "firing" or beer glasses, and stemmed drinking glasses— from liqueurs to goblets and champagnes. Six typical examples are illustrated (Fig. 19a–f).

The export of English and Irish glass to Maryland has frequently been considered by authors on American glass, but the fact that German glass was imported in great quantities has generally been overlooked.[84] By 1794, German glass was mentioned in newspaper advertisements in Baltimore nearly as often as English glass. Many merchants, like Frederick Hammer of Baltimore, specialized in German products. The inventory

of his warehouse, taken in 1818, lists more than 140,000 pieces of glass worth nearly $4,700, apparently all imported from Germany. Included were more than 85,000 tumblers, in sizes ranging from one-half gill to one-half gallon, 12,000 decanters of one-half pint to quart capacity, and 10,000 wineglasses. The decoration on these glasses was described as "flowered," "cut glass with stars, guirlands (garlands), wreaths," "gilt," and "flutes."[85] These descriptions precisely fit the illustrations in the Bohemian catalogues—and the glasses frequently found in Maryland. Hammer, moreover, was one of over two hundred merchants who are known to have sold glass in Baltimore between 1780 and 1820. It should not, therefore, be surprising that so many glasses of Continental origin have been found in Maryland.

While it cannot be stated categorically that Amelung never made such objects, it is proposed that such glass be attributed to Bohemia until a similar documented Amelung glass is found.

(1) THE "BREMEN" GOBLET

Signed and dated (1788) • Colorless, non-lead glass, slight greenish tint
Dimensions: OH. 28.5 cm; (Goblet) H. 22.0 cm, D. (bowl) 12.6 cm; (Cover) H. 7.7 cm, D. (max.) 12.5 cm
Collection of The Metropolitan Museum of Art (Rogers Fund), New York, 1928 (Acc. No. 28.52A,B)

The Bremen goblet (or *Pokal,* as it would be called in Germany) was the first signed example of Amelung's glass discovered. It was found in 1928 in Bremen, Germany, where it may have been sent by Amelung, perhaps to one of the merchants who had invested in the glassworks. Whether those investors ever received any other return on their money is not known. It is, nonetheless, a jubilant toast from Amelung to his backers.

Before other signed examples of Amelung's glass were found, there was speculation that the Bremen goblet was not made in America but was a German commemoration of the New Bremen factory. Clearly, that theory is incorrect, but it does emphasize the fact that Amelung's goblets are Germanic in form and decoration. This goblet is related to *Pokals* made in Kassel about the same time. (Grünenplan is only about seventy-five miles from Kassel, so Amelung may have been familiar with that glass, or some of his workers may have come from there.)

The bowl is engraved with the arms of the city of Bremen within a rich baroque shield, flanked by lion supporters. The design was probably derived from a printed version of the arms. The style of the engraving is consistent with that of other Amelung glasses. The details, though elaborate, are not especially crisp. The lions—amusing, with their rippling manes and rubbery legs—are caricatures of the heraldic beasts they represent. The style of lettering is also consistent with Amelung's earliest glasses: it is generally stiff and not precisely aligned; the curls on the upper-case letters are well done, but are sometimes ragged.

The stem of the goblet is formed of separate hollow knops, a flattened ball above an inverted baluster. The bowl is joined to the stem with two thin disks (mereses); the stem is expanded slightly at its joint with the domed foot.

The cover is engraved with a characteristic foliate spray. Its flange fits inside the bowl of the goblet. The cover seats on a half-round thread trailed around its side. The hollow baluster finial is applied directly to the cover, without a merese. There are rough pontil marks on the inside of the lid and the underside of the foot.

Photographs by George J. Fistrovich. Published by permission of The Metropolitan Museum of Art, New York City, New York.

FIG. 20(a) The "Bremen" goblet—overall, obverse. (b) Composite photo of engraving, obverse. *(Note: the separation of details on this and following composites is due to the curvature of the bowl).* (c) Composite photo of the engraved inscription on the reverse. (d) Photo of the engraved foliate spray on the cover.

A

B

New Bremen Glasmanufactory · 1788
North America State of Maryland

C

D

(2) THE "TOBIAS AND THE ANGEL" TUMBLER

Dated (1788) • Colorless, non-lead glass, slight gray tint
Dimensions: OH. 30.1 cm; (Tumbler) H. 21.4 cm, D. (rim) 14.7 cm; (Cover) H. 9.8 cm, D. (max.) 15.2 cm
Collection of The Corning Museum of Glass (Acc. No. 55.4.37a,b)

An incident from the Book of Tobit decorates the tumbler made in 1788 for Carolina Lucia, wife of John Frederick Amelung. As the popular story is depicted here, the angel leads Tobias, the son of Tobit, on his journey to cure his father's blindness; he will do so by using the gall of the fish he has caught, which is tucked precariously under his arm. A dog playfully bounds ahead of the two. The source of the design may have been a print, but the depiction may be an original composition. Certainly, this scene and the inscription arching above, "Happy is he who is blessed with Virtuous Children . . . ," indicate that Amelung considered his life a happy one. The occasion for the gift is not known.

The central scene is framed by a delicate arrangement of scrolls and simple flowers. The execution of the figures is less satisfactory; the engraver was obviously not at ease with the human anatomy. The angel is too long-waisted, and Tobit's son's left leg looks out of joint. Their heads are also somewhat carelessly engraved.

The cover is engraved with an elaborate double foliate scroll.

The tumbler (it is *not* a "flip" glass—that is a twentieth-century term) is of characteristic tapered form with thick base, but the sides are gently waisted at the center and slightly incurved at the top. The domed cover rests on a trailed ring; the hollow-baluster finial is applied. There are rough pontil marks on the underside of the base of the tumbler and inside the cover.

Photographs by Raymond F. Errett; composite by George F. Fistrovich. Published by permission of The Corning Museum of Glass, Corning, New York.

C

FIG. 21(a) The "Tobias and the Angel" Tumbler—overall, obverse. (b) Composite photo of the engraving, obverse. (c) Photo of the engraved foliate spray on the cover.

A

B

(3) THE "GHEQUIERE" TUMBLER

Signed and dated (June 20, 1788) • Colorless, non-lead glass, gray tint in cover and gray-green tint in tumbler.
Dimensions: OH. 31.2 cm; (Tumbler) H. 20.6 cm, D. (rim) 15.3 cm; (Cover) H. 11.9 cm, D. (max.) 16.4 cm
Collection of the Henry Francis du Pont Winterthur Museum, Winterthur, Delaware (Acc. No. 59.3009a,b); Ex coll. Dr.
Charles G. Fenwick, Baltimore, Maryland (great-grandson of original owner)

This tumbler was made for Charles Ghequiere (d. 1818 or 1819), merchant and president of the Baltimore Fire Insurance Company. It was the second signed specimen to be brought to the attention of students of American glass and was first publicly exhibited at The Baltimore Museum of Art about 1934.

Ghequiere was an importer who sold European glass, among other items. The tumbler may have been presented by Amelung to Ghequiere, along with other examples of his wares, to induce him to sell his glass. We do not know if Ghequiere did, because he never advertised it. Indeed, throughout Amelung's period of operation, he advertised Bohemian window glass. Ghequiere did enter into some business transactions with Amelung because by May 23, 1795, he and two other mercantile firms forced Amelung and Labes to mortgage some land holdings to cover their debts. A year later Ghequiere was listed among the creditors of the firm of Amelung and Labes.[86] Ghequiere died in 1818 or 1819. Neither his will nor the inventory of his estate is itemized, and there is no known contemporary reference to the tumbler.

The engraving on this glass is clean and fresh. Curving, crossed palm (?) fronds and a thorny branch with flowers (rose?) enclose the name of the recipient, "Charles Ghequiere," which is off-center. A finely detailed bird, holding a branch in its beak, stands above a flower, probably a "pink," at the intersection of the two sprays. The glass is further inscribed "Floreat Commercium" ("May commerce flourish") above an elaborate crown and a stylized floral spray.

The reverse bears the name of the factory and the date "20^{the} of June 1788." The significance of the date is not known. The lettering on this side is more crude than on the obverse, but the forms of the letters are consistent. Those on the back, however, are noticeably less graceful and the curls are ragged. "Glasmanufactory" is misspelled, and an error is made on the date, "20^{the}."

When the piece was first exhibited, the remains of gilding were noted in the engraving.[87] Now the only indication that it was gilded is a dark, gummy deposit on parts of the engraving, probably the remains of a fixative which was used to affix the gold leaf. Amelung's engraved glasses may have been gilded frequently, but there is no other evidence to suggest that gilding was commonly done.

A foliate scroll is engraved on the cover.

The tumbler is of the typical form with solid base, slightly waisted sides, and gently incurved rim. The cover is flared and domed and rests on the customary trailed ring. The hollow baluster finial is applied. There are rough pontil marks on the underside of the base and inside the cover.

Photographs by George J. Fistrovich. Published by permission of The Henry Francis du Pont Winterthur Museum, Winterthur, Delaware.

FIG. 22(a) The "Ghequiere" Tumbler—overall, obverse. (b) Composite photo of the engraving, obverse. (c) Composite photo of the inscription, reverse. (d) Photo of the engraved foliate spray on the cover.

A

B

C

D

(4) THE "J.F.C.H." TUMBLER

Dated (1788) • Colorless, non-lead glass, faint gray tint
Dimensions: H. 9.3 cm, D. (rim) 7.7 cm
Collection of The Henry Francis du Pont Winterthur Museum, Winterthur, Delaware (Acc. No. 58.9); Ex coll. Dr. Ira
Hostetter, Lancaster, Pennsylvania; Miss Katharine Woodward, Middleburg, Virginia

The attribution of this small tumbler to the Amelung factory has been based on the similarity of its engraved decoration to that on documented glasses. The style of its lettering is consistent with other specimens dated 1788, although the "H" is different. The identity of the owner (or owners, if the initials should be read as "J.F." and "C.H.") is not known. The date, itself, is identical to those on the B. Johnson case bottles (cat. no. 5). The wreath is not precisely paralleled, but is of a similar character to many. The use of double dashes (=) instead of periods is paralleled on the Tobias and the Angel tumbler (cat. no. 2) and on the B. Johnson case bottles.

The chemical composition of the glass is also similar to documented glasses.

The tumbler has a rough pontil mark on the base.

Photographs by George J. Fistrovich. Published by permission of The Henry Francis du Pont Winterthur Museum, Winterthur, Delaware.

Fig. 23(a) The "J.F.C.H." Tumbler—overall, obverse. (b) Composite photo of the engraving, obverse.

A

B

(5) The "B. JOHNSON" CASE BOTTLES (originally nine)

Dated (1788) • Colorless, non-glass, with various tints, from gray to greenish. Mold-blown, "half-post"
Dimensions (Corning example): H. 18.2 cm, W. 8.9 cm, D. 8.9 cm
Collections: 1. Museum of Fine Arts Boston, H. E. Bolles Fund (Acc. No. 1973.552. Ex. coll. (see Winterthur Museum);
2 and 3. Mr. James C. Brand, Morrilton, Arkansas (two bottles and case). Ex coll. Mrs. Bradley T. Johnson,
Charlottesville, Virginia; 4. The Corning Museum of Glass (Acc. No. 73.4.138). Ex coll. (see Winterthur Museum); 5.
Senator Charles McC. Mathias (on loan to Smithsonian Institution, No. 317890). Ex coll. Baker Johnson, to Catherine
Johnson Ross (his daughter), to Caroline Ross Rogers, to Charles Ross Rogers; Dr. William Crawford Johnson, to Miss
Emily Johnson (his daughter); 6. Colonel Richard P. Ross (on loan to The Maryland Historical Society, Baltimore, No.
DEP 347); 7. The Smithsonian Institution (Acc. No. 62.181). Ex coll (see Winterthur Museum); 8. The Henry Francis du
Pont Winterthur Museum, Winterthur, Delaware (Acc. No. 73.357). Ex coll. Mrs. Bradley T. Johnson, Charlottesville,
Virginia; Mr. James C. Brand, Morrilton, Arkansas, probably ex coll of Mrs. Alfred S. Dashiell (McKearin, American
Glass, Plate 40, No. 2)

Nine square "case" bottles and a walnut chest to hold them were made in 1788 for Colonel Baker Johnson (1747–1811) of Frederick, Maryland. He was the brother of Maryland's first governor, to whom Amelung brought a letter of introduction. As a lawyer, landowner, and businessman, Baker Johnson was, in his own right, a prominent and influential figure of Frederick County. Together with his brothers, Johnson established the Catoctin iron works, paper mills, and had an interest in glassmaking as well.

Fitted into sturdy wood cases, such bottles would have been used to store a variety of liquors, and they could be transported safely without additional packing. They must have been relatively common items at the end of the eighteenth century, for they are frequently advertised for sale. Many were imported from Bohemia. Some were fitted into elaborately inlaid, veneered cases, and in addition to bottles, had a variety of drinking glasses, plates, and funnels. Many were plain, but some were elaborately decorated with gilt flowers. No inventory of Baker's estate was taken, but his brother, Thomas, owned a bottle case worth $1. "2 Cases White Bottles," valued at £1, appear in a Frederick inventory of 1787.[88]

These are the only case bottles which have been attributed to the Amelung factory. A fragment of a similar one (A.S. 125A) was found on the factory site, but it is not known if it was actually made there. These bottles were formed in square molds and were blown by the "half-post" method—the second gather ends on the shoulder. The necks were not ground for stoppers, so they must have been closed with corks.

The bottles match and, because there are exactly enough known to fill the case, it seems likely that we are dealing with a single set which survives in its entirety, not the remains of two or more sets. Each bottle is engraved "B. Johnson/1788" (one is misspelled "Johnsen") within a circle suspended by a ribbon from a

wreath of leaves. Two birds are perched on top of the wreath, at either side of a melon-ribbed ball.

It has been suggested that these bottles were not made at New Bremen but at the Johnson's own Etna glassworks. There is no evidence to support such an attribution. Since Thomas Johnson claimed in 1793 that only one nine-month blast had been finished, the glassworks was presumably not in operation in 1788 and there is no reason to doubt that the bottles were actually made then.[89]

The engraving on these bottles is similar in many details to that found on documented Amelung glass. The "88" of the date was lightly abraded onto the surface, just as was done on all of the other pieces dated "1788" included in this catalogue. The birds are also similar to the ones on the Ghequiere (cat. no. 3) and the Great Seal of the U.S. (cat. no. 9) tumblers. The rope-like strands of leaves are similar in construction to shorter sprigs found on the Repold tumbler (cat. no. 29) and the Repold/Amelung goblet (cat. no. 10), with a rough-ground center and leaves engraved over that (there is no central rib). The engraver's habit of using a double dash (=) instead of a period is paralleled on the Tobias and the Angel tumbler (cat. no. 2) and others. Dissimilar, however, are the forms of the letters of the name; they are cruder and more angular.

Four of the bottles have been analyzed; their chemical compositions tentatively are thought to be different from the "standard" Amelung composition for colorless glass. This is far from conclusive evidence that the bottles were not made at Amelung's factory, but it does suggest that that possibility should not be overlooked. Until glass made at other Frederick County factories and fragments from the other Amelung sites have been analyzed, a different attribution, at present, is not warranted.

Photographs by George J. Fistrovich. Published by permission of The Henry Francis du Pont Winterthur Museum, Winterthur, Delaware. Photograph of case and bottles published by permission of Mr. James C. *Brand, Morrilton, Arkansas, The Museum of Fine Arts, Boston, Massachusetts, and The Corning Museum of Glass, Corning, New York.*

B

A

C

FIG. 24(a) The "B. Johnson" Case Bottles—four bottles and the original walnut case, with spaces for nine bottles. (b) Overall photo. (c) Detail of engraved decoration, obverse.

(6) THE "BOSTON TUMBLER"

Signed and dated (January 23, 1789) • Colorless, non-lead glass, pale gray tint
Dimensions: H. 14.6 cm, D. (rim) 12.0 cm
Collection of Yale University Art Gallery (Garvan Collection), New Haven, Connecticut (Acc. No.
1935.258); Ex coll. Mrs. E. A. Peirce, Waltham, Massachusetts (great-great-granddaughter of the first owner)

Family tradition has traced the history of this tumbler to John Phillips (1770–1823), elected first mayor of the city of Boston in 1822. It was his father-in-law, Thomas Walley (d. 1806), who, as a partner of the Boston Crown Glass Company, probably received the tumbler from Amelung. William Phillips, John's cousin, was chairman of the company.

Although there had been earlier attempts at glassmaking in the Boston area, the Boston Crown Glass Company, founded in 1787, was the first successful factory. Glass may not have actually been produced, however, until 1793. That the Boston company at least responded with a thank-you if not a gift in kind is indicated by an entry in their Receipt Book, dated October 1, 1789: "Receiv'd of John Andrews Treasurer to the Glass Company One pound ten shillings Ling [Sterling] for Cash pd Mr. Deakins of Georgetown for Expence he was at in sending an Express to Mr Amelung at the Town of Fredericks, Maryland. [signed] Gustavus Fellowes" [Receipt Book, Boston Crown Glass Company,

original at Boston Atheneum; microfilm copy at Winterthur Museum 297].

The lettering on this glass is unusually competent for its date. Several letters are curvilinear as those found on glasses dated after 1791, but the forms of certain letters, like the "d" and "e," place the engraving squarely within the earlier group. The "2" is identical to that on the Ghequiere tumbler (cat. no. 3), and the "8" is abraded in the same way as on all the classes dated "1788."

The foliate branch and scrolls on the observe are typical and are crisply executed, but they are not well balanced. The "pink" at the center is similar to the one on the Ghequiere tumbler. The engraved border at the rim, a wide band with serrations below, is also seen on the Great Seal of the U.S. tumbler. The rough-ground pontil mark also does not appear on any other Amelung glass.

Photographs by George J. Fistrovich. Published by permission of Yale University Art Gallery (Garvan Collection), New Haven, Connecticut.

Fig. 25(a) The "Boston" Tumbler—overall, obverse. (b) Composite photo of the engraving and inscription, obverse. (c) Composite photo of the engraved inscription, reverse.

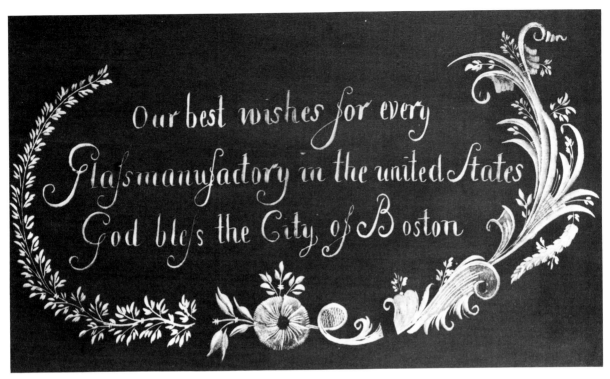

B

Our best wishes for every Glassmanufactory in the united States God bless the City of Boston

C

Made at the Glassmanufactory New Bremen in Maryland the 23 Jan. 1789 by John Fr: Amelung & Comp:

(7) THE "MIFFLIN" GOBLET

Signed and dated (1791) • Colorless, non-lead glass, purple tint
Dimensions: OH. 25.6 cm, D. (rim) 14.1 cm
Collection of the Metropolitan Museum of Art (Rogers Fund), New York, 1937 (Acc. No. 37.101)

When Amelung came to America, he carried a letter of introduction to Thomas Mifflin (1744–1800), President of the Continental Congress. In 1791, when Mifflin became the Governor of Pennsylvania, Amelung presented him a capacious goblet engraved with the Arms of the State. The gift was undoubtedly made to attract Mifflin's influential favor. Only the year before, one of Amelung's glasshouses had burned, sales were slow, and Congress had rebuffed his attempt to gain governmental financing.

The fact that the goblet has survived, despite the loss of its foot, is proof that it was valued by Mifflin and his descendants. Someone turned a new walnut foot for the goblet, probably early in the nineteenth century. It is attached to the stem with plaster-of-Paris. The bottom of the plaster plug is inscribed "Presented/to Gov:/Mifflin/1791/Jany. 1."

The Arms of Pennsylvania engraved on the bowl were copied from the version introduced in 1790. In that year the rococo shield was introduced, further proof that Amelung's rococo-style engraving was popular in America long after it had been supplanted by the neoclassical style in Europe. This particular representation of the Arms was used until 1805, at which time the horses were deprived of their trappings and the stalks of Indian corn were removed.

The representation of the Arms on the bowl of the goblet is reasonably faithful to the printed version from which it was probably taken (d). Many of the alterations would have been necessitated by the shape of the bowl. There may, of course, be a printed version which is even closer than the one illustrated here.

In form, the goblet is similar to all the others associated with Amelung, and it is by far the largest. It has a massive, hollow, inverted baluster stem—as shown by the x-ray photograph (e). It originally had a glass foot which was probably domed, and must also have had a cover, which has since been lost.

The lettering on the reverse is typical of glasses dated between 1791 and 1793. The curls of the letters demonstrate the engraver's mastery of tight curves.

Photographs by George J. Fistrovich; x-ray photo by The Metropolitan Museum of Art. Published by permission of The Metropolitan Museum of Art, New York City, New York.

A

Fig. 26(a) The "Mifflin" Goblet—overall, obverse.

B

C

FIG. 26(b) Composite photo of the engraving, obverse. (c) Composite photo of the engraved inscription, reverse. (d) The Arms of Pennsylvania, as used from 1790 to 1805. From James Evelyn Pilcher, *The Seal and Arms of Pennsylvania*, Harrisburg, 1902. (e) X-ray photograph of the stem, showing the baluster knop; the foot is missing. (f) Inscribed plaster plug on the underside of the wood foot.

D

E

F

(8) THE "GUEST" TUMBLER

Signed and dated (1791) • Colorless, non-lead glass, tumbler of dark greenish-gray tint; cover of pale greenish tint
Dimensions: OH. 28.7 cm; (Tumbler) H. 21.7 cm, D. (rim) 15.7 cm; (Cover) H. 8.0 cm, D (max.) 15.9 cm
Collection of The Henry Francis du Pont Winterthur Museum, Winterthur, Delaware (Acc. No. 69.139a,b)
Ex coll. Mr. and Mrs. Robert A. Metz, Wynmor, Chestnut Hill, Pennsylvania (collateral descendants
of the original owner, John Guest)

When the goblet bearing the Arms of Pennsylvania was made for Governor Thomas Mifflin (cat. no. 7), Amelung may have had this covered tumbler prepared for the Philadelphia merchant, John Guest (1768–1817). Born in Burlington, New Jersey, Guest became the owner of a far-flung mercantile empire. By the early nineteenth century, he had established branches in Philadelphia, Baltimore, New York City, Charleston, Pittsburgh, and London. No wonder, then, that Amelung was anxious to secure his support. At the present time, there is no evidence that Guest ever sold Amelung's glass.

The decoration on the Mifflin and Guest glasses is sufficiently close to suggest that they were done simultaneously. The minor differences between them are probably due to the requirements of their forms, for in both cases they handsomely fill the spaces available. The representation of the Arms of Pennsylvania is nearly identical to that on the Mifflin goblet.

There are a few more flowers on the tumbler, and the shield has rococo embellishments; otherwise, the differences are unimportant. In one case, a flower at the bottom right masks a particularly large bubble; it is balanced by a similar flower at the left. The lettering of the inscription is also similar; the date differs slightly in that the tail of the "9" does not intersect the "7."

The cover does not fit well. Its color is also slightly different from the base, so it may actually have been made for another tumbler. There is no reason to doubt that it was made at New Bremen. The hollow baluster finial is characteristic, as is the customary trailed ring. It is engraved with a balanced floral spray. There are rough pontil marks on the inside of the cover and on the base of the tumbler.

Photographs by George J. Fistrovich. Published by permission of The Henry Francis du Pont Winterthur Museum, Winterthur, Delaware.

B

FIG. 27(a) The "Guest" Tumbler—overall, obverse. (b) Composite photo of the engraving, obverse. (c) Composite photo of the engraved inscription, reverse. (d) Photo of the engraved foliate spray on the cover.

A

VIRTUE *LIBERTY* *AND* *INDEPENDENCE*

New Bremen Glassmanufactory.
1791

C

D

(9) THE "GREAT SEAL OF THE U.S." TUMBLER

Signed and dated (1792) • Colorless, non-lead glass, strong grayish-tan tint
Dimensions: H. 20.7 cm, D. (rim) 15.3 cm
Collection of Mr. and Mrs. George M. Kaufman, Norfolk, Virginia; ex coll. Mr. and Mrs. Albert J. Henry, Newport,
Rhode Island

It is unfortunate that we do not know for whom this, the most resplendently nationalistic of all of Amelung's known glasses, was made. Its history before World War II has been lost. Because of its engraved subject, it is reasonable to suppose that it was made for a person of national prominence.

The Great Seal was adopted by the Federal Government and was used in 1789. The Seal was used in numerous ways on official government documents and a variety of coins. The representation on this tumbler was copied from such a source, but the specific one has not been identified. Interestingly, the version on the tumbler is the reverse of the official Seal. Amelung's engraver has also taken certain liberties with the design: there are six arrows instead of thirteen, the olive branch looks more like a palm frond,

and the Seal is framed with rococo scrolls. The latter relates the engraving to other Amelung glasses.

The lettering of the inscription is beautifully fluid and controlled. For grace and thinness of line, these letters are the high-point of engraving on Amelung's known glasses. As in the Mifflin goblet (cat. no. 7), the tail of the "9" intersects the "7" in the date.

The tumbler is said to have had a cover similar to the one on the Tobias and the Angel tumbler (cat. no. 2). Unfortunately, it was broken and thrown away many years ago.

There is a rough pontil mark on the base.

Photograph by Raymond F. Errett; composites by George J. Fistrovich. Published by permission of Mr. and Mrs. George M. Kaufman.

A

FIG. 28(a) The "Great Seal of the U.S." Tumbler—overall, obverse. (b) Composite photo of the engraving, obverse. (c) Composite photo of the inscription, reverse.

B

C

(10) THE "REPOLD/AMELUNG" GOBLET

Dated (October 16, 1792) • Colorless, non-lead glass, light gray tint
Dimensions: H. 17.6 cm, D. (bowl) 10.0 cm
Collection of The Corning Museum of Glass (Acc. No. 50.4.49); Ex coll. Miss Margaret B. Waesche,
Washington, D.C. (a Repold descendant)

This goblet was apparently given to Metha (or Metta) Repold (d. 1826) by Carolina Amelung on October 16, 1792 ("d. [donatio?] 16 Octo[ber] 1792"). George Repold (d. 1811), Metha's husband, was an influential merchant with whom Amelung dealt in Baltimore.

Five glasses which belonged to the Repolds have been attributed to the Amelung factory: this goblet, the G.M.R. tumbler (cat. no. 29) and three G.R. wineglasses (cat. no. 22). When George Repold died, the inventory of his household goods included,

". . . 1 doz. decanters	$6.
1½ doz. half pint tumblers	1.12½
1 d°. d°.	1.50
3 doz. wine glasses	3.00
2 goblets 3	6.-
1 doz. Galley [jelly?] glasses	1.- "90

This goblet may have been one of the two valued at $3.00 each.

Also noted in the probate record are debts due his estate from Frederick Amelung, Amelung and Labes, Labes and Co. and, even John von Lengerke of Bremen—one of Amelung's backers. In 1795, Repold forced Labes to mortgage some of his properties to guarantee his debt to Repold's firm[91] along with Ration and Konecke and Charles Ghequiere.

The engraved decoration on this goblet is unusual in that two different cartouches are used.

The side inscribed "Metha Repold" is richly ornamented with bold scrolls and a corpulent cornucopia, almost baroque in feeling. The inscription on the opposite side, on the other hand, is framed with delicate, graceful, foliate sprays. The foliate scrolls above the inscriptions are related in form, but there is a difference in handling.

The lettering, on the other hand, is consistent on both sides and is delicate and well-executed. The "A" in "Amelung" is unusual and, indeed, duplicated only on the goblet made for John Frederick Amelung. The "R" in "Repold" is also unusual. The date line is less competent and is choppy, especially the abbreviation "Octo." and the "2" in "1792." The cramped placement of the line suggests that it may have been added as an afterthought, if not at a later date. The former is the more likely, or is just another example of the engraver's occasional inability to plan inscriptions, the most obvious example of which is the Ghequiere tumbler (cat. no. 3). The style of lettering of both names and date is typical of glasses dated between 1791 and 1793.

The bowl is broken and repaired. At one time metal staples held the pieces together.

There is a rough pontil mark on the underside of the foot.

Photograph by Raymond F. Errett; composites by George J. Fistrovich. Published by permission of The Corning Museum of Glass, Corning, New York.

FIG. 29(a) The "Repold/Amelung" Goblet—overall, obverse. (b) Composite photo of engraving, obverse. (c) Composite photo of engraved decoration, reverse.

A

C

B

(11) THE "MAUERHOFF" GOBLET

Signed and dated (1792) • Colorless, non-lead glass, strong grayish-tan tint
Dimensions: H. 20.1 cm, D. (bowl) 10.9 cm
Collection of The Toledo Museum of Art (Acc. No. 61.2); Ex coll. F. Bodenheim, Amsterdam

The identity of "G. F. Mauerhoff" has so far eluded researchers. Because the glass was found in Europe, Mauerhoff may have been European, perhaps one of Amerlung's backers, merchants, or friends. The name does not appear in any of the factory records which have survived, and it has not yet been noted in American newspapers.

The detailed geographic inscription on this glass also suggests that its owner was not thought to be conversant with American geography and the location of New Bremen. While this does not necessarily mean that Mauerhoff lived in Europe, it is interesting to note that only one other glass was as specific—the Bremen goblet, which was made for Amelung's Bremen merchants.

The style of engraving is typical of that found on Amelung glasses dated between 1791 and 1793. The elaborate scrolled frame is heavily, but crisply, executed. Unusual is the extensive use of polished engraving: the banded orb, at the top right, the terminals of the uppercase letters, and throughout the scrollwork. These polished areas give the engraving a scintillating lightness. The style of lettering is also paralleled on other Amelung's glasses, but the "2" is angular and crude in comparison with the other letters. It is duplicated, however, on the Ghequiere (cat. no. 3) and Boston tumblers (cat. no. 6). The bird, atop the scroll at the left, is also found on other glasses, as are the fruits and flowers.

Photographs by George J. Fistovich. Published by permission of The Toledo Museum of Art, Toledo, Ohio

C

Fig. 30(a) The "Mauerhoff" Goblet—overall, obverse. (b) Composite photo of engraving, obverse (c) Composite photo of inscription, reverse.

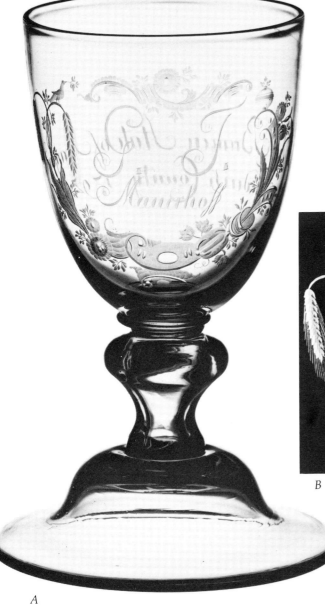

A

B

(12) THE "STENGER" FLASK

Dated (1792) • Colorless, non-lead glass, dark gray-green tint
Dimensions: H. 17.1 cm, W. 10.2 cm, D. 7.2 cm
Collection of The Corning Museum of Glass (Acc. No. 55.4.277)

Liquor flasks were known as pocket bottles in the eighteenth century. Appraisers of one Frederick County estate recorded "one pocket Pottle" in a household inventory of 1789.[92] This flask, the only one bearing engraved decoration which relates closely to documented Amelung glasses, was presumably made for Francis Stenger (or Stanger). When discovered, it was in the possession of descendants of Francis Stanger who also had a *fraktur* marriage certificate, dated March 11, 1803, for Francis Stanger and Elizabeth L. Campbell (collection of The Henry Ford Museum).[93] Six members of the Stanger family came to America in 1768 to make glass for Caspar Wister. In the nineteenth century several Frederick Stangers are recorded as glassblowers: one of them worked in Baltimore in 1810. Francis's association with the American glass industry has not been determined.

Like the Repold/Amelung goblet, this flask is engraved with two enframement styles: one is composed of light, airy, rococo, foliate sprays; the other is a circular medallion formed by two thin, willow-like sprays of leaves with simple, four-petalled flowers at top and bottom. The lettering of the name is of the typical style; the "2" in the date is angular, as has already been observed on the Ghequiere and Boston tumblers

and the Mauerhoff goblet. The foliate scrolls on the obverse are similar in character to those on the "C. Amelung" side of the Repold/Amelung goblet. The familiar "pink," found on many other dated glasses, is again placed at the intersection of the sprays.

The reverse side is engraved with a bottle, plow, trowel and square, within the thin foliate wreath. The interpretation of these symbols is not clear, but Helen McKearin has logically suggested that, "The emblems may have been intended to indicate Stanger's occupation, place of residence, and fraternity—the bottle for glassmaker, the plow for New Jersey, as one appears in the state's coat of arms, the trowel and square for a Free Mason."[94] The wreath is not duplicated on any other signed or dated specimens, but it is related to the wreath on the J.F.C.H. tumbler (cat. no. 4). It is paralleled on several glasses attributed to New Bremen.

Flasks of similar form and engraved decoration are found in Germany.[95]

The neck of this flask is ground for a stopper. There is a rough pontil mark on the base.

Photographs by Raymond F. Errett. Published by permission of The Corning Museum of Glass, Corning, New York.

FIG. 31(a) The "Stenger" Flask—overall, obverse. (b) Overall, reverse.

A

B

(13) THE "TRISLER" GOBLETS

Dated (1793) • Colorless, non-lead glass, (A) pale gray-green tint, (B) pale purplish tint
Dimensions: (A) H. 22.3 cm, D. (bowl) 12.5 cm; (B) H. 21.6 cm, D. (bowl) 12.0 cm
Collection of The Corning Museum of Glass (Acc. No. 55.4.34A,B); Ex coll. Dr. Grace Thomas, Frederick, Maryland,
from Trisler descendants in Wytheville, Virginia

This pair of goblets belonged to George Trisler (1768–1845), a native of Frederick-Town. Trained as a printer by Mathias Bartgis, Frederick's first printer, Trisler edited a Winchester, Virginia newspaper for a number of years. He then entered the firm of Baltimore merchant Henry Schroeder, an importer of German and Irish goods and son-in-law of George Jacob Schley (no. 18). It was probably after his marriage in 1794 that Trisler returned to Frederick and opened a shop. The significance of the date 1793 is not known.

The Trisler goblets are the latest dated pieces which are confidently attributed to the New Bremen factory. In them, one can witness that, when necessary, the engraver was able to repeat complicated arrangements of foliate sprays. There are, to be sure, differences in minor details, like the number of leaves and in the ways some leaves curl, but in general they are the same. The only glaring difference occurs in the use of two different forms of "s" in the name "Trisler," but this inconsistency has been noted on other Amelung glasses.

The overall character of these delicate sprays is the same as the framing of "C. Amelung" on the Repold/Amelung goblet (cat. no. 10). The incorporation of the date within a circle at the intersection of the foliate sprays is successful, and one wonders why it was not used again.

It is surprising that the feet on these goblets are so different: one is boldly domed, the other conical. The difference must not have been important to Trisler for a closer match could, presumably, have been made before they were engraved. (The straight conical foot occurs on no other documented goblet, nor on any whose attribution to New Bremen is generally accepted.) The stems also differ slightly, one being more bulbous than the other.

Nevertheless, there is no overriding factor that suggests that they were made at different times. Analysis of the glass (discussed elsewhere) shows that they are chemically identical.

Both goblets originally had covers; but one was broken and the other was lost.[96]

There are rough pontil marks on the feet of both goblets.

Photographs by Raymond F. Errett; composites by George J. Fistrovich. Published by permission of The Corning Museum of Glass, Corning, New York.

FIG. 32(a) The "Trisler" Goblets—overall, obverse. (b) Composite photo of engraving, obverse. (c) (another)—overall, obverse. (d) Composite photo of engraved decoration, obverse.

A

B

C

D

(14) THE "J. AMELUNG" GOBLET

Probably 1791–1793, possibly 1792 • Colorless, non-lead glass, faint gray tint
Dimensions: H. 17.0 cm, D. (bowl) 10.1 cm
Collection of Mrs. Graham John Barbey, Astoria, Oregon, a direct descendant of Amelung's oldest daughter, Frederica (on
loan to The Maryland Historical Society, No. DEP. 337); Ex coll. Frederica Amelung Sommerkamp, to her daughter
Amelia Sommerkamp Bredemeyer, to her daughter Helena Bredemeyer Patterson, to her daughter Ethel Patterson
McCallum, to her sister's daughter Ethel Bailey Weddell, to her daughter Ann Murray Barbey

This goblet made for John Frederick Amelung is, befittingly, the most elaborately engraved. The scrollwork surrounding his name surpasses that on all the other known glasses in its richness of detail. It is, nonetheless, characteristic. Compare it, for example, with the engraving on the Repold/Amelung goblet (cat. no. 10). The individual elements in the framing of the name "Metha Repold" are similar, even though the overall effect is not as crisp. Likewise, the scrolls above the names on these two glasses are closely related but inverted.

The lettering on both sides of this goblet is consistent with glasses dated between 1791 and 1793, although the "earlier" forms of the "e" and "d" are used alongside the "later" ones. Perhaps significantly, the elaborate "A" is duplicated only on the Repold/Amelung goblet. The tiny floral sprig on the "J" is a delightful ornament, but it is unparalleled on other glasses. The general quality of the lettering is so close to the later group that a date consistent with that group is proposed for this glass; it may have been made at the same time as the Repold/Amelung goblet.

The lengthy inscription on the reverse is said to be the Amelung family motto. It has been translated to read: "Seek Virtue and when you find Her leave everything else to Providence."[97]

There is a rough pontil mark underneath the foot.

Photograph by Raymond F. Errett; composite by George F. Fistrovich. Published by permission of Mrs. Graham John Barbey.

FIG. 33(a) The "J. Amelung" goblet—overall, obverse. (b) Composite photo of engraving, obverse. (c) Composite photo of engraved inscription, reverse.

A

B

Suche Jugend und wann du die findest, so überlasse alles übrige der Vorsehung.

C

(15) THE "C.G.C." GOBLET

Ca. 1785–1795 • Colorless, non-lead glass, faint gray tint
Dimensions: H. 21.1 cm, D. (bowl) 11.7 cm
Collection of the New Orleans Museum of Art (Acc. No. 418); Ex coll. Mr. Melvin P. Billups, New York City

In form and decoration this goblet, made for "C.G.C." (who has not been identified), relates closely to several dated or inscribed New Bremen glasses. The airy, foliate frame is closest to one on the Repold/Amelung goblet (cat. no. 10), but this one is simpler. The spray above the initials is suprisingly sketchy.

Because the letters on this glass are not among those which change dramatically from the ear-lier group to the later, it is not possible to date this glass accurately. Their workman-like quality, however, does suggest that it may date from the later period.

Photograph by Raymond F. Errett (The bowl has been broken since photography); composite by George J. Fistrovich. Published by permission of the New Orleans Museum of Art, New Orleans, Lousiana.

B

FIG. 34(a) The "C.G.C." Goblet—overall, obverse. (b) Composite photo of engraving, obverse.

A

(16) THE "KÖNIG" GOBLET

Ca. 1785–1795 • Colorless, non-lead glass, strong gray tint
Dimensions: H. 19.8 cm, D. (bowl) 10.6 cm
Collection of The Maryland Historical Society, Baltimore, Maryland (Acc. No. 51.125.1); Ex coll. Mrs. E. H. Morse,
Baltimore (great-great-granddaughter of August König)

August König (d. 1801) was a wealthy Baltimore merchant of German extraction. In his store he sold everything from a child's circus on wheels to harpsichord strings, and carried a large stock of glass: seed glasses, burning glasses, show glasses, and toilet glasses. A 1792 newspaper advertisement proves that he imported, "direct from manufactories," colorless and green glass "Philas."[98]

The engraving on this glass is confident and clean, but it lacks the control in some of the tight curls, as seen on the 1791–1793 glasses. The "A"

is fluid and is similar to that on the Boston tumbler (cat. no. 6). The style of the foliate sprays is not particularly indicative of a date; they are related to those on the Ghequiere tumbler (cat. no. 3) and the Repold/Amelung (cat. no. 10) and Marshall goblets (cat. no. 17). The familiar "pink" is seen at the intersection of the foliate sprays.

Photographs by George J. Fistrovich. Published by permission of The Maryland Historical Society, Baltimore, Maryland.

B

FIG. 35(a) The "König" Goblet—overall, obverse. (b) Composite photo of engraving, obverse.

A

(17) THE "MARSHALL" GOBLET

Ca. 1792 • Colorless, non-lead glass, the goblet with grayish-tan tint; the cover of a paler, grayish tint
Dimensions: OH. 27.3 cm; (Goblet) H. 19.9 cm, D. (bowl) 10.6 cm; (Cover) H. 8.2 cm, D. (max.) 11.0 cm
Collection of the Wachovia Historical Society, Winston-Salem, North Carolina (Acc. No. G-105 and C-173)

Frederic William Marshall (1721-1802) was a guiding figure of the Moravian settlements in America. A native of Stolpen, Germany, Marshall came to Pennsylvania in 1761 to supervise the financial affairs of the Moravians there. Two years later the Directorial Conference of the Unity of Brethren in Europe appointed Marshall agent for the Unity in North Carolina and Oeconomus of Wachovia, the 100,000-acre tract the Moravians owned in that colony. Because of his role in the planning and construction of the town of Salem in Wachovia, Marshall was known as the "Father of Salem." During the Revolutionary period, Marshall was responsible for safeguarding the property of the Moravians.

The extensive records of the North Carolina Brethren provide a detailed picture of Marshall's activities. During the period when Amelung's glassworks was in operation, Marshall did not travel into Maryland. The goblet was almost certainly brought to him as a gift by his daughter, Anna Dorothea (b. 1754), who came "after a safe and quick trip from Pennsylvania" to visit her parents, arriving in Salem on June 17, 1792.[99]

A date of ca. 1792 for this goblet is consistent with the details of engraving. The lettering is fluid and the curls are clean. The "F" and "M" are graceful and are similar to those on the Mauerhoff goblet (cat. no. 11). The "ll" seems first to have been lightly outlined, then filled in with a broader wheel—the only indication of such an approach on any of Amelung's glasses.

The foliate scrolls relate to those on several glasses, including the König goblet (cat. no. 16). The bird and the familiar "pink" have been noted on many glasses. The bird on the Mauerhoff goblet and Ghequiere tumbler (cat. no. 3) are closely related, and on the latter, it perches atop a similar "pink."

The cover is of typical form, with a hollow baluster finial and trailed ring. It has an engraved stiff foliate spray but it is related to the spray on the cover of the Guest tumbler (cat. no. 8). The lid is, however, chemically different from the goblet, so it may not have been made or engraved at the same time.

The bowl of the goblet is unusually deep; otherwise the form is typical. There are rough pontil marks underneath the foot and inside the cover.

Photographs by George J. Fistrovich. Published by permission of the Wachovia Historical Society, Winston Salem, North Carolina.

FIG. 36(a) The "Marshall" Goblet—overall, obverse. (b) Composite photo of engraving, obverse. (c) Detail of the engraved foliate spray on the cover.

A

B

C

(18) THE "SCHLEY" GOBLET

Ca. 1785–1795, possibly 1791–1793 • Colorless, non-lead glass, pale gray tine
Dimensions: OH. 29.2 cm; (Goblet) H. 21.5 cm, D. (bowl) 11.9 cm; (Cover) H. 8.6 cm, D. (max.) 12.4 cm
Collection of The Henry Francis du Pont Winterthur Museum, Winterthur, Delaware (Acc. No. 59.47a,b); Ex coll. George
S. McKearin, Hoosick Falls, New York, who acquired it from a great-great-great-great-grandson of George Jacob Schley

George Jacob Schley (1737–1811) was another local patron of the Amelung glassworks. Son of the founder of Frederick-Town, Schley kept a tavern and engaged in various other business activities. Appraisers of his estate probably described this object when they wrote, "1 large Goblet, $1.25."[100]

The elaborately engraved rococo framework on the bowl has certain affinities with the decoration on the J. Amelung goblet (cat. no. 14)—such as the plinth at the left. The most prominent feature of the decoration, the elaborate shield at the bottom, has no parallel. The meaning of the device within, a fish swimming below a cloudy sky through which the rays of the sun are breaking, is obscure. Perhaps it is a pun on the name "Schley" (a "Schlei" is a fish of the carp family which is found in Europe; perhaps that fish, also known as a "tench," was regarded as a badge, since the fish is noted for its tenacity to life). Because there is nothing else amusing about the goblet, any thought that it is simply a joke may be dismissed. The scrolls and flowers are related to those on a number of glasses.

The lettering is characteristic of the group dated between 1791 and 1793.

The foliate spray on the cover is crude and unexceptional. It does, however, relate to the sprays on the covers of the Guest tumbler (cat. no. 8) and the Marshall goblet (cat. no. 17).

The form of the glass is typical, but the relationship of the lid to the bowl is excellent. The line of the bowl carries smoothly into the cover, and its dome relates well to the dome of the foot.

The quality of the glass, especially its lack of obvious tint, is perhaps the best of the surviving New Bremen glasses. It suggests that Amelung was capable of producing a material which could stand comparison with European glass. Unfortunately, Amelung rarely seems to have produced such a satisfactory material.

There are rough pontil marks underneath the foot and inside the cover.

Photographs by George J. Fistrovich. Published by permission of The Henry Francis du Pont Winterthur Museum, Winterthur, Delaware.

FIG. 37(a) The "Schley" Goblet—overall, obverse. (b) Composite photo of engraving, obverse. (c) Detail of the engraved foliate spray on the cover.

A

B

C

(19–21) UNDECORATED GOBLETS

Ca. 1785–1795
(FIG. 38) Colorless, non-lead glass, dark grayish-tan tint
Dimensions: H. 20.6 cm, D. (bowl) 11.0 cm
Collection of The Maryland Historical Society, Baltimore, Maryland (Acc. No. 60.51.1); Ex coll. Mrs. Walter W. Kohn,
Baltimore, Maryland
(FIG. 39) Colorless, non-lead glass, faint gray tint
Dimensions: H. 17.0 cm. D. (bowl) 9.8 cm
Collection of The Corning Museum of Glass (Acc. No. 51.4.50)
(FIG. 40) Colorless, non-lead glass; dark gray-green tint
Dimensions: H. 20.3 cm, D. (bowl) 8.9 cm
Collection of The Corning Museum of Glass (Acc. No. 55.4.42)

The attribution of these glasses to the New Bremen factory is based on a number of factors: their forms, histories of origin or discovery, and their materials. Two are straightforward examples of the forms already illustrated; both have histories of ownership in Baltimore. Chemical analysis shows that the material is similar to "standard" Amelung.

The third glass (Fig. 40) also has a history of ownership in Baltimore. From the neck down, it certainly has the appearance of an Amelung glass; the bowl is, however, distinctly different from anything documented to the factory. The base of the bowl incorporates a group of air beads which are arranged in a circle of eight, around a single bubble in the center. Such decorative air beads are frequently found in German glass, especially from Lauenstein. But a fragment of a stem and bowl which contains a similar pattern of bubbles was found on the factory site, suggesting that they may have been made there (A.S. 152A). Such evidence is, however, suspect because the piece may have been cullet. Chemical analysis does show a similarity of this glass to documented Amelung pieces.

The attribution of this piece to New Bremen is considered tenuous.

All of these goblets have rough pontil marks underneath their feet. The foot of the second goblet (Fig. 39) has been trimmed.

Photographs by Raymond F. Errett and George J. Fistrovich. Published by permission of The Maryland Historical Society, Baltimore, Maryland, and The Corning Museum of Glass, Corning, New York.

Fig. 39. Undecorated Goblet.

Fig. 38. Undecorated Goblet.

Fig. 40. Undecorated Goblet, with air beads in the base of the bowl.

(22) THE "G.R." WINEGLASSES (three)

Ca. 1785–1795 • Colorless, non-lead glass, strong gray tint
Dimensions (Corning example): H. 10.6 cm, D. (bowl) 5.5 cm
Collections: The Corning Museum of Glass (Acc. No. 50.4.48 and 79.4.337, gift of Mr. Jerome Strauss, State College,
Pennsylvania); Greenfield Village and Henry Ford Museum (Acc. No. 59.28.148); Ex coll. Miss Margaret B. Waesche,
Washington, D.C. (a descendant of the Repolds)

The G.R. wineglasses belonged to George and Metha Repold of Baltimore (cat. no. 10). In the inventory of George's estate "3 doz. wine glasses" were listed against a total value of $3.00; these three may be all that remain from that group.

In form they are duplicated by numerous fragments excavated at the factory site. (See Noël Hume section.) The G.R. wineglasses have plain, conical feet, but a large number of the fragments had folded feet. Both types may have been popular concurrently.

The engraving is simple. The initials are smoothly executed. The surrounding wreath, with four simple flowers interspersed, is similar to that found on the Stenger flask (cat. no. 12), the covers of the W.A.G. tumblers (cat. no. 25), the Liberty tumbler (cat. no. 27), and other pieces.

There are rough pontil marks underneath the feet.

Photograph by Raymond F. Errett; composite by George J. Fistrovich. Published by permission of The Corning Museum of Glass, Corning, New York.

FIG. 41(a) The "G.R." Wineglass—overall, obverse. (b) Composite photo of engraving, obverse.

A

B

(23) THE "F.C.S.A." TUMBLER

Ca. 1785–1795 • Colorless, non-lead glass; enameled and gilt
Dimensions: H. 10 cm, D. (rim) 6.9 cm
Collection of Tacoma Art Museum, Tacoma, Washington, gift of Mrs. Lowell Thomas Murray, Tacoma, Washington; Ex coll. Mrs. Ethel Amelung McCallum, a great-great-granddaughter of Amelung through Frederica's marriage to Dr. Philip Sommerkamp; given to Mrs. Murray, also an Amelung descendant

Within the range of Amelung glass, this small tumbler is unique: it is the only known, surviving piece which is decorated with enameling and gilding. The script initials F.C.S.A. and the scrolled frame around them are gilt; they are backed with blue enamel on the inner surface of the glass. The rim is also gilt. The forms of the letters are not precisely paralleled on any other glass. The "A" is similar to those on the A.G. (cat. no. 24) and W.A.G. (cat. no. 25) tumblers and to the "H" on the J.F.C.H. tumbler (cat. no. 4).

Originally, there were said to have been three such glasses, each with the initials of John Frederick Amelung's daughters. Only this one, with the initials of the oldest daughter, Frederica Christina Sophie Amelung, seems to have survived. The others are said to have existed into this century but have since disappeared.

Information and photograph from Helen and George S. McKearin's Two Hundred Years of American Blown Glass, *p. 282. Photograph published by permission of the Tacoma Museum of Art, Tacoma, Washington.*

FIG. 42. The "F.C.S.A." Tumbler—overall, obverse.

(24) THE "A.G." TUMBLER

Ca. 1785–1795 • Colorless, non-lead glass, greenish tint
Dimensions: H. 20.6 cm, D. (rim) 14.9 cm
Collection of The Henry Francis du Pont Winterthur Museum, Winterthur, Delaware (Acc. No. 59.3004); Ex coll. Richard
Loeb, Hampton, New Jersey; William T. H. Howe, Cincinnati, Ohio

Although no documentation exists, Anthony Grosz has been named as the original owner of this tumbler. No one of that name has been traced in Maryland. In Frederick County alone during the period of New Bremen's operations, there were at least six people whose initials were A.G.

The wreath of simple foliage and flowers surrounding the initials is unlike any others. The elements, however, are to be found on a number of them. Compare, for example, the sprays on the covers of the Marshall goblet (cat. no. 17) and the Guest tumbler (cat. no. 8), where all of the details are used. Also related are the foliate spray on the lid with the Stover sugar bowl (cat. no. 33) and the spray, at the right, on the L.S. tumbler (cat. no 30).

Of the letters, the "A" has no precise parallel; but related letters are found on the F.C.S.A. (cat. no. 23), W.A.G. (cat. no. 25), and J.F.C.H. (cat. no. 4) tumblers. The "G" is typical of the form found on Amelung glasses. The periods are formed by oval cuts, capped with short, straight cuts; similar periods are used on the M.T. bowl (cat. no. 38).

There is a rough pontil mark underneath the base.

Photographs by George J. Fistrovich. Published by permission of The Henry Francis du Pont Winterthur Museum, Winterthur, Delaware.

FIG. 43(a) The "A.G." Tumbler—overall, obverse. (b) Composite photo of engraving, obverse.

A

B

(25) THE "W.A.G." TUMBLERS (three)

Ca. 1785–1795 • Colorless, non-lead glass; the large ones of yellowish-brown tint, the smaller of gray tint
Dimensions: (Left) OH. 30.2 cm; (Tumbler) H. 20.9 cm, D. (rim) 13.8 cm, (Center) H. 12.8 cm, D. (rim) 9.7 cm.
(Right) OH. 29.6 cm; (Tumbler) H. 20.3 cm, D. (rim) 14.0 cm
Collection of The National Museum of American History, Smithsonian Institution, Washington, D.C. Ex coll. Hope
Goddard Iselin, Providence, Rhode Island

The original owners of these tumblers were probably William and Abigail Goddard. William Austin Goddard's *Descendants of Edward Goddard* (1833) states that William Goddard published a newspaper, the *Gazette,* in Providence, Rhode Island, beginning in 1762. He later moved to New York City, lived briefly in Philadelphia, and moved to Baltimore in 1773. In 1775 Goddard was appointed surveyor of Post Roads and Comptroller of the General Post Office (where Amelung's son's father-in-law, Alexander Furnival, was Postmaster). He married Abigail Angell on May 27, 1786. If the tumblers were a wedding present, they would be the earliest known datable Amelung glasses. Goddard remained in Baltimore until 1792 when he returned to Providence. The tumblers descended to Hope Goddard Iselin in Rhode Island.

As will be immediately obvious, these pieces share several characteristics of form with documented tumblers, especially in their covers, where the customary finial and trailed ring are noted. The engraving appears to be a bit flatter, but the motifs of the foliate scrolls are closely paralleled by those on the C.G.C. (cat. no. 15) and Trisler (cat. no. 13) goblets, the Stenger flask (cat. no. 12) and on the Ghequiere tumbler (cat. no. 3). The pendant flower, suspended from the

spray on the right, is not precisely duplicated on other glasses, but it is not unexpected considering that Amelung's engraver placed a long pendant of flowers on the Schley goblet (cat. no. 18), in roughly the same position. The crowns are slightly different in execution, that on the center tumbler having crosshatching inside while the others do not. Crowns are found on four pieces attributed to New Bremen. Those on the Ghequiere tumbler (cat. no. 3) and the "M.T." bowl (cat. no. 38) come the closest to matching the one on the small tumbler. The initials are the only unusual note, for they do not conform to the general style of letters found on other Amelung vessels. The "A" relates to that found on the A.G. tumbler (cat. no. 24) and the F.C.S.A. tumbler (cat. no. 23).

The engraving on the covers is a simple circle of willow-like branches, with four-petaled flowers interspersed. It is essentially the same as is found on the "G.R." wineglasses (cat. no. 22) and other pieces.

There are rough pontil marks on the bases and inside the covers.

Photograph by Raymond F. Errett. Published by permission of The Smithsonian Institution, Washington, D.C.

Fig. 44. The "W.A.G." Tumblers—overall, obverse.

(26) THE "DIE JUNO" TUMBLER

Ca. 1785–1795 • Colorless, non-lead glass
Dimensions: OH. 33 cm; (Tumbler) H. 18.9 cm, D. (rim) 14.6 cm; (Cover) H. 11.7 cm, D. (max) 14.6 cm
Collection of The Baltimore Museum of Art (Acc. No. L.34.50.1); Ex coll. Mrs. Miles White, Jr.,
Baltimore Maryland

The "Die Juno" tumbler apparently celebrates a Danish brig which plied the West Indies trade. In the representation on the tumber the flag it flies is the swallowtail of the Danish Royal Navy. The port records for Baltimore are, unfortunately, incomplete. It is known, however, that a "Brig Juno" entered Baltimore in 1793, 1794, and 1795. Perhaps on one of those visits, the master of the Brig ordered a tumbler to be decorated with a representation of his ship. No direct connection between the Brig Juno and New Bremen or the Amelungs has been found.

The engraved foliate sprigs framing the scene on the left are related to those found on other glasses attributed or documented to Amelung, but the scrolls on the right are not. The engraving, in general, lacks the precision of Amelung's best, but perhaps this was a "rush" job to meet a sailing date.

The lettering of the name of the ship matches that of other glasses. Although there are too few letters to be certain of a date range, they do suggest a date in the 1780's.

The cover is of the typical form, but the placement of the finial is rather ungainly. The engraved foliate scroll on the cover is not repeated on other glasses but some individual elements are found elsewhere: for example, the sprays on the covers of the Marshall goblet cat. no. 17), the Guest tumbler (cat. no. 8) and, particularly, the Ghequiere tumbler (cat. no. 3).

There are rough pontil marks on the base of the tumbler and inside the cover.

Photographs by Raymond F. Errett. Published by permission of The Baltimore Museum of Art, Baltimore, Maryland.

FIG. 45(a) The "Die Juno" Tumbler—overall, obverse. (b) Detail, foliate spray at left. (c) Detail, foliate spray at right. (d) Detail of engraved foliate spray on cover.

A

B

C

D

(27) THE "LIBERTY" TUMBLER

Ca. 1785–1795, possibly 1788–1789 • Colorless, non-lead glass, faint gray tint
Dimensions: H. 16.2 cm, D (rim) 12.0 cm
Collection of The Corning Museum of Glass (79.4.333), gift of Mr. Jerome Strauss, State College, Pennsylvania

The jubilant proclamation on this tumbler has no apparent historical significance, since it must have been made several years after Independence was won. Perhaps it was made to commemorate the ratification of the Constitution in 1788. Amelung's workers marched with the painters and glaziers in the "grand procession" in Baltimore and carried "Glass Trumpets."[101] Unfortunately, nothing is known of the history of this piece before it appeared on the market.

The style of engraving is consistent with other pieces associated with New Bremen. With its simple oval wreath, it reflects a neoclassical taste that is unusual in Amelung decoration. The simplicity of the wreath is an effective foil for the strength of the sentiment. In form, it is closely paralleled by the wreaths on the G.R. wineglasses (cat. no. 22), and other glasses. The style of lettering relates the glass to other pieces dated 1788 and 1789. It is possible, of course, that it is earlier.

The tumbler has a rough pontil mark underneath the base.

Photographs by Raymond F. Errett. Published by permission of The Corning Museum of Glass, Corning, New York.

Fig. 46(a) The "Liberty" Tumbler—overall, obverse. (b) Composite photo of engraving, obverse.

A

B

(28) THE "FEDERAL" TUMBLER

Ca. 1785–1795, probably 1788–1789 • *Colorless, non-lead glass, grayish tint*
Dimensions: H. 15.2 cm, D. (rim) 11.8 cm
Collection of Mr. Frank T. Innes, Chester, New Jersey

This tumbler, discovered just *after* the first printing of this publication went to press, lends credence to the theory that the "Liberty" tumbler (cat. no. 27) was made "to commemorate the ratification of the Constitution in 1788." With the inscription, "Federal," this tumbler assuredly celebrates this event.

Besides the forms of the letters in the inscription, the engraved foliate wreath punctuated with four stylized floral sprays links the "Liberty" tumbler to the "Federal" tumbler. The same wreath appears in the "G.R." wineglasses (cat. no. 22) and the "Stenger" flask (cat. no. 12). The style of lettering is also consistent with that on the "Liberty" example (although here the lettering is more carefully executed) and with

engraving on other pieces attributed to the New Bremen Glass Manufactory.

Spectrographic analysis, conducted at the Winterthur Museum in 1976, also demonstrates a close relationship between this tumbler and the 39 other examples of Amelung glass analyzed there. Unfortunately, this tumbler has no traceable history; it was found in a New Jersey antiques shop.

The tumbler has a rough pontil mark under the base.

Published in *Journal of Glass Studies,* XX, 1978, p. 123; Jean Taylor Federico and Frank T. Innes, "A Newly Discovered Amelung Tumbler," *The Glass Club Bulletin,* No. 125, March 1979.

Photograph published by permission of the owner.

FIG. 47. The "Federal" Tumbler—overall, obverse.

(29) THE "GMR" TUMBLER

Ca. 1790–1795, possibly 1792 • Colorless, non-lead glass, dark greenish-tan tint
Dimensions: H. 20.1 cm, D. (rim) 15.0 cm
Collection of The Corning Museum of Glass (Acc. No. 55.4.291); Ex coll. Miss Margaret B. Waesche,
Washington, D.C. (a descendant of the Repolds)

One of the most interesting glasses attributed to New Bremen is the tumbler made for George and Metha Repold. Their initials are inscribed on the obverse, surrounded by an elaborate frame of foliage, flowers, and scrolls.

The details of the engraving are found on many other glasses—the "pink" at the bottom, the ears of wheat, and the simple, multi-petaled flowers. The composition is somewhat unusual. There are no known Amelung glasses with the second swag of flowers at the bottom, or the foliage-winged flower above the typical scroll at the top.

The letters are carefully and competently engraved. The curves are smooth and the curls are finished with polished circles. They relate most closely to the lettering on the Mauerhoff goblet (cat. no. 11), and on the G.R. wineglasses (cat. no. 22)—which were also made for the Repolds.

The extraordinary feature of this tumbler is the decoration on the reverse: a naive representation of a country landscape, which is in sharp contrast to the elegant flowers and foliage on the other side. The scene includes a house, trees, and birds, depicted without perspective. The house appears to have its front and side on the same plane. The birds, three on the ground and two in the air must have been four feet tall, if we are to judge by the house. The trees at the left are likewise fanciful; that on the right has three trunks. The ground, grass, and shrubs are only summarily drawn. This is the only time Amelung's engraver is known to have attempted such an ambitious design. It is amusing to our eyes, but it was undoubtedy considered a remarkable achievement when it was made. It is still extraordinary in the annals of the American glass.

The inventory of George Repold's estate, mentioned in the discussion of the "Repold/Amelung" goblet (cat. no. 10), does not list any tumblers which may reasonably be identified as this tumbler.

There is a rough pontil mark on the base of the tumbler.

Photographs by George J. Fistrovich. Published by permission of The Corning Museum of Glass, Corning, New York.

FIG. 48(a) The "GMR" Tumbler—overall, obverse. (b) Composite photo of engraving, obverse. (c) Composite photo of engraved scene, reverse.

A

B

C

(30) THE "L.S." TUMBLER

Ca. 1785–1795 • Colorless, non-lead glass, gray-green tint
Dimensions H. 20 cm, D. (rim) 14 cm
Collection of the Connecticut Historical Society, Hartford (Acc. No. A-761); Ex coll. Mr. George Dudley
Seymour, New Haven, Connecticut (purchased in 1923)

The motifs on this tumbler indicate that the original owner was a Freemason. Unfortunately, who "L.S." was, or even where he lived, is unknown.

Its engraved details place this tumbler securely within the family of Amelung glasses. The foliate wreath around the initials has many parallels: its closest relative is on the J.F.C.H. tumbler (cat. no. 4), but similar ones are on the Stover sugar bowl (cat. no. 33), and the Schley (cat. no. 18) and Repold/Amelung (cat. no. 10) goblets.

The foliate sprays around the Masonic symbols are also allied to those on other glasses. In particular, that on the left parallels the sprays of the Ghequiere (cat. no. 3) and Great Seal of the U.S. (cat. no. 9) tumblers and of the C.G.C. goblet (cat. no. 15) with the same, simple, flower at the intersection of the two sprays. The spray on the right is not precisely paralleled, but it does have similarities to the A.G. (cat. no. 24) tumbler, and the sprays on the covers of the Stover sugar bowl (cat. no. 33), the Marshall goblet (cat. no. 17) and the Guest tumbler (cat. no. 8). The Masonic symbols have no direct parallel.

There is rough pontil mark on the base of the tumbler.

Photographs by Raymond F. Errett, Published by permission of the Connecticut Historical Society, Hartford, Connecticut.

FIG. 49(a) The "L.S." Tumbler—overall, obverse. (b) Detail, foliate spray at left. (c) Detail, foliate spray at right.

A

B

C

(31) THE "C.G." SUGARBOWL

Ca. 1785–1795 • Transparent, dark amethyst, non-lead glass
Dimensions: OH. 20.4 cm; (Bowl) H. 11.3 cm, W. 18.1 cm; (Cover) H. 10.6 cm, D. (max) 10.5 cm
Collection of The Henry Francis du Pont Winterthur Museum, Winterthur, Delaware (Acc. No. 59.3011a,b)

The sugar bowl given "To Mis. C.G. In Washington Cty." was the first colored piece of Amelung glass discovered, and it was by far the most fanciful. It was found in 1939 "in a farmhouse just a few miles over into Washington County . . ." (from Frederick County).[102] When published it caused a great deal of excitement, and it continues to do so; it is certainly one of the most dramatic and elaborate pieces of eighteenth-century American glass known.

The bowl was supposedly owned by Catherine Geeting or Geeding of Washington County, Maryland. Since she was married in 1808 to Daniel Thomas, there was perhaps an older "CG" for whom the piece was originally blown.

The bowl was initially associated with the New Bremen factory on the basis of the similarity of the engraving to that found on documented and attributed pieces. Related wreaths, with flowers interspersed, are found on the Liberty tumbler (cat. no. 27), the covers of the W.A.G. tumblers (cat. no. 25), and the G.R. wineglasses (cat. no. 22). The closest parallel is found on the amethyst glass cream jug (cat. no. 34). The similarity of the glass and the engraving suggests that they may have been produced at the same time, but there is no historical evidence to connect the two. The graceful spray engraved on the cover is similar to the sprigs found on the Trisler goblets (cat. no. 13).

The lettering is somewhat rough, perhaps because it had to be done on a complex form. The style of the letters suggests, but does not prove, an association with the 1791–1793 group.

The bowl has a wide, bulbous body which tapers sharply above and below the rounded mid-section. The disk foot is applied. A ring is trailed below the rim and there are two loop handles with elaborately pincered trailing. The domed cover fits over the rim of the bowl and rests on its trailed ring. The ball finial is decorated with an elaborate, swanlike bird with a long, curved neck, clipped wings and tail; four leaflike ornaments spring from the ball finial, below the bird.

At first glance, the construction of the bowl and lid seems atypical. But, if they are thought of as being inverted (that is, if the bowl were to be compared to the cover of, say, The Ghequiere tumbler and the cover of the sugar bowl to the tumbler), they are of the "standard" construction.

The attribution of this sugar bowl to the New Bremen factory is strengthened by its chemical similarity to documented Amelung glasses and to fragments of amethyst glasses excavated at the factory site. In addition, several of those fragments are from objects of related form.

Because there are close European parallels, the form cannot be considered characteristically Amelung. A covered "butter dish" illustrated in the 1763 catalogue of glass made at the Nøstetangen factory in Norway is identical in its construction but not ornamentation. It was available in mauve glass. A covered bowl of similar form, in the collection of the Germanisches Nationalmuseum in Nuremberg, has an equally fantastic bird finial.

There are rough pontil marks on the foot of the bowl and inside the cover.

Photographs by George J. Fistrovich. Published by permission of The Henry Francis du Pont Wintherthur Museum, Winterthur, Delaware.

FIG. 50(a) The "C.G." Sugar Bowl—overall, obverse. (b) Composite of engraving, obverse. (c) Composite of engraved foliate spray on cover. (d) "Butter dish with lid," Nøstetangen, Norway, ca. 1763. From Ada Buch Polak, *Gammelt Norsk Glass*, Oslo, 1953, p. 145.

A

C

D

B

(32) SUGAR BOWL COVER

Ca. 1785–1795 • Transparent, dark amethyst, non-lead glass
Dimensions: H. 3.8 cm, D. (rim) 11.4 cm
Collection of The Bayou Bend Collection, The Museum of Fine Arts, Houston; Ex coll. Mr. John T. Gotjen, Warren, Rhode
Island; Colonel M. Robert Guggenheim, Washington, D.C.; Mrs. John A. Logan, Washington, D.C.

Although this may have been used as a small bowl, judging by the wear on the flat "base," it is more likely that it was *made* as a cover for a sugar bowl. There is additional wear on the rim, which *may* be the result of its long use in that manner. The appearance of a pontil scar *inside* the bowl, in addition to a scar on the "base," is further evidence for its initial function as a lid, because no *bowl* attributed to the Amelung factory has a pontil mark inside. The scar on the base is probably the remains of a finial which was broken off.

The engraved decoration on the side of the cover is closely related to that on many pieces associated with the New Bremen factory: the "Trisler" goblet dated 1793 (cat. no. 13), the "König" goblet (cat. no. 16), the "Schley" goblet (cat. no. 18), and the "C.G." amethyst sugar bowl cover (cat. no. 31). Indeed, it is most closely related to the form of the cover on the "C.G." bowl.

Published in *Journal of Glass Studies*, XXVI, 1984, pp. 157–158.

"J.T.G." (Absentee Auction, Jan. 1985), David and Linda Arman, No. 9, pp. 13–14.

Photographs by John T. Gotjen. Published by permission of The Museum of Fine Arts, Houston, Texas.

Fig. 51. Sugar Bowl Cover—overall.

(33) THE "STOVER" SUGAR BOWL AND COVER

Ca. 1785–1795 • Colorless, non-lead glass
Dimensions: OH. 17.2 cm; (Sugar bowl) H. 10.2 cm, D. (rim) 10.5 cm
Collection of The Corning Museum of Glass (79.4.309 A, B), gift of William G. Bushwaller and Mrs. Regina B. Cole. Ex
coll. Mrs. August J. Raggi, Frederick, Maryland; Mr. J. Quynn Rodock, Mrs. Raggi's brother

The Stover sugar bowl is one of two known engraved sugar bowls which are attributed to the New Bremen factory. That the form was made at the factory is suggested by the discovery of fragments of similar decorated handles, feet, and covers at the factory site (Noël Hume section, Fig. 38, 39). Also, Amelung sold several sugar dishes to the Annapolis firm of John and Samuel Davidson in 1791; the merchants sold sugar dishes, perhaps Amelung's, for 5/4 to 8/10 each in 1792 and 1793.[103]

The bowl was apparently made for Philip Stover (d.1813) of Frederick-Town. When Stover died no glass was itemized in the inventory of his estate.

The engraving on the bowl is simpler than that on the C.G. sugar bowl (cat. no. 31), but they are related. The wreath is similar to the one on the C.G. bowl, and also to those on the G.R. wineglasses (cat. no. 22), the covers on the W.A.G. tumblers (cat. no. 25), and the Liberty tumbler (cat. no. 27). The sprig on the reverse side of the bowl likewise has readily identifiable parallels. The lettering relates the sugar bowl to the Amelung glasses dated between 1791 and 1793, but not exclusively so.

The cover, which fits the opening of the bowl, may originally have been made for another object. It will be noted that the bowl has a trailed ring on which the lid was undoubtedly meant to rest. The existing cover rests on the rim of the bowl. In form it resembles lids found on goblets. Its engraved spray is related to those on the Schley (cat. no. 18) and Marshall (cat. no. 17) goblets and the Guest tumbler (cat. no. 8).

The bowl now has one handle, but it is obvious that it once had two. The missing one probably matched the other. The conical foot is applied; it has a rough pontil mark. The cover has a rough pontil mark on the inside.

Photographs by Raymond F. Errett. Published by permission of The Corning Museum of Glass, Corning, New York.

FIG. 52(a) The "Stover" Sugar Bowl—overall, obverse, with cover. (b) Overall, reverse, without cover. (c) Detail of engraving, obverse. (d) Detail of engraved foliate spray on cover.

A

B

C

D

(34) SUGAR BOWL

Ca. 1785–1795 • Colorless, non-lead glass, strong greenish tint
Dimensions: OH. 21.2 cm; (Bowl) H.10.8 cm, W. 20.2 cm; (Cover) H.13.1 cm, D. (max) 12.5 cm
Collection of The Henry Francis du Pont Winterthur Museum, Winterthur, Delaware (Acc. No. 52.279a,b);
Ex coll. Said to have belonged to the Stevens family who took it from Maryland to New York State; a great
granddaughter of the first owner gave it in 1909 to Nancy Boyington, Marshall, Michigan; then to her
sister, Mary Edgerton, Marshall, Michigan, who sold it to Mrs. James Bryant, Marshall, Michigan;
to Mr. Ralph N. Hamilton, Battle Creek, Michigan, May 28, 1928; to Mr. and Mrs. James R. Gabell, Dayton
Ohio, about 1945; to Mr. Henry Francis du Pont, Winterthur, Delaware, September, 1952.

This covered sugar dish is celebrated for its elegant form and, especially, its flamboyant swan finial. The bird is constructed on the familiar hollow baluster finial. The arched neck, flaring wings, and arched tail feathers are separately applied to the top of the finial. Four leaves project from the bottom of the baluster and curve gently downward. The form and construction of the bird on the finial are the same as that on the C.G. sugar bowl (cat. no. 31), but this one is more graceful.

The domed cover is flattened on the top, like the C.G. cover, and it rests on a ring trailed below the rim of the sugar bowl. The handles on the bowl have pincered trailing which ends in smooth curls. The applied disk foot has a rough pontil mark underneath, as does the cover.

The green tint of the glass adds to the attraction of the object—at least to modern eyes. It is surprising that so much effort was expended in the creation of a bowl that was of a material Amelung could only have considered as inferior quality.

Photograph by George J. Fistrovich. Published by permission of The Henry Francis du Pont Winterthur Museum, Wintherthur, Delaware.

FIG. 53. Sugar Bowl—overall.

(35) SUGAR BOWL

Possibly ca. 1785–1795 • Yellowish-green, non-lead glass
Dimensions: OH. 20.7 cm; (Bowl) H. 10.9 cm, W. 17.2 cm; (Cover) H. 11.3 cm, D. (rim) to 10.3 cm
Collection of the Smithsonian Institution, Washington, D.C. (Acc. No. 69.15a,b)

The bird on the finial of this sugar bowl is constructed differently from those on the C.G. (cat. no. 31) and pale green (cat. no. 34) sugar bowls. There, the wings, tail, and neck were formed from separate gathers; here, the wings were pincered from one gather, and the neck and tail were applied to that. The bird lacks the grace of the one on the pale green bowl, and it sits atop a very different knop: two solid ball knops, instead of the hollow baluster, or the single ball knop on the C.G. cover. Four applied, clipped leaves were attached to the top tall knop and curled down and in toward the base of the finial. The lid is also smoothly domed, unlike the complex curves found on the other sugar bowl covers.

In construction the bowl shares the characteristics of the other bowls: a trailed ring below the rim serves as a seat for the cover; the handles have trailed and crimped decoration; and the conical foot is applied. There are rough pontil marks on the foot and inside the cover.

With so few sugar bowls attributed to New Bremen, it is impossible to be certain which details of construction and proportion are significant. It is possible only to note that there are differences between this and the other sugar bowls; at the present time it is not advisable to make attributions on those features.

Because this bowl is not made of the colorless glass used for most of the tablewares analyzed, it is not yet possible to make any conclusions on the basis of its chemical compositions.

Photograph by George J. Fistrovich. Published by permission of the Smithsonian Institution, Washington, D.C.

Fig. 54. Sugar Bowl—overall.

(36) SUGAR BOWL

Poss. ca. 1785–1795 • Colorless (bowl: brownish-amber tint; cover: greenish tint)
Dimensions: OH. 18.9 cm; (Cover) H. 10.1 cm, D. (rim) 10.1 cm; (Bowl) H. 10.0 cm, W. 19.0 cm
Collection of the Museum of Early Southern Decorative Arts, Winston-Salem, North Carolina (gift of Thomas A. Gray);
Ex coll. Mrs. Pauline Leiter, Hagerstown, Maryland, collector, who sold it to Richard H. and Virginia A. Wood, dealers
in Baltimore, Maryland, who sold it to Mr. Gray in 1980.

The form of the handled bowl is essentially that of the four other sugar bowls illustrated here. The two applied loop handles, with curled lower terminals, and pincered additional trailings are also related. So is the trailed ring seat for the cover. These are, however, undoubtedly duplicated by bowls made concurrently in northern Europe. The covered butter dish from the Nøstetangen, Norway, factory is the closest identified parallel, but the handles are placed quite differently.

The domed cover is rather squarish when compared with the others shown previously. However, the drawn ball finial on short stem is paralleled in the "C.G." sugar bowl cover (cat. no. 31). The downturned rib-twisted "arms" have no exact parallel in the other attributed Amelung sugar bowls, but three of them have four decorative frills applied below the bird finial. None has the rib-twisted post for the bird that is seen in this example. Unfortunately, only one wing of the original (presumably) bird finial has survived. It is a curved form with sheared rim to indicate feathers. Its closest parallel is the bird finial on the greenish sugar bowl at Winterthur (cat. no. 34).

Photograph published by permission of the Museum of Early Southern Decorative Arts, Winston-Salem, North Carolina.

Fig. 55. Sugar Bowl—overall.

(37) CREAM JUG

Ca. 1785–1795 • Transparent, dark amethyst, non-lead glass
Dimensions: H 12.0 cm, D. (foot) 5.4 cm
Collection of The Henry Francis du Pont Winterthur Museum, Winterthur, Delaware (Acc. No. 59.3010)

This cream jug, said to have been found near Hagerstown, Maryland, has no known parallel among surviving Amelung glasses. Feet from vessels of a similar size, perhaps cream jugs or mugs, were found at the Amelung site. they were in green, blue, and amethyst glass (see Noël Hume section, Fig. 38). In material, this jug also relates to the C.G. sugar bowl (cat. no. 31).

The engraved wreath on the front is reminiscent of other attributed glasses. In particular, one should note its striking similarity to the wreath on the C.G. sugar bowl; closely related are the wreaths on the Liberty (cat. no. 27) and L.S. (cat. no. 30) tumblers, the G.R. wineglasses (cat. no. 22). The only parallel for the star in the center is a somewhat cruder six-pointed star on the L.S. tumbler.

The glass is striated with lines of darker and lighter color. The handle and disk foot are applied. There is a rough pontil mark underneath the foot.

Photographs by George J. Fistrovich. Published by permission of The Henry Francis du Pont Winterthur Museum, Winterthur, Delaware.

Fig. 56(a) Cream Jug—overall. (b) Composite photo of engraving.

A

B

(38) THE "MARGARET THOMAS BOWL"

Poss. ca. 1789 • Colorless, non-lead glass, gray tint
Dimensions: H. 10.8 cm, D. (max) 20.3 cm
Collection of the Smithsonian Institution, Washington, D.C. (Acc. No. 392, 709); Ex coll. Mr. W. Dan Quattlebaum,
Pasadena, California; Mrs. Rachel Russell, New Market (?), Maryland (a great-granddaughter of Margaret Thomas
Brooke, of Montgomery County, Maryland)

Family tradition identifies the original owner of this bowl as Margaret Thomas (1768–1797) of Montgomery County, Maryland. She is said to have married in 1789; it is assumed that the bowl was made just prior to that.[104]

The roughly-hemispherical bowl rests on a flattened, trailed foot ring; there is a rough pontil mark in the center. A foliate wreath, with a crown above, enclosing the script initials "M.T.", is engraved on one side. The leaves on the wreath are attached to the main stem by short stems—unlike the representations of wreaths on other New Bremen glasses, where the leaves are connected directly to the main stems. The four-petaled flower at the intersection of the two sprays is found on a number of glasses. The crown is nearly identical to that on the Ghequiere tumbler (cat. no. 3) and is similar to the crown on the smallest W.A.G. tumbler (cat. no. 25). The letters are different from any found on Amelung glasses, although the somewhat hesitantly elaborated letters on the J.F.C.H. tumbler (cat. no. 4) have a similar feeling.

Photographs by George J. Fistrovich. Published by permission of the Smithsonian Institution, Washington, D.C.

FIG. 57(a) The "M.T." Bowl—overall, obverse. (b) Detail of engraving.

A

B

(39) COVERED URN (?)

Ca. 1785–1795 • Pale yellow-green, non-lead glass
Dimensions: OH. 38.7 cm
Collection of The Metropolitan Museum of Art (Rogers Fund), New York, 1933 (Acc. No. 33.108a,b)

This covered urn is strikingly different from the other illustrated pieces attributed to the New Bremen factory. In form it is a giant rummer with cover. Its use is not known; it has been suggested that it was a sweetmeat bowl. It relates to documented pieces in its cover, with its trailed ring which seats on the rim of the bowl and its hollow baluster finial. Dissimilar are the shape of the stem and foot, the pointed ovoid bowl. Here, too, the finial is mounted on a merese, rather than directly on the cover.

The person who made this piece obviously had considerable talent, but his material was not of comparable quality. Rather than using the decolorized glass from which most of the other pieces (discussed here) were made, he used a bubbly, light green glass. In color it relates to bottle glass. Perhaps the object was made for the gaffer's own use rather than as an object intended for sale.

In any case, at least two were made: a related bowl, without a cover, was owned by the Frederick County Historical Society. It was stolen in 1975 and has not yet been recovered.

There are rough pontil marks under the foot and inside the cover.

Neither of the bowls has any documented history, and neither has been analyzed chemically.

Published by permission of The Metropolitan Museum of Art, New York City, New York.

FIG. 58. Covered Urn (?)—overall.

(40–41) "CHECKERED-DIAMOND" PATTERN

Pocket Bottle: colorless, non-lead glass
Dimensions: H. 15.6 cm, W. 11.9 cm, D. 6.0 cm
Collection of The Corning Museum of Glass (Acc. No. 50.4.54)
Salt (?) Dish: transparent, dark blue, non-lead glass
Dimensions: H. 7.1 cm, D. (bowl) 6.6 cm
Collection of The Corning Museum of Glass (Acc. No. 50.4.56)

Salt (?) dishes and pocket bottles molded in the so-called "checkered-diamond" pattern have been found in Maryland and have frequently been attributed to New Bremen. Fragments of similar flasks were found at the site, suggesting that some may have been made there (Noël Hume section, Fig. 40). Unfortunately, New Bremen was not the only glasshouse where the pattern was used. A few flasks of this pattern have been attributed to Midwestern factories[105] and "checkered-diamond" mugs and pocket bottles were blown in Europe. It is possible that Amelung brought the idea, and possibly the molds, for the "checkered-diamond" pattern when he came to America. A fragment with "checkered-diamond" molding was excavated at Grünenplan, in a seventeenth-century context.

The flask is of the typical flattened-pear shape. The mold featured eight diamonds in a horizontal row. There is a rough pontil mark on the base.

The salt (?) dish has the characteristic "double ogee" bowl, drawn stem, and applied foot with rough pontil mark. It was patterned in a mold having seven diamonds in a horizontal row.

Examples are known in colorless and blue (salts).

Neither of these pieces has been analyzed chemically.

Photographs by Raymond F. Errett. Published by permission of The Corning Museum of Glass, Corning, New York.

FIG. 60. "Checkered-Diamond" Salt (?) Dish—overall.

FIG. 59. "Checkered-Diamond" Pocket Bottle—overall.

(42) CANDLESTICK

Ca. 1785–1800, possibly made in the vicinity of Frederick, Maryland
Colorless, non-lead glass, gray tint
Dimensions: H. 20.9 cm, D. (foot) 11.6 cm
Collection of James B. Burger; Ex coll. Miss Josephine Etchison and Marshall Lingan Etchison, Frederick, Maryland

Found locally, this candlestick exhibits certain similarities with documented Amelung glasses. Obvious are the inverted baluster at the base of the stem and the modified baluster above it. Significant, too, is the broad domed foot, although it has a folded rim, a feature not found on the documented goblets. (It is found on fragments of wine glasses excavated at the site.) The candle socket, with an applied and tooled gather at its base, has no parallel, since there are no documented Amelung candlesticks.

The analysis of the material used in this candlestick shows that it is not the same as the "standard" Amelung glass. It is not, therefore, attributed to the New Bremen factory, but it may have been made at one of the other factories which operated in Frederick County.

Photograph by George J. Fistrovich. Published by permission of James B. Burger.

FIG. 61. Candlestick—overall.

(43) THE "C.H." RUMMER

Ca. 1785–1795 • Colorless, non-lead glass, grayish tint
Dimensions: H. 12.1 cm, D. (bowl) 7.8 cm
Collection of the Historical Society of York County, York, Pennsylvania (Acc. No. 1986.130), gift of Mrs. Josephine S. Appell

This object illustrates another form of drinking vessel that can be attributed to the Amelung factory. Small in stature, with a deep bowl and short stem, the glass is best described as a rummer.

Introduced about 1770, the rummer was in fashion well into the nineteenth century. The written and pictorial evidence of the period indicates that its generous bowl was used to hold a wide range of alcoholic beverages.

English and Irish rummers often have a pronounced ovoid bowl. In Amelung's version, however, the bowl has the same rounded shape and proportion of the larger presentation goblets. Here, too, a merese separates the bowl from the stem. Unlike the familiar inverted balusters of the goblets, the solid stem is short and waisted. The applied foot is very flat compared with the high domed feet of other New Bremen stemware.

This rummer helps substantiate the Amelung attribution of the very large urn (cat. no. 39), which is similar in form. Blown of bubbly green glass, the urn is much cruder than the gray-tinted colorless rummer with wheel-engraved decoration.

Although simple, the engraved decoration of the rummer exhibits the usual Amelung elegance. The initials are carefully executed, and the "C" parallels those seen on several other glasses. The "H" differs from those of both the "Tobias and the Angel" tumbler (cat. no. 2) and the "J.F.C.H." tumbler (cat. no. 4), but it is fluid and clearly modeled on the "Round Hand"-style alphabet Amelung's engraver preferred. Typical of New Bremen decoration is the asymmetrical wreath surrounding the letters. It combines a rather tight branch on the left with more exuberant foliage on the right, much in the manner of the "Boston" tumbler (cat. no. 6).

The rummer is believed to have belonged to a member of the Harding family of Frederick County, Maryland, although the exact owner has not yet been identified.

Photographs by George J. Fistrovich. Published by permission of the Historical Society of York County, York, Pennsylvania.

Fig. 62(a) The "C.H." Rummer—overall, obverse. (b) Detail of engraving.

A

B

VI. BIBLIOGRAPHY

Abraham, Evelyn. "The Glass of New Geneva and Greensboro." *The Antiquarian,* XVII, August 1931, pp. 15–17.

Amelung, Friedrich. *Familiennachrichten.* Dorpat, Lithuania: 1887, 1890, 1894 (Written, in part, by Franziska Amelung, b. 1789, daughter of Anton C. F. Amelung, niece of John Frederick Amelung).

Amelung, John F. *Remarks on Manufactures, Principally on the New Established Glass-House near Frederick-Town, in the State of Maryland.* Printed for the Author, 1787.

Anon. "Amelung Glass Factory Excavated." *Archaeology,* 16, No. 1, Spring, 1963, pp. 63–64.

Anon. "An Amelung Goblet." *Antiques,* LXXXI, No. 2, Feb. 1962, p. 221 (the "Mauerhoff" goblet).

Anon. "An Amelung Pokal and Its Owner." *Antiques,* LXXIII, No. 3, Jan. 1958, p. 80 (the "Marshall" goblet).

Anon. "American Glass Bowl." *Antiques,* LV, No. 2, Feb. 1949, pp. 108–109.

Anon. "America's Oldest Glass Works Crumbling to Earth in Maryland." *Washington Post,* Feb. 16, 1935, p. 1.

Anon. "Another Glass Rarity at Corning." *Antiques,* LXIX, No. 3, March 1956, p. 262 (the "Trisler" goblets).

Anon. "Another Inscribed Amelung Glass." *Antiques,* XXXIII, No. 2, Feb. 1938, pp. 80–81 (the "Mifflin" goblet).

Anon. "A Dated Tumbler with Amelung Characteristics." *Antiques,* LVIII, No. 3, Sept. 1950, pp. 204–205.

Anon. "The Editors' Attic: Amelung Exhibition in Maryland. . . ." *Antiques,* LXII, March 1952, p. 268.

Anon. "The Editors' Attic: By Amelung? . . ." *Antiques,* LIV, Sept. 1948, p. 189.

Anon. "Major John Adlum/His Amelung Glass." *The Now and Then,* 9, new series, 1941, pp. 315–317.

Anon. "Rare Glass Presented." *Frederick News,* March 24, 1960 (The "Kohn" goblet).

Anon. "Search Launched for Washington Goblets." *Collectors News,* XXI, No. 1, May 1980, p. 60.

Anon. "A Visit to the Amelung Mansion." *The Glass Club Bulletin* (The National Early American Glass Club), No. 89, March 1969, pp. 7–9.

Beutin, Ludwig. *Bremen und Amerika.* Bremen, Germany: Carl Schünemann, 1953.

Boicourt, Jane. "Drinking Through the Ages." *Antiques,* LXIII, No. 4, April 1953, pp. 351–353.

Breen, Robert G. "Glass Factory Found." *The Sun,* (Baltimore), Nov. 29, 1962, p. 16.

The Corning Museum of Glass. *Glass from the Corning Museum of Glass.* Corning, N.Y.: 1974, p. 87 (the "Tobias and the Angel" tumbler).

Davidson, Marshall. "An American XVIII Century Presentation Goblet." *Bulletin of the Metropolitan Museum of Art,* XXXII, Sept. 1937, pp. 215–216 (the "Mifflin" goblet).

Davidson, Marshall B. "The American Wing's Fifteen Finest—A Portfolio." *American Heritage,* XXXI, No. 3, April/May 1980, pp. 15–31.

Davidson, Ruth. "He Saw Amelung's Goblets Presented." *Antiques,* LXXXV, April 1964, p. 448.

———. "New Light on American Glass." *Antiques,* LXXXIII, No. 1, Jan. 1963, p. 112.

Delaplaine, Edward S. "Amelung Glass in Frederick." *The Post* (Frederick, Md.), Jan. 30, 1969.

———. *John Frederick Amelung, Maryland Glassmaker.* Frederick, Md.: *Frederick News Post,* 1971 (originally appeared on Jan. 23, Jan. 30, Feb. 5, Feb. 13, 1971).

Faust, Albert Bernhard. *The German Element in the United States.* New York: The Steuben Society of America, 1927.

Gaines, Edith. "An Amelung Goblet." *Antiques,* LXXI, No. 2, Feb. 1957, p. 163 (the "C.G.C." goblet).

Gardner, Charles B. and Rhea Mansfield Knittle. "Deming Jarves' Reminiscences of Glassmaking." *Antiques,* XXVIII, No. 1, July 1935, pp. 13–16.

Gest, Neil C. and Parke G. Smith. "The Glassmaking Kramers." *Antiques,* XXXV, No. 3, March 1939, pp. 118–121.

Gregory, Linda. "Amelung: Glass with Class." *News-Post* (Frederick, Md.), July 1, 1975, "Bicentennial Supplement," p. 9.

Heacock, William. "Is It Amelung?" *The Glass Collector,* No. 5, Winter 1983, p. 43.

Heissenbuttel, Orva W. "Two-Bit Find Attributed to Amelung." *The Glass Club Bulletin,* No. 136, Winter 1981–1982, pp. 7–8.

Hubbard, Donald, Lillie B. Jenkins and Elizabeth M. Krumrine, "Amelung Glasses Compared with Some Modern Commercial Glasses." *The Scientific Monthly,* LXXV, No. 6, Dec. 1952, pp. 327–338.

(Keyes, Homer Eaton). "The Editors' Attic: Add to Amelung." *Antiques,* XXVII, No. 1, Jan. 1935, pp. 7–8 (the "Boston" tumbler).

———. "A Masterpiece of Early American Glass." *Antiques,* XXXVI, Aug. 1939, pp. 58–59.

———. "Safe Clues in the Amelung Quest." *Antiques,* XXVI, No. 3, Sept. 1934, pp. 88–91.

Knittle, Rhea Mansfield. "Bowls & Pans: A Guide for Collectors." *Antiques,* XXI, No. 6, June 1932, pp. 264–268.

———. *Early American Glass.* Garden City, N.Y.: Garden City Publishing Co., Inc., 1927.

———. "Rex Absolutus of the Monongahela." *Antiques,* XIII, April 1928, pp. 290–292.

Kramer, Leroy. *Johann Baltasar Kramer, or "Baltzer"*

Kramer, Pioneer American Glass Blower. Chicago, Illinois: printed for the author, 1939.

Lanmon, Dwight P. "The Baltimore Glass Trade, 1780 to 1820." *Winterthur Portfolio* 5, 1969, pp. 15–48.

———. "The Importation of Glass into the United States, 1780 to 1820." *Annales du 5ᵉ Congrès International d'Etude Historique du Verre,* 1970, pp. 233–245.

Dr. Lührs to Mrs. Paul Amelung, A.l.s. Fairfield, Conn., 3 Nov. 1975 (concerning records of the Amelung family in the Staatsarchiv Bremen, in Germany).

The Maryland Hall of Records, Annapolis.
Frederick County Land Records
Frederick County Orphan's Court Records
Frederick County Circuit Court Records
Chancery Papers
Fisher Account Book No. 14370

The Maryland Historical Society, Baltimore. *Amelung Glass,* Baltimore: for the Society, 1952.

———. Amelung Glass. 1952. (exhibition catalogue).

The Maryland Historical Society, Baltimore.
Glassware Account Books, MS. 393
Brantz Mayer Papers, MS. 581
Friese Account Books, MS. 933
Kohlenburg Papers, MS. 1559
Baker Johnson Letters, MS. 1656
McPherson-Johnson Papers, MS. 1714

McKearin, George S. "This Is How It Happened." *Antiques,* LVIII, No. 4, Oct. 1950, pp. 290–293.

McKearin, George S. and Helen. *American Glass.* New York: Crown Publishers, 1941.

McKearin, Helen. "Early American Glass." *Antiques,* XL, No. 2, Aug. 1941, pp. 83–86.

McKearin, Helen and George S. *Two Hundred Years of American Blown Glass.* New York: Crown Publishers, Inc., 1949.

Michael, George. "Amelung Glass." *The Wooden Nutmeg,* V, No. 16, Dec. 3, 1982, p. 17.

Montgomery, Florence M. "An Amelung Sugar Bowl." *Journal of Glass Studies,* I, 1959, pp. 89–93.

Noël Hume, Ivor. "[Final report concerning the] archaeological excavations on the site of John Frederick Amelung's New Bremen glass manufactory, 1962, 1963." Unpublished typescript, 1963.

———. "Preliminary report on archaeological excavations at the site of John Frederick Amelung's New Bremen glass manufactory near Frederick, Maryland," Unpublished typescript, 1962.

———. "The Search for New Bremen and the Glass of John Frederick Amelung." *Antiques,* LXXXV, March 1964, pp. 310–313.

Norman-Wilcox, Gregor. "On Attributing American Blown Glass." *Antiques,* XXXVI, No. 2, Aug. 1939, pp. 72–75.

Oland, Dwight D. "The New Bremen Glass Manufactory." *Maryland Historical Magazine,* 68, No. 3, Fall 1973, pp. 255–272.

Papert, Emma. *The Illustrated Guide to American Glass.* New York: Hawthorn Books, Inc., 1972.

Pazaurek, Gustav E. "A German View of Early American Glass, Part I." *Antiques,* XXI, No. 4, April 1932, pp. 164–167; "Part II," XXI, No. 5, May 1932, pp. 225–227.

Perrot, Paul N. "The Melvin Billups Glass Collection, Part I." *Antiques,* LXXXVIII, No. 3, Sept. 1965, p. 342 (the "C.G.C." goblet).

Quattelbaum, W. Dan. *Early American Glass: Informal Sketches with Special Notes on Amelung.* Pasadena, Calif.: for the Author, n.d., pp. 12–15.

Quynn, Dorothy Mackay. "Johann Friedrich Amelung at New Bremen." *Maryland Historical Magazine,* XLIII, No. 3, Sept. 1948, pp. 155–179.

Records of Marriages and Burials in the Monocacy Church, in Frederick County, Maryland, and in the Evangelical Lutheran Congregation in the Town of Frederick, 1743–1811. Washington: National Genealogical Society, 1972, tr. and ed., Frederick S. Weiser.

Roosma, Maks. "The Glass Industry of Estonia in the 18th and 19th Century." *Journal of Glass Studies,* XI, 1969, pp. 70–85.

"R.R." "Accessions and Notes: A Recent Purchase of American Glass." *Bulletin of the Metropolitan Museum of Art,* XXIII, June 1928, pp. 166–168 (the "Bremen" goblet).

Stohlman, Martin and Elizabeth. "Amelung Glassworks." *The Antiques Journal,* 19, No. 1, Jan. 1964, pp. 8–12, 17.

———. "Excavating and Collecting Amelung Glass." *Antiques,* LIV, No. 4, Oct. 1948, pp. 253–255.

Stone, Mrs. Frank Pelham. "The First Glass Factory in America." *The Patriotic Marylander,* III, No. 2, 1916, pp. 88–93.

Stow, Charles Messer. "Amelung and Contemporary Maryland Glassblowers." *The Antiquarian,* XV, Dec. 1930, pp. 58–60.

[Strauss, Jerome]. *Glass Drinking Vessels from the Strauss Collections.* Corning, N.Y.: The Corning Museum of Glass, 1955, pp. 115–116 (No. 291, 292—the "Liberty" tumbler and a "G.R." wineglass).

Tacke, Eberhard. *Bilder aus der Geschichte der Gemeinde Grünenplan und der Glasindustrie im Hils.* Grünenplan, Germany: 1949.

The Toledo Museum of Art. *Art in Glass.* Toledo, Ohio: 1969, p. 87 (the "Mauerhoff" goblet).

Vaughan, Mary L. "Excavation Reveals Manufactory." *The Sunday Star* (Washington, D.C.), Oct. 21, 1962, pp. D-1, 5.

Watkins, C. Malcolm. "An Amelung Discovery." *Antiques,* LXIX, No. 6, Dec. 1952, pp. 488–489 (the "Trisler" goblets).

———. "Collectors' Notes: Maryland Glass with the Aura of Amelung." *Antiques,* LXV, April 1954, p. 312.

Weddell, Kennard, "The Amelung Saga." Mimeographed, n.d.

Williams, T. J. C. and Folger McKinsey. *History of Frederick County Maryland.* Baltimore: Regional Publishing Company, 1967, reprint of 1910 edition, I, pp. 268, 325, 536, 647.

Willnow to Mrs. Paul Amelung A. L. S., Fairfield, Conn., 12 Nov. 1975 (concerning records of the Amelung family in the Niedersächsisches Hauptstaatsarchiv, Hannover, Germany).

Wilson, Kenneth M. "Amelung and the Minor Glassworks." *Discovering Antiques*, No. 57, 1971, pp. 1366–1368.

———. "Amelung Find- and Puzzle." *Antiques*, LXXXVI, No. 3, Sept. 1964, p. 315 (the "L.S.-Masonic" tumbler).

———. "A 'New' Amelung Tumbler." *Antiques*, XC, Sept. 1966, pp. 334–336 (the "Great Seal of the U.S." tumbler).

———. "The New Bremen Excavation." *The Glass Club Bulletin* (The National Early American Glass Club), No. 69, March 1964, pp. 1–6.

———. "Serendipity and an Amelung Tumbler." *Connecticut Historical Society Bulletin*, 29, No. 2, April 1964, pp. 33–42.

Winchester, Alice. "Editorial." *Antiques*, LXI, No. 5, May 1952, pp. 412–413 (the "König" goblet).

VII. APPENDICES

APPENDIX I

SUMMARY OF LAND TRANSACTIONS

Summary of Land Transactions

Date of Indenture	Buyer	Seller	Price	Tract Name	Acres	Total Belonging to Amelung (and Labes)	Land Record (Maryland Hall of Records)
20 Nov. 1780	Conrad Foltz	William Murdoch Beall	£500 total	"Tobacco Hook" and "I don't care what"	71 acres said to be 51¼ acres (actual: 51 acres)	—	WR 2, f. 778-780.
26 Nov. 1780	Conrad Foltz	James Marshall	"divers good causes and considerations" and 5/-	"Gantt's Garden"	Said to be 1577¾ acres (actual: 1376 acres)	—	WR 2, f. 780-782.
30 Nov. 1784	J. F. Amelung	Foltz's executors	£1,000 total	"Tobacco Hook" and "I don't care what"	71 acres said to be 51¼ acres (actual: 51 acres)		WR 5, f. 520-522.
30 Nov. 1784	J. F. Amelung	Foltz's executors	£1,000	"Gantt's Garden"	Said to be 1577¾ acres (actual: 1376 acres)		WR 5, f. 522-524.
30 Nov. 1784	J. F. Amelung	Abraham Faw	£700	"Adam's Bones"	194 acres	1692 acres	WR 5, f. 524-527.
12 Aug. 1785 (Resurveyed 26 April 1786, Patented 18 Dec. 1787)	J. F. Amelung	(Resurvey)	£7/10/- for 324 acres of "vacant" land	"New Bremen" (contains: "Tobacco Hook," "I don't care what," "Gantt's Garden" and 324 acres of "vacant" land)	1822 acres	2016 acres	Patents IC #C, IC #D
21 Mar. 1787	Abraham Faw	J. F. Amelung	5/-	"Adam's Bones"	35 acres	1981 acres	WR 7, f. 201.
ca. 1788 or 1789 (officially: 25 March 1795)	J. F. Amelung	Thomas Johnson	"in compliance with an agreement heretofore made" and 5/-	"Resurvey on right and good reason"	560 acres	2541 acres	WR 13, f. 155-156.
30 Aug. 1792	George Ramsberg	J. F. Amelung	£46/15/-	"New Bremen"	(two parts)—14½ and 2½ acres	2524 acres	WR 11 f. 105-106.
11 Feb. 1793	John Darnall	James Marshall and J. F. Amelung	£100	"New Bremen"	100 acres		WR 11, f. 652-653.
25 June 1793	J. F. Amelung	Abraham Faw	£264/12/-	"Resurvey on right and good reason"	378 acres	2802 acres	WR 12, f. 150-151.

Date	Pledged			Amount	Acres	Land Record
1 July 1793	"New Bremen" / "Adam's Bones"	James Labes	J. F. Amelung	£12,000 total	said to be 1822 acres (actual: 1705 acres) / 194 acres	WR 12, f. 151-155.
1 July 1793	"Resurvey on right and good reason"	James Labes	J. F. Amelung	£264/12/-	378 acres	WR 12, f. 155-156.
1 July 1793	"The Resurvey of the Hope"	James Labes	Henry Darnall	£200	16¼ acres	WR 12, f. 156-157.
1 July 1793	"New Bremen"	Henry Darnall	J. F. Amelung and James Labes	£200	16¼ acres / *2802 acres*	WR 11, f. 640-641.
4 Sept. 1794	"New Bremen"	George Ramsberg	George Ramsberg	£41/17/6	16¾ acres (2 parts) / *2785¼ acres*	WR 12, f. 560-561.
18 Sept. 1795	"Resurvey on right and good reason"	J. F. M. Amelung	J. F. Amelung	"Consideration of natural love and Affection" and 5/-	560 acres / *2225¼ acres*	WR 13, f. 547-548.

MORTGAGES

Date	Given by/to	Pledged	Amount/Due	Paid by	Date	Land Record (Maryland Hall of Records)
16 June 1792 interest due from [1 Dec. 1791]	State of Maryland to J. F. Amelung	George Schnertzel and James Labes — securities (in lieu of bond with Thomas Johnson, Benj. Ogle and George Schnertzel, securities)	£1,000	George Schnertzel, (assigned to Abraham Faw, 1799)	1797	Chancery Papers, #1767
17 Jan. 1794	Abraham Usher to James Labes	"New Bremen" and "Adam's Bones" — said to be 2016 acres; and personal bonds from Labes and Amelung (actual: 1864 acres)	£1,000 due 17 Jan. 1797	Sale of property		WR 12, f. 249-250
26 Mar. 1794	Abraham Faw to James Labes	"New Bremen," "Adam's Bones" and "The resurvey on right and good reason," said to contain 2394 acres (actual: 2242 acres)	£750 plus bills with merchants, account of Amelung and Labes, paid by Faw, and other debts			WR 12, f. 484-485
23 May 1795	Ration & Konecke, George Repold, and Charles Ghequiere to James Labes	"New Bremen" and "Resurvey on right and good reason"	£250 debt £211 debt £26 debt	Sale of property		WR 13, f. 643-645

Auction sale of land belonging to James Labes, insolvent debtor, 10 December 1798 [MHR, Chancery Papers, #3252, "Report of Samuel Moale," Dec. 18, 1798]

TRACT:
"NEW BREMEN"

Lot Number	Buyer	Size	Price
1	Balis Combes	9 acres	£15/19/6
2	John Wilson	44 acres	£50/12/-
3	Abner Ritchie	120½ acres	£111/-/-
4	Abner Ritchie	93 acres	£97/13/-
5	Philip Singstock	105 acres	£241/10/-
6	George Schnertzell	156½ acres	£215/3/9
7	George Schnertzell	133½ acres	£190/4/9
8	Adam Krammer	82 acres	£102/10/-
9	George Schnertzell	134½ acres	£309/7/-
10	Ignatius Davis	129 acres	£306/7/6
11	George Schnertzell	113 acres	£163/17/-
12	Abner Ritchie	89 acres	£46/14/6
13	Peter Volkman	112 acres	£112/-/-

"Resurvey on the Hope"

14	George Schnertzell	16¼ acres	£10/19/4½

"Adam's Bones" and part of "Resurvey on Right and Good Reason"

15	Peter Volkman	282 acres	£760/-/-

An Island on Monocacy River

16	Welham Harding	6 acres	£6/1/6
Total			£2697/0/0½

APPENDIX II

John Frederick Amelung's *Remarks on Manufactures . . .* (1787)

Published by permission of the Charleston Library Society

REMARKS
on
MANUFACTURES,
PRINCIPALLY
ON THE
NEW ESTABLISHED
GLASS-HOUSE,
NEAR
FREDERICK-TOWN,
IN THE STATE OF
MARYLAND.

By JOHN F. AMELUNG.

PRINTED for the AUTHOR.
M,DCC,LXXXVII.

REMARKS, &c.

AT this juncture of affairs, every well-wisher of his country, ought to rejoice, when he is informed, that not only great men, but great associations also, do their utmost, to favour and assist the establishment and progress, of the Manufactures of their country.

Now, I take the liberty to address the Public—till this time I had no courage for it—I was certainly persuaded that the time would arrive, when necessity would force this country to establish Manufactures, and by this means, bring the balance of trade in favour of the United States, but imagined, that period still farther of.—I experienced on my arrival, with what coolness Manufacturers of foreign parts were received here, and how little they were encouraged.—I found instead of encouragement, that the best plan for establishing Manufactures, did not meet with the least confidence——Alas!—this was very discouraging—but notwithstanding, did not get afraid—I continued my path, and have now the pleasure to see, that the idea I had formed of the public spirit of the free Americans, when in Europe, was just; it only wants to be stirred up, when beginning to blaze, and then nothing is impossible.

The sensible, and this I flatter myself, is the greater part of this nation, seem to be fully persuaded, that it is impossible for a country to flourish and become powerful, without country Manufactures—as mathematically certain as this truth is in itself, yet it has often been disregarded.

Self-interest and chicane, often originate obstacles, and really have given rise to them; for instance, would not a self-interested merchant, who, to a great profit, import foreign goods, overlook the benefit of the Public? Would he think so nobly, as to prefer his country, to his own advantage, so far as to resolve to quit importing one or the other article out of true patriotism, and assist and favour a Manufactory

factory, which makes the fame. This, though much to be wished for the common good, is only to be expected of a few namely, the true friends of their country.—

For such a general way of thinking, we must look back to the times of the patriotic Romans and Greeks. But we are not at a loss of more modern examples, even in this country.—If we review with attention, the history of the European States, which all serve as a proof how highly necessary Manufactures and Commerce are for a country, the foregoing observations are fully confirmed and put out of all doubts.

It is hoped a few remarks will not be disagreeable to the reader.

Was not France at the highest top of fortune under the administration of a Colbert? This great man, assisted with all his power, Manufactures and Commerce. What encouragement did not this Minister, crowned with immortal fame, give to all foreign, principally English, and German Manufacturers?

What immense sums of money, which amounted to millions, did he not expend, to establish and assist Manufactures, of which France had the raw materials, and was obliged to import them from other parts.—His penetrating eagle-look, and all-piercing eye, made him expect success, and his expectation was not deceived.

What was afterwards the reason of the deep and sudden fall of France? A spirit of persecution, driving off a number of good Manufacturers, who carried with them, their arts into other countries, and depopulated theirs: England, Holland, and Germany, made in their turn, use of this favourable opportunity, and replanted the artizans of France with great expence, and generous encouragement, in their respective countries; by which they increased considerably their power and grandeur.

What makes Spain, notwithstanding its immense tracts of fine land, and great quantities of raw materials so weak? Bigotry, suppression of religion, and envy towards every Manufacturer. The most striking instance of this, is quite new, in the following anecdote.

OLIVADES, a man who, with foreigners, changed into a paradise the wilderness of Sierra Leona, (an uninhabited part of Spain, but blessed with a fine climate) drew in the space of ten years, several thousands of different religions there. His expectations were very nearly fulfilled, and his plan promised the best success; but how did he in reality succeed?—Alas! all the world knows it; all the world law it. Astonishment overcame every good and well thinking citizen of Spain and Europe; they drop a tear of sorrow.

OLIVADES was in consequence of these prejudices arrested, and was obliged to fly in the greatest danger of his life—but found protection in enlightened France. After long ten years work, returned to its former uncultivated state; the holy inquisition took share in this disgraceful business; the industrious foreigners were plagued and surprised, and at last obliged to disperse themselves, and the growing paradise became a chaos.

What makes the small dominions of the King of Prussia so formidable and well settled? Is it not Manufactures of all kinds, which by his wisdom and generosity are strongly assisted? A number of industrious workmen of the different nations of Europe, settling in his dominions, where, when they understand useful trades, they find a generous reception and a liberal assistance; to mention instances thereof, is as unnecessary as tedious—they are innumerable, and well known to the world. The public papers of this country, have mentioned some of the most remarkable.

All the Princes of Europe, small and great, are fully convinced, that useful and necessary Manufactures, are of a very great advantage to their country and to their people.

All able Manufacturers are always certain to find a good reception, even in case that his plan the first year, should meet with difficulties and losses, he is assisted; then there is no Manufactory in the world, which, by its first establishment, has not encountered great difficulties.

The present Duke of Brunswick, one of the greatest Princes in Europe, if we look on him as a hero, a politician, and as a father of his country, establishes new Manufactures, assists the old, and notwithstanding he found his country, which is but small, at his accession to government, deeply indebted, it does not deter him therefrom. He oversees with a piercing eye the whole; although, that the fruits of his labour, do not shew themselves directly in their full lustre, and his expectations are not immediately fulfilled, still the succeeding age will fully enjoy them. At

At leaſt ſo much is obvious, that every Manufacture increaſes the number of inhabitants, and, as ſoon as they are able to export their commodities, bring the money of other countries in circulation, or at leaſt keep the money for that article which it is making in the country; certainly advantages of great importance.

The Empreſs of Ruſſia, without doubt, the greateſt Princeſs of this age, has laid a duty of one hundred per cent. on all imported glaſs, becauſe ſhe has the raw materials of which it is made in her country, which has occaſioned already ſeven Glaſs-Houſes to be erected in her dominions, when at her coming to the Throne, not a ſingle one did exiſt.

To ſay any thing about Great-Britain would be ſuperfluous; every one in this country, knows what premiums and encouragements ſhe has granted to Manufacturers; and what tender care ſhe takes of them, as a mother of her darling child.—We know what advances the Parliament of Ireland, and other great men in that Kingdom, have lately made to new Manufactures.

North-America, is, in regard to her liberty and ſituation, happy; bleſſed with raw materials, which partly are, and more will be diſcovered, but as yet very backward in Manufactures, which are but in their childhood; the ſpirit of this neceſſary branch, ſeems only to enliven a very few.—At the firſt view, one would ſuppoſe, that the public ſpirit which reigns in theſe States, ought to be very favourable to new eſtabliſhed Manufactures, but till now, I have found it quite the reverſe; unaccuſtomed to graat particular privileges, to any citizens, who perhaps are of more utility to the community than others, notwithſtanding it may daily happen, that in private matters we have acted againſt this rule, yet to my knowledge, no man who has had ſenſe and fortune enough to make any progreſs in Manufactures, got any public preference and encouragement whatſoever. This point deſerves to be looked into with judgment, knowledge, and impartiality; and the judicious encouragement thereof, is what I take to be the life and ſpirit of Manufactures.

Manufactures are, as already obſerved, yet in their infancy, but what mother would not cheriſh a child of which ſhe can promiſe herſelf great (perhaps her only) hopes to be nouriſhed and taken care of in her old days; nurſe it with all tenderneſs

derneſs, and do all in her power for its growth and proſperity? Will ſhe not love it in preference to a number of others? Manufactures cannot ſubſiſt without particular neceſſary privileges. Every judge of foreign Manufactures knows what privileges the European governments have granted them; often were they extravagant; for inſtance,

The firſt Looking-Glaſs Manufactory at St. Aubin, in France, obtained through the great Colbert, the privilege, and ſtill has it, that all her Manufacturers are nobleſſe.

The Venetian Glaſs-Houſe at Murano, the mother of the before-mentioned in France, and one of the oldeſt in the world, has ſtill greater liberties; it is moſtly independant, has her own courts of juſtice, and the Manufacturers enjoy, by a law of the Senate, very great liberties. By the famous marriage of the Doge of Venice with the Adriatic See, their gondolo, or pleaſure-boat, has the preference, to go before that of the Doge, called Bucentaur, and other more eſſential privileges.

Little as I will ſpeak in favour of thoſe extravagant privileges, which perhaps the Governments in thoſe countries, where they were granted, thought neceſſary for their ſucceſs; ſtill am I perſuaded, that no manufactory of any conſequence can ſucceed in this country, when Government does not grant, according to its utility and conſequence, ſome real aſſiſtance for its beginning, and ſome privileges for the encouragement of foreign Manufacturers.

Such privileges ought not to be very expenſive to Government: A Manufactory of conſequence, will bring a number of induſtrious workmen into the country; for inſtance, a Glaſs Manufactory, which eaſily can be ſuppoſed I have in view, as I am thoroughly acquainted with the ſame, and it can not be eſtabliſhed to any advantage, when not directly in the beginning, a number of neceſſary workmen are employed: The Manufacturers muſt be brought from Europe, and their loſs through death or other accidents, muſt the firſt ſix years be replaced from thence, which time is required to inſtruct a good workman.

On the continent of Europe, every Manufacturer has the privilege, that he is exempted from war ſervice and taxes, and none can be arreſted or taken to public ſervices, if the owners of the Manufactory conſents not to it; then if one man is wanting

(o)

wanting, the chain of buſineſs is broke, and it is the ſame as if a wheel is taken out of a clock, the whole work is at a ſtand. In caſe of a civil arreſt, the owner is anſwerable for the man; in criminal caſes, the law continues in full force againſt the delinquent.

As a Manufacturer enjoys ſo many privileges in deſpotic Governments on the continent of Europe, how many more muſt there not naturally be expected in the free and independent States of America? By not finding them, will he not return to a country, where, as a Manufacturer, he is really free, principally as he is ſure, that thoſe privileges are never encroached upon, or taken from him? Wherefore, it ſeems to me, very neceſſary to grant thoſe and other privileges to Manufacturers here; as they are not expenſive to the State, a relief from taxes might perhaps bear the appearance of leſſening the income of the State; but how little is this loſs, in compariſon to the advantages which Manufactures are of, and beſides that, if no encouragement draws foreign Manufacturers here, no taxes can be expected from them.

Manufacturers in Europe, enjoy ſtill a much greater aſſiſtance; if their capital is not ſufficient to carry their Manufactory on a large and extenſive plan, the Prince, in whoſe dominions they are ſettled, advances them in general, upon five or more years without intereſt, the neceſſary amount; this I believe, will be wanted in this country: Some will ſuppoſe that ſuch a loan out of the public funds, is a real expence to the State, as the intereſt is loſt for ſome years; but that only appears ſo, even if one does not draw the great benefit which Manufactures give in compariſon. This ſeeming loſs is very eaſy made up, by laying duties on the importation of the like goods, as are manufactured in the country, which, at the ſame time, operates in favour of the Manufactures. It is naturally ſuppoſed, that the public hold the firſt mortgage on the property of ſuch a Manufactory as receives a loan, and ought not the ſame to be more than one half of the real value, and then is the public, for their advance, ſufficiently ſecured.

Still another great encouragement for beginning Manufactures would be, if patriotic citizens would aſſiſt foreign ones with their good advice—give them protection againſt impoſitions (which often is the caſe with foreigers, who are ſtrangers to the laws and language of this country.) If ſuch noble thinking

(9)

thinking men would aſſiſt them in the diſcovery of raw materials, which are wanted to carry on the work, and if they would be above the common prejudices that the foreign goods would be better than the home manufactured, and would by uſing them, through their good example, perſuade others to follow them, even if the Manufactory had not arrived to the greateſt perfection. Great men, even courts of Kings and Princes, on the Continent of Europe, have but lately given excellent patterns hereof, which without law, or perſuaſion, made the Manufactures of thoſe countries increaſe, and what adventurer would not, with the warmeſt thanks, acknowledge ſuch an aſſiſtance?

Every part of the Continent of Europe, which has Manufactures, has a Board of Superviſors, which conſiſt of different Members of Government, who by order of their Prince, are moſtly or only employed to look into the different branches of Manufactures, and return their reports, either to thoſe above them, or to the Prince himſelf. Every member is obliged to get as much knowledge as poſſible in the Manufacturing line; every Manufacturer brings his well grounded complaints before this Board, and wo unto them, if they do not render him a ſpeedy redreſs. How ſuch a Board may take place in this State, I do not know, and leave this to the judgment of men of more knowledge and underſtanding; I only hint it. In Germany, Manufactures are carried on in three different ways.

FIRST. Thoſe, who work only for account of Government, who chuſes and pays all the workmen of it.

SECOND. Such as are firſt eſtabliſhed for account of Government, but afterwards farmed out for a certain annua[l] rent, in ſuch, the Farmer of the Manufactory chuſes his own workmen, by paying his rent, and giving ſecurity not t[o] neglect the buildings; he is quite independent.

The third and laſt, are thoſe who are eſtabliſhed at th[e] expence of the Manufacturer, thoſe get in general the grea[t] teſt privileges and aſſiſtance; and the owners, if they ar[e] honeſt and induſtrious men, are certain of the eſteem an[d] protection of their Prince.

I know by experience, that one of the wiſeſt Princes no[w] in Europe, preferred a plain but induſtrious Manufacture[r] at his Levee, ſpoke with ... above an hour, when at th[e] fame

fame time, he did not look at a number of the greateſt and richeſt of the Nobility of his dominions, whoſe principal occupation is to oppreſs their farmers and hunt foxes; no-thing elſe could be the reaſon of ſuch proceedings, of this wiſe Prince, than that he was perſuaded that the Manufac-turer who maintained a number of his ſubjects, retained the money in his dominions, and brought more into it, was bet-ter worth his eſteem than thoſe proud idlers. This Prince knows the true ſpirit of encouraging Manufactures.

It would be eaſy for me to become tedious, I only beg the Public's per-miſſion to ſay ſomething about the Glaſs-Houſe, eſtabliſhed by me, and brought to a tolerable degree of perfection.

I made the beginning to a complete Glaſs-Houſe, in the year 1785, and advertiſed it in the public papers.

In the beginning of the year 1784, a company was formed between ſome of the moſt capital houſes in Bremen and the ſubſcriber, to eſtabliſh a Glaſs-Houſe in one of the moſt con-venient parts of the United States of America; we got ac-quainted with Mr. Benjamin Crocker, from Baltimore, who was at that time in Bremen, and from what we learned from him, we choſe this State for its eſtabliſhment, with flattering expectations to meet here with encouragement in this great enterpriſe, that the principal materials, as wood and pot-aſh, were to be had in abundance, which I have ſince found, like-wiſe, that the prices of Glaſs as ſoon as the Manufactory was well eſtabliſhed, were more advantageous in compariſon, than thoſe in England and Germany, which they really are. The principal point was, and which we had the greateſt rea-ſon to expect, that the Government of this State would en-courage and aſſiſt to their utmoſt a Manufactory, which drew a number of induſtrious workmen into it, as the great ſum of money, which for this neceſſary article is ſent abroad remains in the country; principally, as little elſe but the produce of his country is uſed at it. It ought to be preferred to a number of other Manufactures to which the raw materials muſt be drawn from other parts, and as for the purchaſe of f fifteen thouſand pounds is in circulation in this country; it certainly deſerves the patronage of the Public.

Upon

11

Upon theſe grounds a contract was made, between the beforementioned Merchants and me; a capital of ten thou-ſand pounds ſtipulated for this enterpriſe, and all poſſible preparations made to get the neceſſary workmen—a veſſel fitted out for their tranſportation; we got inſtruments for three different Glaſs Ovens; in ſhort, every thing that could be moſt effectual to forward this great enterpriſe—a number of Glaſs Makers and Workmen from different parts of Germa-ny, to whom we applied, informed us, that they would engage themſelves, and really did, to go to this part of the world.

Every thing went well till the hard winter, which in the year 1784, was much ſeverer in Germany than here, put very great obſtacles in our way—partly by the Manufacturers, which with great expences I had engaged in Bohemia, Thuring, and other parts of Germany, could not travel ſoon enough; ſome were on the road half ſtarved for the common want, and thoſe who arrived, could not be directly tranſported, as the rivers were frozen up—during this delay, this buſineſs, with a number of additions and enlargements, were made known; ſome Engliſh Merchants, and ſea Captains, who were at that time in Bremen, wrote to England about it, and this jealous Nation, who look on the glaſs trade as an important one, deſired the Government of Hanover, to do all that was in their power to fruſtrate a plan which they feared, would be to their loſs, and greatly to the benefit of this country.—Brunſwick, Heſſe, and other neighbouring Princes of the Roman Empire, were called upon to join for that pur-poſe—now all poſſible obſtacles were partly by intrigue, partly by force and deſpotic behaviour thrown in my way—the work-men I had engaged were detained, and nothing left untried to oppoſe me—this affair had made ſuch a rumour, that I was obliged to go off with as many workmen as I could collect in a ſhort time, under thoſe diſagreeable circumſtances—As I would not expoſe myſelf and family, to the rage which then took place, as it was known that before this ſtorm broke out, I had all the hands which were wanted engaged, and had ſup-ported the greateſt part through the long and tedious winter.

I am aſſured by good authority, that the brig Fame in which myſelf and ſome of the moſt neceſſary workmen came over, was to be taken by ſome Engliſh ſhip of force, but this plan was defeated owing to the extraordinary quick paſſage of twenty-ſix hours through the Channel.

I had letters of recommendation from thofe great men, Franklin and Adams, and the American Conful at Paris, to the firft men in this country, *viz.* to his Excellency General Mifflin, Prefident of Congrefs, Thomas Johnfon, Efq. William Paca, Efq. and Charles Corroll, of Carrollton, Efq. and a great number to the firft mercantile houfes, which would be too tedious to mention; all thofe letters will prove that I had the character of a worthy and honeft man in Germany, and kept the fame until I left it.

After a tedious and difagreeable paffage of fixteen weeks, I arrived with fixty-eight hands, the laft day of Auguft, 1784, in Baltimore—I had left an Agent behind, who arrived here, the 22d of November following, with fourteen hands more, which he had brought with great difficulties through Friefland, Holland, and embarked them at Amfterdam.

My firft occupation after my arrival was, to look out for a Seat to eftablifh the Glafs-Houfe, to which Meffrs. Crockets and Harris, at Baltimore, and Mr. Faw, at Frederick-town, have rendered me all poffible affiftance, and I have fo far fuccee- ded, that I have purchafed an advantageoufly fituated tract of land on Patowmack, not far from the mouth of Monocafey, of two thoufand one hundred acres, which except a fmall balance, is paid—on this land I have erected all the neceffary buildings for the Manufactory, as glafs ovens for bottles, window and flint glafs, and a dwelling houfe for one hundred and thirty-five now living fouls—I have made a beginning of glafs making; the goodnefs of the glafs is fuch that the gentlemen in Baltimore, Frederick, and Elizabeth-town, to whom I have fold my glafs are contented; by inquiry it will be found, that my glafs is cheaper, and of a better quality, than a great deal of what is imported. In my opinion, if a Manufactory can give fuch proof, it certainly deferves the attention of Government and the patronage of the Public.

I am now building another glafs oven, as I expect in a few months more Glafs Makers from Germany, having fent in October 1785, an Affiftant there to engage and bring them over. I expect to have every thing ready, to fet them directly (by their arrival) to work—Befides the before mentioned fifteen thoufand pounds, which the eftablifhment of the Glafs-Houfe has already coft, more money will be required to put every thing belonging to it in proper order. Perfuaded

Perfuaded that no greater happinefs can be for the fucceeding generations, than to give them a good education in their younger years, and imprefs religion and morals early in their breafts; for this purpofe, I have (directly after my fettlement here) eftablifhed a German School, the mafter, a worthy man, is fully acquainted with his duty, and has a yearly falary from me, a commodious houfe, in which every Sunday divine fervice is kept, a garden, fome land, and free fire wood. The inhabitants, who fend their children to this fchool, pay a trifle to him.

I am now about eftablifhing an Englifh School, for which purpofe I have built a houfe on my land, and as I advance, I intend to put the fame upon fuch a footing, that children may get a complete education in the fame, as in the Englifh, German, and French languages, writing, ciphering, mufic, to play on the harp, harpfichord, flute, and violin; I have the mafters for this purpofe already here, and will contribute all that is in my power to make the charges eafy, and will pay attention to the education and morals of thofe children, who will be fent to this School.

If any patriot, or friend to mankind, chufes to have nearer information, will affift a Manufactory, which fhews fo great profpects with his advice, knows Fullers earth, which will ftand the fire, or is acquainted with Glafs Makers, who underftand their bufinefs, he will pleafe to addrefs himfelf, or direct them to me. I always fhall very thankfully acknowledge fuch a fervice, and not only pay any expences which might have been occafioned thereby, but give a premium, according to the utility fuch information may be to me.

I laftly recommend this Manufactory to the kind patronage of every true friend of this Country, and to the Public in general, perfuaded that if I have fuccefs, and it comes to perfection, it will be advantageous to this and the neighbouring States.

JOHN FREDERICK AMELUNG.

NEW-BREMEN, near
Frederick-Town.

This Pamphlet was publish

a Years after my Arrival here & Since
that time a great Deal of Alterations
happened, and as the quality of
of Goods ± expended &, & of the Value
of the Manufactory have increased
three times this Sum, not only in
regard to the Number of People
also in making articles of Soap
Wares and which is increasing every
Day —

I also have Purchased one thousand
Acres of Land more, and erry'd an
other Glasshouse on that Spot all
which is paid —

The quality of Glass is coming to
Perfection from degree to degree
almost every Month, owing to the
Experience I have acquired since these
6 Years Past which enabled one
to be better acquainted with the Manu
facture here consequently making
a better Use of it, then in the be=
ginning & therefore do not in the
least Doubt if a Moderate assistance

should given me, the Glassmaker
turn quite Equal the imported
in a short time —

This one will likewise be very know
more from Boston to Charlestown
in Parton.

Feb: 1790.

1. February 13, 1789, Julian P. Boyd, Lyman H. Butterfield, et al., eds. *The Papers of Thomas Jefferson,* vol. 14, Princeton: Princeton University Press, 1958, p. 547.

2. Quoted in Jacob E. Cooke, "Tench Coxe, Alexander Hamilton, and the Encouragement of American Manufactures," *William and Mary Quarterly,* 3rd ser., vol. XXXII, No. 3, July 1975, 372.

3. Phineas Bond to the Duke of Leeds, *American Historical Association Annual Report* for the year 1896, vol. 1, Washington: Government Printing Office, 1897, 630–631.

4. J. C. Harrington, *A Tryal of Glasse,* Eastern National Park and Monument Association, 1972; a revision of *Glassmaking at Jamestown America's First Industry,* Richmond: Dietz, 1952.

5. Arlene Palmer, "Glass Production in Eighteenth-Century America, The Wistarburgh Enterprise," *Winterthur Portfolio 11,* Charlottesville, Va.: University of Virginia Press for the Henry Francis du Pont Winterthur Museum, 1976, pp. 75–101.

6. October 1748–May 1749, Account Book, United Glass Company, 1743–1767, pp. 51–58, Wistar Papers, Historical Society of Pennsylvania.

7. Thomas Lepper of a New York glasshouse advertised such personalized bottles, but none has been documented. *New York Gazette,* Nov. 18, 1754.

8. William Franklin to Lord Hillsborough, *Documents Relating to the Colonial History of the State of New Jersey,* reprinted in William A. Whitehead et al., eds., *The Archives of the State of New Jersey 1631–1800,* 1st ser., 31 vols., Newark, 1880–1906, 10: 29–32.

9. Wistar to Daniel Taylor & Bros., Bristol, May 12, 1760, Richard Wistar Letterbook, microfilm 220, Joseph Downs Manuscript and Microfilm Collection, Winterthur Museum Libraries.

10. Account Book, United Glass Company, p. 10.

11. For example, the advertisement of Richard Wistar, *Pennsylvania Chronicle,* July 31, 1769.

12. *South Carolina Gazette,* July 8, 1771; Letter to the Lords Commissioners for Trade and Plantations, Jan. 21, 1767, *Minutes of the Provincial Council of Pennsylvania,* reprinted in *Colonial Records of Pennsylvania,* vol. 9, Harrisburg: Theo. Fenn & Co., 1852, p. 354.

13. Wistar to Daniel Taylor, Oct. 21, 1760, Richard Wistar Letterbook.

14. Benjamin Franklin to William Franklin, March 13, 1768, ed. William B. Willcox, *The Papers of Benjamin Franklin,* 18 vols. to date, New Haven: Yale University Press, 1972, 15: p. 77; see Arlene Palmer, "Benjamin Franklin and the Wistarburg Glassworks," *Antiques,* 105, No. 1, Jan., 1974, pp. 207–210.

15. *Pennsylvania Journal and Weekly Advertiser,* July 5, 1769.

16. Tower and Leacock hoped Benjamin Franklin, in London, could arrange for glassworkers to emigrate. Franklin to Tower and Leacock, August 22, 1772, BF 85. 56 [ms. no.], American Philosophical Society.

17. William Logan to Cornelius Fry, May 17, [1773], Smith Papers, Library Company of Philadelphia.

18. I. Daniel Rupp, *A Collection of 30,000 Names of . . . Immigrants in Pennsylvania from 1727–1776,* Philadelphia: Kohler, 1876, p. 408.

19. Will of Conrad Foltz, 1784, Frederick County Wills, G.M. #2, pp. 112–114, Maryland Hall of Records, Annapolis, Microfilm WK 427–428.

20. The information in this section on the Amelung family history has been derived from Friedrich Amelung, *Familiennachrichten,* Dorpat, Lithuania: 1887, 1890, 1894.

21. Eberhard Tacke, *Bilder aus der Geschichte der Gemeinde Grünenplan und der Glasindustrie im Hils,* Grünenplan, Germany, 1949, is the principal source for information about Grünenplan and the Amelungs' activities there.

22. *Ibid.,* p. 65.

23. Dr. Luhrs, State Archives, Bremen, Germany to Mrs. Paul Amelung, Fairfield, Conn., Nov. 3, 1975.

24. "Answer of John Frederick Magnus Amelung," Chancery Papers, No. 1767, Maryland Hall of Records (hereafter MHR).

25. Edward S. Delaplaine, *John Frederick Amelung, Maryland Glassmaker,* Frederick, Maryland: *Frederick News Post,* 1971, p. 3.

26. Frederick County Land Records, W.R. No. 5, f. 520–527, MHR.

27. *Maryland Journal and Baltimore Advertiser,* Feb. 11, 1785. The advertisement was dated Feb. 9, 1785.

28. Phineas Bond to the Duke of Leeds, Nov. 10, 1789, *American Historical Association Annual Report,* 1, p. 654.

29. *Maryland Journal and Baltimore Advertiser,* Feb. 11, 1785.

30. *Maryland Gazette, or the Baltimore Advertiser,* April 7, 1789.

31. *Maryland Journal and Baltimore Advertiser,* Feb. 11, 1785.

32. Bond to the Duke of Leeds, Nov. 10, 1789, AHA, etc., p. 654; *The North Carolina Chronicle; or Fayetteville Gazette,* May 24, 1790.

33. Capt. Jacob Good, 1783, Frederick County Inventories, GM No. 2, ff. 102–106, MHR.

34. *Federal Intelligencer and Baltimore Daily Gazette,* March 25, 1795.

35. Dorothy Mackay Quynn, "Johann Friedrich Amelung at New Bremen," *Maryland Historical Maga-*

zine, 43, No. 3, Sept., 1948, pp. 155–179; *Federal Intelligencer and Baltimore Daily Gazette*, March 25, 1795.

36. The teacher at Grünenplan, Johann Martin Feuerhacke, died in February 1784, at the very time when Amelung was planning to emigrate to America. Tacke, pp. 73–79. A "George Feuerhacke" is known to have been at New Bremen and is said to have come with Amelung in 1784. Although no documented relationship has been found, it is tempting to suggest that George Feuerhacke may have been Johann Martin Feuerhacke's son. George was a glassblower, as he was one of the five Amelung glassblowers to seek employment, post-New Bremen, with John Nicholson in Philadelphia (see *Journal of Glass Studies*, XXI, p. 108).

37. Patents, IC #D, f. 81–83, MHR.

38. "Answer of John Frederick Magnus Amelung," March 23, 1801, Chancery Papers, No. 1767, MHR.

39. "Answer of James Labes," Feb. 25, 1804, Chancery Papers, No. 1767, MHR.

40. *Remarks*, ms. notes, p. [14].

41. "Answer of John Frederick Magnus Amelung," March 23, 1801, Chancery Papers, No. 1767, MHR. On January 6, 1804, an announcement was printed in the *Republican Advocate* (Frederick-Town, Maryland) that on 18 January an auction of "PART of the effects of Frederick M. Amelung, a bankrupt—a tract of land, near Frederick-Town, part of the re-survey on Right and Good Reason, containing 560 acres, clear of older surveys; on said land is erected an extensive Glass Manufactory, with the necessary buildings and ovens; 14 or 15 dwelling houses; barn, stables, +c." [The same advertisement also appeared in the *Frederick-Town Herald* on January 7,1804.]

42. Petition of John Frederick Amelung, May 26, 1790, to Congress, quoted in Quynn, p. 168.

43. *Remarks*, ms. notes, p. [13–14].

44. J. P. Brissot de Warville, *Nouveau Voyage dans les Etats-Unis . . . fait en 1788*, Paris, 1799, p. 269.

45. Feb. 13, 1789, Boyd, *Jefferson*, 14:547.

46. *Remarks*, ms. notes, pp. [14–15].

47. *Maryland Chronicle or The Universal Advertiser*, Nov. 15, 1786. A nearly identical advertisement appeared in the *Virginia Gazette and Winchester Advertiser*, July 11, 1787.

48. *Maryland Journal and Baltimore Advertiser*, May 22, 1789. On March 17, 1789, James Labes advertised [*Maryland Journal and Baltimore Advertiser*; *The Maryland Gazette; or, the Baltimore Advertiser*] "10 by 12, 8 by 10, 7 by 9, and 6 by 8 Window-Glass; and a Quantity of hollow Glass Ware, in small Packages assorted; containing Quart, Pint, Half-Pint, Gill and Half-Gill Tumblers and Wine-Glasses. . . . at the Glass-House. . . ." Andrew Keener, the Baltimore merchant, also advertised "A general Assortment of GLASS, . . . amongst which are, 6 by 8, 7 by 9, 8 by 10, 9 by 11, and 10 by 12 Window-Glass; Quart, Pint, Half-Pint, Gill, and Half-Gill Tumblers; Wine Glasses; Quart, Pint, and Half Pint Decanters, exact Measure; Goblets; Glass Cans, with handles, of different Sizes; Phials assorted; and green Bottles, from Pint to Gallon; with sundry other useful Glass Ware. . . . This GLASS is all AMERICAN MANUFACTURE, very little inferior in Quality to any imported, . . ." [*Mary-*

land *Journal and Baltimore Advertiser* and *The Maryland Gazette; or, the Baltimore Advertiser*, March 14, 1788.]

49. *City Gazette, or the Daily Advertiser*, Charleston, April 25, 1789, and in the *Virginia Herald*, Fredericksburg, April 9, 1789.

50. *Massachusetts Magazine or Monthly Museum*, IV, No. II, Dec. 1792, p. 759.

51. Petition of John Frederick Amelung to U.S. Congress, May 26, 1790, quoted in Quynn, pp. 167–168.

52. Laws of the Maryland Assembly, May session, 1788, quoted in Quynn, p. 167; "Bond of John Frederick Amelung. . . ," "Schnertzell's Case," and "Assignment of Bond," Chancery Papers, No. 1767, MHR. "An act for the benefit of John Frederick Amelung . . ." was announced as having been passed at the 27 May 1788 meeting of the General Assembly in the *Maryland Journal and Baltimore Advertiser* and in *The Maryland Gazette; or, the Baltimore Advertiser* on June 3, 1788.

53. Laws of the Maryland Assembly, May session, 1788; Petition of John Frederick Amelung to U.S. Congress, May 26, 1790, quoted in Quynn, pp. 167–168.

54. T. J. C. Williams, and Folger McKinsey, *History of Frederick County Maryland*, 1910; reprint ed., Baltimore: Regional Publishing Co., 1967, p. 136; *The Times & Patowmack Packet*, Georgetown, April 21, 1790.

55. *The Times & Patowmack Packet*, May 12, 1790, and in the *State Gazette of North Carolina*, Edenton, May 28, 1790. There is also a letter (from the Claude W. Unger Collection, Historical Society of Pennsylvania) addressed to "Messrs. Andrew Clow & Co. Merchants Philadelphia," which reads in part: "I have sent by Dr. McGaw a sample of Perlash such as I make, please have it inspected, and Inform me what you Can Give for such. Mr. Emelong who owns the Glass house in Maryland says it is the best he has seen in America, and has purchased a Considerable Quantity from me, but his late Misfortune by fire, prevents him, I am told, from having such a demand for it as he formerly had, for which reason, (if the p[lan?] suits) I would wish to send a few Tuns to Philad[elphi]a soon, or Next fall, which—?—time might answer best for Exportation. [signed] Wm Henderson, Green Castle, June 25th 1790."

56. Quoted in Quynn, pp. 168, 170.

57. Quoted in Quynn, p. 169. On June 11, 1790, *The Maryland Journal and Baltimore Advertiser* noted "The House toook [sic] up the report of the committee on the petition of J. F. Amelung, proprietor of the Glass-House at New-Bremen, in Maryland, praying the aid of Congress to enable him to proceed in the business of Glass-making. The committee had reported that there should be a loan of 8000 dollars to him. The House, after considerable debate, rejected the report."

58. "Complaint of Abraham Faw," Jan. 11, 1800, "Amelung & Labes Account with Faw, Feb. 6, 1794," Chancery Papers, No. 1767, MHR.

59. *Familiennachrichten*, p. 364.

60. "Answer of John F. M. Amelung," March 23, 1801, Chancery Papers, No. 1767, MHR.

61. *The Federal Intelligencer and Baltimore Daily Gazette*, March 23, 1795, p. 2.

62. Frederick County Land Records, WR No. 13, f. 547–548.

63. "Petition of Labes, and Amelung and Labes as Insolvent Debtors," May 23, 1796, Chancery Papers, No. 3252, MHR. James Labes had previously advertised "THE great many losses the subscriber has suffered in the Glass Manufactory, obliges him to petition the next session of assembly, for an insolvent law to be passed in his favour, for debts contracted under the firm of Amelung and Labes. . . ." [*Maryland Journal, and Baltimore Universal Daily Advertiser*, Sept. 28, 1795.

64. *Ibid.*

65. Frederick County Land Records, WR No. 15. f. 272–274; *Federal Gazette and Baltimore Daily Advertiser*, Dec. 8, 1798.

66. *Familiennachrichten*, pp. 356, 74.

67. *Federal Gazette and Baltimore Daily Advertiser*, Nov. 21, 1798.

68. *Frederick-Town Herald*, April 18, 1812.

69. Frederick County Commissioners, Land Assessment Book, No. 19268, 1798, f. 57, 63, 115, MHR; "Adam Kohlenberg and George Chris[n] Gabler," Chancery Papers, No. 3252, MHR.

70. Frederick County Inventories, RB No. 3, f. 443, MHR.

71. *Maryland Gazette and Frederick-Town Weekly Advertiser*, Feb. 26, 1793; *Maryland Journal and Baltimore Advertiser*, Nov. 15 and Nov. 29, 1793; Land Assessment Book No. 19268, 1798, f. 115; Jedediah Morse, coll. and comp., *The American Gazetteer*, Boston: S. Hall et al., 1797.

72. Notice of B. S. Pigman, *Frederick-Town Herald*, May 28, 1814; Roger & Thomas Perry, glassmanufactory, Cumberland County, Md., United States Census of Manufactures 1820. M 1599, DMMC. The only glassworks listed in the 1820 Census were those of the Perrys and that of John F. Friese in Baltimore.

73. *Frederick-Town Herald*, Jan. 7, 1804.

74. Johann David Schoepf, *Travels in the Confederation* [*1783–1784*], tr. and ed. Alfred J. Morrison, I, Philadelphia: William J. Campbell, 1911, p. 327.

75. *Federal Gazette and Baltimore Daily Advertiser*, June 27, 1800. An advertisement of the intended opening of the factory on July 1 also appeared in *The Telegraphe And Daily Advertiser* (Baltimore), June 28, 1800. A note that the ". . . Baltimore Glass Manufactory . . . have now on hand, at their factory on the south side of the basin, a general assortment of Hollow White Glass—also a quantity of Porter and Claret Bottles, and a large assortment of Glass Pots, which are deemed superior to any other ware for the use of pickling and preserving. . . ." appeared in *The Telegraphe And Daily Advertiser* (Baltimore) on August 16, 1800.

76. *Federal Gazette and Baltimore Daily Advertiser*, Aug. 31, 1802. An announcement of the dissolution of the partnership of Frederick M. Amelung, Alexander Furnival, Jacob Anshutz, and Louis Repperd was printed in the November 8, 1802 issue of *The Telegraphe And Daily Advertiser* (Baltimore).

77. Philip R. J. Friese, Glassworks Ledger, *Friese Account Books*, 2 MS 933, Maryland Historical Society. On June 8, 1803, Frederick Magnus Amelung was declared a bankrupt in the *Federal Gazette and Baltimore*

Daily Advertiser: the same announcement was printed in the June 9, 1803, issue of *The Telegraph And Daily Advertiser* (Baltimore). In an advertisement dated December 22 [1803?], Amelung stated his intention of operating the signal flags (used to notify merchants of the imminent arrival of their ships) at the Observatory (which Amelung owned) on Federal Hill above the harbor (*American and Commercial Daily Advertiser*, Baltimore, July 9, 1804). An announcement of the intention to divide Frederick M. Amelung's "estate and effects of the said bankrupt" among his creditors was printed in the *American and Commercial Daily Advertiser* on April 2, 1808.

78. Adeline Pepper, *The Glass Gaffers of New Jersey*, New York: Charles Scribner's Sons, 1971, p. 48.

79. *Friese Account Books*, 2, p. 161.

80. Dwight P. Lanmon, "The Baltimore Glass Trade, 1780 to 1820," *Winterthur Portfolio 5*, Charlottesville, Va.: University of Virginia Press for the Henry Francis du Pont Winterthur Museum, 1969, pp. 15–48.

81. *Federal Gazette and Baltimore Daily Advertiser*, Aug. 15, 1800.

82. *The Daily Advertiser*, New York, Jan. 1, 1791.

83. *American and Daily Advertiser*, Baltimore, Dec. 25, 1800.

84. See Dwight P. Lanmon, "The Baltimore Glass Trade, 1780 to 1820," *Winterthur Portfolio 5*, Charlottesville, Va.: University of Virginia Press for the Henry Francis du Pont Winterthur Museum, 1969, pp. 15–48.

85. Hammer Account Books, MS. 423.1–.3, Maryland Historical Society.

86. Frederick County Land Records, WR No. 13, f. 643–645; "Petition as Insolvent Debtors" and "List of Debts," Chancery Papers, No. 3252, MHR.

87. Homer Eaton Keyes, "Safe Clues in the Amelung Quest," *Antiques*, 26, No. 3, Sept. 1934, p. 89.

88. Frederick County Inventories, 1807, HS No. 4, f. 27; inventory of Robert Owen, GM No. 2, f. 29–30, MHR.

89. *Maryland Journal and Baltimore Advertiser*, Nov. 15, 1793.

90. Baltimore City Inventories, WB No. 27, f. 194–197, MHR.

91. Repold's action was taken in association with Ration and Konecke and Charles Ghequiere. Frederick County Land Records, WR No. 13, f. 643–645, MHR.

92. Margaret Mathews, Frederick County Inventories, GM No. 2, f. 88, MHR.

93. Illustrated in George S. and Helen McKearin's *American Glass*, New York: Crown Publishers, 1941, plate 37, no. 3.

94. Helen and George S. McKearin, *200 Years of American Blown Glass*, Garden City, N.Y.: Doubleday, 1950, p. 328.

95. Roland Mars, *Kunst-Auktion*, no. 22, Würzburg, Germany, March 22, 1975, Lot 2634.

96. C. Malcolm Watkins, "An Amelung Discovery," *Antiques*, 69, No. 6, Dec. 1952, p. 489.

97. Helen and George S. McKearin, *Two Hundred Years*, p. 252. The correct version of the motto should be: "Suche Tugend und wann du Sie findest . . ."

98. August König, Baltimore City Inventories,

1801, No. 21, f. 328, MHR: *Maryland Journal and Baltimore Advertiser,* Aug. 21, 1792.

99. Information supplied by Old Salem, Inc.

100. Frederick County Inventories, R.B. No. 3, MHR.

101. *Maryland Journal and Baltimore Advertiser,* May 6, 1788.

102. Ms. catalogue of the glass collection of Henry Francis du Pont, prepared by Neil C. Gest, Aug. 21, 1939, Winterthur Museum.

103. Davidson Account Books, Ms. 381, Vol. C., Maryland Historical Society.

104. "American Glass Bowl (ca. 1789) attributed to the New Bremen Glasshouse of John Frederick Amelung from the collection of W. Dan Quattlebaum," *Antiques,* 55, No. 2, Feb. 1949, pp. 108, 109.

105. McKearin, *Two Hundred Years,* p. 4.

ARCHAEOLOGICAL EXCAVATIONS
ON THE SITE OF
JOHN FREDERICK AMELUNG'S
NEW BREMEN GLASSMANUFACTORY
1962–1963

Ivor Noël Hume

I. PREFACE

EXCAVATIONS BY THE CORNING MUSEUM OF GLASS were carried out on the site of John Frederick Amelung's New Bremen Glass Manufactory in 1962 and 1963. Like far too many archaeological projects, the time that has elapsed between completion of the digging and the publication of the report has been of considerable duration. The delay, however, was not due to a failure to complete the manuscript but rather to an unwillingness on the part of all concerned to admit that further more conclusive digging was less than a viable proposition.

The Corning Museum's original intent had been to mount a test excavation on the Amelung site to obtain specimens of glass and factory waste that would be helpful in identifying yet-to-be-found or disputed New Bremen products. It was never envisaged that the entire factory site should be explored. Nevertheless, even an excavation with limited goals had to be conducted by an archaeologist possessing some knowledge both of glass technology and of the period, and in 1962 the Museum had no archaeologist on its staff with experience in digging on eighteenth-century American sites. For that reason this writer was invited to direct the fieldwork as Colonial Williamsburg's contribution to the project. Completing the research triad was the Smithsonian Institution's Division of Cultural History, which took responsibility for a preliminary site survey, for the provision of much equipment, and for the services of several valuable staff members. It was expected that the Smithsonian Institution would participate in publishing the final report.

Inevitably, shared responsibilities have both advantages and disadvantages. Although the three organizations worked hard and harmoniously throughout the time allotted to each season's fieldwork, it thereafter became extremely difficult to bring the principals together again to make a collective decision as to what more, if anything, should or could be done on the site.

As the following report explains in detail, the initial test excavation not only yielded a large quantity of glass and refractory debris, it also revealed one corner of a sophisticated factory building which, once exposed, could not be ignored, and which could not be described or interpreted without considerably more digging. Thus it was that a second season's work on the site was agreed upon. The major excavation of 1963 succeeded in its intended goals by clearing the factory building discovered in the previous year. Nevertheless, a careful study of information derived largely from the historical evidence indicated that the excavated structure was but one of several, and therefore its place and relative importance in Amelung's master plan remained unclear.

There was convincing evidence that the building had been destroyed by fire, but it was uncertain whether it had been rebuilt on the same foundation, if at all. If so, was its successor of similar design? Was it larger or smaller, and did it incorporate new features learned from the previous experience? Was the excavated structure at any time Amelung's main glasshouse? Was it the oldest of his buildings? The evidence of its own foundation suggested that it was not. Where, then, was the first glasshouse? If the sites of all the manufactory buildings could be explored, would it be possible to determine which were used in the making of bottles, window glass, table glass—or were all three produced under the same roof? These were but a few of the questions posed but unanswered at the end of the second season's digging. It was evident that determining *what* Amelung's workers made, and *where* and *how* they made it were very different questions. The "what" had been sufficiently well answered as a result of the 1962 and 1963 diggings, to keep glass historians, chemists, and curators busy for some time to come; but the solutions to the other puzzles remained buried in the ground—out of reach without a major expenditure of funds and manpower, and the Corning consortium could afford neither.

At a conservative estimate the team would have had to reassemble for four or five seasons to find and investigate only the industrial buildings. After that study the question would almost certainly have been asked: What about the workers and their domestic life? Were they not part of the Amelung story? To that one could only answer—unquestionably. The documentary evidence shows that Amelung employed as many as 500 workers, many of them living in a well-serviced community that he had built on his property. New Bremen was one of the fledgling United States' first "planned communities" and unlike earlier Germanic ventures in Pennsylvania and North Carolina, the bond was economic rather than religious. Certainly, therefore, the whole sociological, industrial, architectural, and artistic story of New Bremen needed to be told. But to do so would require a commitment on the part of the triad of such duration that it would be virtually open ended. There should be no more half measures; having accomplished its original limited purposes, any new digging would have to be the beginning of a commitment to a total investigation of the site.

For reasons no longer clear, a member of the Smithsonian team later returned to the site and by private agreement with the landowners embarked on the excavation of a domestic structure close to Amelung's brick mansion. The excavation proved that the newly found structure had continued in use for some time after the glass manufactory closed in 1795, but neither the full plan of the building nor its life span was determined before the archaeologist realized that he had bitten off more than he could chew and so abandoned the project. This incident only served to demonstrate the magnitude of the problem and made the consortium leaders more certain that publication of the existing evidence should be the limit of this commitment. Meanwhile, thanks to the efforts of then Maryland Congressman, Charles McC. Mathias, Jr., attempts were being made to secure state and federal protection for the site, a task fraught with difficulty because the property was not in the hands of a single landowner.

The report on the two seasons' fieldwork was completed on December 24, 1963, but only a selection of what were initially seen to be key artifacts was described. It was hoped that this section would be revised when the vast quantity of material retrieved from the site could be thoroughly studied by the Corning Museum's glass scholars. Before that could be done, the enormous task of numbering the fragments had to be undertaken, an unscheduled project for which the Corning Museum was ill prepared. Consequently, the collection was set aside to await a propitious moment. Alas, the moment that finally came was one of disaster; almost the entire Amelung assemblage was submerged along with the Museum's unparalleled collections in the Chemung River flood of 1972. This, the aftermath of Hurricane Agnes, resulted in the loss of labels, the mixing of archaeological groups, and severe damage to many of the glass artifacts, but thanks to the skill and dedication of the Corning Museum's staff the loss of data was kept to a minimum. Subsequently, the damage to the iron items has been arrested by re-treatment in Colonial Williamsburg's archaeological laboratory. In sum, therefore, the principal loss was one of time, three more years passing before the Amelung artifacts could be reassessed and the pre-flood *status quo* restored.

In the more than twelve years that have elapsed since the last spoil heap was pushed back into the excavations, the craft and discipline of historical archaeology have moved forward by leaps and sometimes overly precocious bounds. What in 1963 was misleadingly termed "historic site" archaeology blossomed (not without some opposition) into the less presumptuous but more accurately termed "historical archaeology" in 1967, when an American Society for Historical Archaeology was founded at a meeting held in Dallas, Texas. In the same year the Society for Post-Medieval Archaeology was established in Britain; and more recently, in 1972, a national Society for Historical Archaeology came into being in Australia. The excavation of historical sites around the world, both terrestrial and underwater, is no longer cause for either surprise or amusement among traditionally trained antiquaries.

In 1962 the premier studies in historic sites archaeology in America were confined to the accomplishments of the United States National Park Service at Jamestown and elsewhere, to the long established program at Colonial Williamsburg, and to a few reports by the latter's staff published by the Smithsonian Institution. No textbooks were available to describe the techniques of historical archaeology, nor were there any books devoted to the artifacts to be found on American historical sites. Furthermore, there was a gulf of disagreement and misunderstanding between those architecturally oriented archaeologists who were concerned almost entirely with restoration projects and the anthropologically trained university prehistorians whose courses provided the would be student of historic sites archaeology with his academic credentials. Fortunately these differences have long since diminished and the corpus of information covering the archaeological study of American colonial and later life has grown year by year. Furthermore, it is now widely recognized that archaeologists who limit their interest to one facet of a site's potential do the past a disservice. Indeed, one has a moral obligation to extract, record, and correctly interpret every nuance that the digging reveals; no longer can archaeologists restrict themselves to digging for architectural information, for museum objects, or for the evidence of a single period if, in reaching it, the legacy of others is to be destroyed.

The Corning triad could not be faulted on any of those counts; nevertheless, it is important to recognize that the report was written before historical archaeology had come of age and its language reflects both the agony of caesarian birth and the limits of contemporary knowledge. Like the foundation and artifacts uncovered on the site, the report stands as a page of Amelung history. The temptation to "bring it up to date" and to make its author appear less hesitant than he was, has been resisted, and the manuscript is now presented more or less as written. One major change has been made, however, thus minimizing a somewhat tangled skein of reasoning linking an undated documentary reference to Amelung's "heavy well known Loss by Fire" to a pane of window glass in his house upon which, in German, were engraved the words "Thinking on the 7th May 1790." The present writer had argued that as it was possible to see the excavated factory building through the window on whose pane the inscription was engraved, and as the factory unit seemed to have been destroyed by fire, the "thoughts" were the product of that disaster and were probably written on the morning after the fire. Thanks to subsequent archival research by Mr. Richard Muzzrole, late of the Smithsonian Institution's staff, two hitherto overlooked newspaper references came to light to prove the theory correct, and establish that the fire occurred on May 6, 1790. Those newspaper reports are now incorporated into the text. In addition, uncertainties over the presence or absence of lead in the illustrated glass specimens (resulting from the use of the sometimes misleading hydrofluoric acid test) have been replaced by positive identifications provided by the more sophisticated techniques now in common use. With these exceptions and the newly-studied historical evidence of the factory (parts I–IV, Lanmon/Schwind), all else is as it was.

I.N.H.

April 25, 1975

II. INTRODUCTION

Just as American historical societies have long concerned themselves with preserving the tangible relics of the leading figures of national and local history, so American industries and students of technology are developing a similar enthusiasm for preserving both the products of their predecessors and the places where they worked. As examples, one may point to the support given by the steel industry to the excavation and reconstruction of the Saugus Ironworks in Massachusetts, and to the contributions towards reconstruction and operation of the early glasshouse at Jamestown by members of Glass Crafts of America. It was in this spirit that The Corning Museum of Glass allocated funds for the archaeological excavation and study of an eighteenth-century American glass factory.

The choice of the Amelung site was made by Mr. Paul N. Perrot, then Director of the Corning Museum of Glass, and he chose it for three reasons: first because workers from New Bremen subsequently moved north and west carrying their skills and stylistic influences with them; second, because the life of the factory was believed to have been comparatively short (1784–1795) enabling excavated specimens to be closely dated, and third, because the site lay in open country and had not been mutilated by subsequent urban construction.

Some months after the decision to dig at New Bremen had been made, a fourth reason for doing so presented itself. The tract was predominantly under two ownerships, one of which intimated that the land might be offered for sale as a housing development. At the close of the second season's digging, in the fall of 1963, that possibility had acquired added substance and a sign offering lots on the tract was set up beside the approach to the site.

In the summer of 1961 The Corning Museum of Glass (hereinafter referred to as Corning) approached the Smithsonian Institution to determine whether or not the Museum of History and Technology would be prepared to provide practical assistance in mounting an archaeological exploration of the Amelung site. Mr. Malcolm Watkins, curator of the Division of Cultural History, gladly offered his support, as also did Mr. Paul Gardner, curator of Ceramics and Glass. The Director and Secretary of the Smithsonian subsequently approved these curators' recommendation and the proposed excavation thereupon became a joint Corning-Smithsonian project. At that time neither possessed a staff member trained in the field of historical American archaeology. Consequently Mr. Watkins contacted Colonial Williamsburg and asked whether it would permit me to participate in planning the excavation. Permission was duly granted and I visited the site for the first time on February 16, 1962, with Messrs. Perrot, Watkins, Gardner, and John Pearce, then assistant curator in the Smithsonian's Division of Cultural History.

The group met with Professor and Mrs. William R. Quynn, owners of the brick mansion built by Amelung, and we also walked over the supposed factory site which lay on land then owned partly by Mr. Vernon Yingling and in part by Mr. Charles Smith. The ground lay under a blanket of wet snow that chilled the team's ability and enthusiasm for undertaking anything but the most cursory examination of the area. Once indoors and suitably revived, all agreed most vehemently that here was a splendid project which should merit most favorable consideration. The only resolution actually adopted was that I should prepare an outline of requirements for a preliminary excavation which would determine the extent of the factory site as well as its potential archaeological importance.

On the basis of the outline,[1] plans were made for an exploratory excavation to be mounted in October 1962, the work to comprise nothing more than a few strategically placed test trenches. Corning would finance the operation and share with the Smithsonian the task of providing personnel and equipment. It was later decided that I should direct the fieldwork.

In the course of the late summer Mr. Perrot made the necessary agreements with the various owners of the site[2] and the access routes to it. At the same time the Smithsonian undertook the essential preliminary surveying of the site, a task directed by Mr. Pearce and carried out by the independent surveying firm of Thomas B. McNeill of Chillum, Maryland.

When work began, the fieldstone foundations of three buildings were to be seen flanking a narrow defile which ran west from the supposed main factory area. These remains were traditionally believed to be those of glassworkers' homes, while the depression was thought to mark the line of the old road along which the finished glassware had been transported. The main factory building or buildings was thought to lie beside this roadway more or less due south from the surviving Amelung residence. But all that could be seen were two tree and grass covered mounds, the most easterly of which extended to the almost clifflike edge of a decline which dropped to the flood plain of Bennett's Creek and the channel of a long-disused millrace. Neither mound bore any resemblance to a building and no traces of walls protruded from them.

On the evidence of the terrain, I concluded that if one or other of the mounds had to have been the site of a factory structure, it could only have been the most westerly of the two, the other being much too close to the edge of the cliff. I therefore deduced that the latter represented part of Amelung's waste dump and that the bulk of his refuse had been pushed over the cliff.[3] To test this theory I proposed that east/west trenches should be cut through both mounds to enable us to examine each in section. When these were dug in October 1962, I was proved to be quite wrong; the west mound was a waste heap and the east mound was part of the southeast corner of a substantial factory building.

The 1962 excavation ran from Saturday, October 13th to Saturday the 20th, and by Sunday the 14th it had been determined that the east trench spanned a complex of walls that had clearly been part of an industrial structure. The original plan to dig widely distributed test trenches across the entire site was consequently revised and work was concentrated in the area of the east mound which, by the end of the week, had been completely removed. Exposed beneath it was a massive stone structure which was later deduced to have been a pair of fritting ovens. Extending west and north from this unit were clay-bonded stone walls whose extremeties were not reached, but which were undoubtedly exterior walls of the factory building.

On the final day a test hole beneath the roadway passing north of the two fritting ovens (factory units #A and B on the plan) exposed an area of brick flooring which showed extensive burning. The hole was quickly backfilled without determining the purpose of the floor, though there was every confidence that we had encountered part of another of the factory's major units. In addition to the clearance of the southwest corner of a large factory structure, the 1962 excavations included a test cut through the millrace which showed it to have been open in the Amelung period; a test cut into the cellar filling of the most easterly of the two old foundations south of the road; and the digging of sixteen test holes in the Yingling field north of the road, plus seventeen more in the Smith meadow to the south of it. None of the test holes yielded any significant information, though most of them contained fragments of glass which proved only that the factory waste was well scattered.[4]

The recovery of considerable quantities of vessel glass from Amelung's waste heap (the west mound) and the exposure of the extremely substantial fritting oven foundations were together sufficient cause to consider the first season's work a success and to plan its continuation in 1963. After the vast quantity of artifacts (including much slag and cullet of no consequence) had been washed and studied, an interim report was prepared summarizing the history of the Amelung factory, discussing the methodology and results of the 1962 digging, and drawing some tentative conclusions from it.[5] The principal deduction made in the report, that the factory building was likely to be similar to a plan shown in Diderot's encyclopaedia having three ancillary units in the corners and one melting furnace in the center,[6] provided the basis for all planning for the proposed 1963 excavation. Unfortunately, this premise—like my 1962 guesses—proved to be wrong.

The factory foundations revealed in the first week's digging showed that the building had measured in excess of 54'1" × 53'7" and therefore was larger than Diderot's total area of approximately 57'6" × 45'0".* But because the corner of a seemingly comparable ancillary structure was found at the west edge of the excavated area it was supposed that the total width of the building would not be more than approximately sixty feet. Acting on this assumption it was proposed that the 1963 excavation would clear the remainder of the factory using the grid system rather than the trenching method which is satisfactory only when exploratory cuts are all that is required.

The presumed area of the factory was laid out in a 10'0" grid before digging began in 1963, but the usual device of numbering the squares along right angled base lines (the method used in 1962 to place test holes within the surveyed 50'0" grid pattern) was dropped in favor of numbering the squares consecutively with a single Arabic numeral. This quite orderly system became something less than systematic when it was discovered that the factory building was more than twice the supposed size, causing the 10'0" grid to be extended in all directions beyond the limits of the originally numbered series.

As the 1963 excavation progressed it became increasingly obvious that the original conception of a single working furnace in the center of a rectangular structure with three or four secondary ovens in the corners was by no means the extent of this factory unit. The pattern did develop in this manner at the commencement of the digging but it was then found to repeat itself to the west in an even more substantial form. Consequently the format for the excavation had to be drastically increased, though no additional time was available. Although it was obvious that the remains represented more than one period within the nine year span of the Amelung venture, it was necessary to concentrate on exposing the extremities of the building rather than devoting the time to a careful, though destructive study of each individual feature.

*Ed. Note: Even though the *Journal of Glass Studies* uses metric measurements, the Amelung factory was built using the English measuring system of feet and inches; feet and inches are used throughout this article to describe the factory.

In all, the building was found to measure 112'9" × 65'9" and to have been divided into two unequal parts. The easterly complex comprised a central working furnace (#3) with the previously described pair of fritting ovens to the southeast; a rectangular room at the northeast with a firebox to the south of it (probably the wood-drying room, #4); lastly, situated on the dividing wall line north of Unit #3, another secondary oven which may have been the pot arch. (#5).

The westerly section of the factory contained a larger melting furnace (#8) with four wings protruding from it, each of which had doubtless supported a small oven chamber which could have served for a variety of glass-making needs—fritting being the most likely. At the southwest corner were two small rooms which may have been used for packing and temporary storage of products (#7A and 7B); at the northwest corner were two more rooms (#6A and 6B) which were probably devoted to the making of crucibles, quantities of good plastic clay being found on both floors piled in one corner. Along the west wall was a series of four abutting ovens (#9A, B, C and D), each with a firing channel angled in the same manner as those of the presumed fritting ovens (Units #1A and 1B) found in the building's southeast corner in 1962.

A total of two main melting furnaces, nine ancillary ovens, one drying room, and four small rooms, was ultimately contained within the one massive structure. Most of these units contained re-used materials, and some were constructed over burned clay, cullet, and finished glass, all clearly indicating that the individual ovens (if not the entire building) were rebuilt or extensively repaired in its years of operation. This important consideration will be more thoroughly explored in the section devoted to the dating evidence.

Fragments of cullet and shaped glass were found all over the factory area, and the concentrations and distributions suggested that table glass came from the east section and bottles from the west. The premier glass items were found in a drainage ditch running outside the north wall of the glasshouse and dipping eastward towards the escarpment. Objects recovered included wineglass stems, stoppers, bottle fragments, and pieces of tumblers. From the bottom of a burned barrel (Feature #10) set into the factory floor, were recovered pieces of two repairable tumblers (Fig. 42) and an ogee-bowled glass with the remains of a domed foot (Fig. 39, No. 10). These were the most complete items of table glass found in the entire excavation, the bulk of the pieces being confined to single fragments from innumerable vessels.

A small number of iron tools and structural items was found in and over the destruction debris of the building; these comprised numerous fragments from blowing irons, a small iron wedge, a hammer and chisel-like tool used for breaking up old pots, part of an iron instrument which may have been used to rake frit, two cast iron ties, a furnace grating bar, and a large flat slug which probably served as a counterweight, perhaps to raise hot oven ports. Also recovered was a worn stone ball, possibly one of many tumbled in a barrel to grind old glass into cullet, or quartz to be used in frit.

The history of the New Bremen lands has not been pursued through the nineteenth century. We need only note that apart from laying the Fleecy Dale Road through and over the excavated factory site, there were few changes in the physical appearance of the property. There is archaeological evidence that the excavated glasshouse was dismantled and that rubble from it (or from another glassmaking structure) was later laid along the north edge of the road line, overlying the west melting furnace (Unit #8) and suggesting that a property boundary was established running through the building soon after it was taken apart. Occupation continued in the two structures south of the road, and also, perhaps, in a third which stood to the west, north of the road. This last building, though of similar construction to the others, did not appear on the Brown Plat[7] (Fig. 1), and so may be of later date.

It is reasonable to assume that the site of the factory building excavated in 1962 and 1963 remained undisturbed by domestic occupation or industry (other than plowing) from its abandonment until the present time. Because no evidence of secondary usage was found within the building and overlying the glassworking strata, it is presumed that the building was dismantled soon after it burned or ceased to serve its original purpose.

One cannot conclude this summary without recalling something of the site's archaeological history prior to the Corning-Smithsonian excavations. The approximate location of the Manufactory site has been known for many years, and ever since the Metropolitan Museum ac-

quired the now-celebrated Bremen Goblet in 1928, there has been widespread popular interest in Amelung's products. This enthusiasm manifested itself at New Bremen by the advent of collectors from Washington and elsewhere who took their sandwiches and their shovels and amused themselves digging holes around the area in search of glass fragments. As it happened these minor vandalisms did no real damage to the site and were, to a degree, quite helpful, in that they taught collectors something about the types of glass produced there.

The indiscriminate looting of an archeological site should never be condoned on the grounds that it does yield artifacts—no matter how informative they prove to be. Just as surely as thunder follows lightning, small larcenies are followed by larger, and the Amelung site was no exception. In the summer of 1948 a collector from Baltimore brought a bulldozer onto the site and, according to the Baltimore *Sun,* she ". . . had the trees and their roots cleared out of the way, pressed her excavation on down to a depth of 30 feet, and discovered that she had hit the site of the initial Amelung factory, one that had burned and was rebuilt at a different spot."[8] When questioned about this operation in 1962 the lady inferred that her principal discoveries came from a depth of fourteen feet, though she had previously published an account which placed them from four to twelve feet down.[9] Test cuts on the edge of the bulldozed area in 1962 reached bottom at 2'7", and one can only suppose that the machine had cut through an adjacent cellar, or perhaps part of another major factory unit south of the one excavated in 1962–1963.

The same collector who used the bulldozer also dug numerous holes in various unrecorded parts of the site and recovered considerable quantities of glass. The Baltimore *Sun* noted that "A certain hillside in Frederick County is pitted all over with little holes she has dug. . . ."[10] Writing in the *Scientific Monthly* in December, 1952, Dr. Donald Hubbard expressed the opinion that the bulldozing episode had been responsible for ". . . . destroying forever the possibility of ascertaining the original furnace and factory layout, which may have been perfectly obvious prior to this enthusiastic research."[11] Fortunately, the factory building which is the subject of this report, was actually unharmed. Although he bemoaned the use of the bulldozer, Dr. Hubbard went on to assure collectors that

"Patient digging beyond the reaches of the denuded area, however, will reward the individual with specimens of the furnace and pot refractories and with ample cullet samples of the many types of glass produced by the versatile Amelung enterprises." Unfortunately, such authoritative encouragement tends to promote the idea that the recovery of artifacts, shorn of their context, is a legitimate pursuit. I disagree. Some measure of the purely "collector's" approach was provided by the Washington collector who had previously dug holes on the site, when he visited the excavations after the factory building had been uncovered. He announced, "What I'd like to do would be to get these old foundations out of here and get on down to where the glass is!" It is immaterial that the foundations generally went much deeper than the glass waste scattered around them. The point is simply that the man's attitude was that of many collectors who have yet to learn that archaeological sites, properly excavated, can yield more than an assemblage of museum specimens. I can only hope that the excavation of the Amelung factory will have served to illustrate that archaeology can make a very real and worthwhile contribution to our knowledge of early American life and industry, and that it can provide data that is frequently absent from the documentary sources.

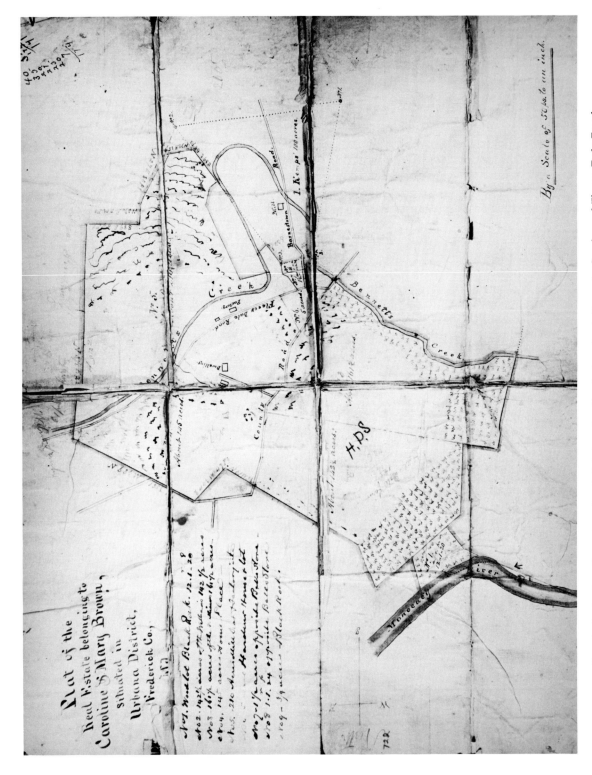

FIG. 1. A nineteenth-century land plat showing the factory tract, Bennets Creek, and Fleecy Dale Road.

154

III. THE ARCHAEOLOGY OF THE NEW BREMEN SITE

THE FOUNDATIONS

As outlined in the introduction, the Corning-Smithsonian excavations were undertaken in two stages, a preliminary exploratory sortie in October 1962 followed by the total clearance of one major structure in the fall of 1963. The results by no means represent the sum of New Bremen's archaeological potential, but they have provided confirmation of the magnitude of the original venture, as well as yielding large quantities of glass which illustrate the range of Amelung's products.

It is unnecessary to give details of the measurements of each trench or to enumerate each artifact from each and every grid square. This would only serve to obscure the salient facts and conclusions. All key measurements can be derived from the site plan (Fig. 2), and the majority of the artifacts are both repetitive and uninformative. As for the techniques of excavation, it is only necessary to repeat that the site was initially laid out in a carefully surveyed fifty foot grid anchored to east/west and north/south baselines. The first season's work began as a series of test trenches and grew into an area excavation which retained certain key balks within the grid. The second year's work was more formally planned and laid out in a carefully plotted ten foot grid whose squares were numbered in advance in Arabic figures. It later transpired that the area to be dug was much larger than had been supposed; the grid was thereupon extended in a variety of directions and in doing so demonstrated the disadvantages of giving the squares single numbers instead of letters and numbers projected from the baselines.

Owing to time limitations, toward the end of the work it was found necessary to take certain short cuts. Some grid squares were not entirely excavated—notably those which extended beyond the north wall of the factory and the ditch that ran beside it. Experience had shown that the ground beyond the ditch was largely barren and had been disturbed almost to the natural grade in the course of plowing.

As always happens, numerous key features lay partially beneath the balks, many of which were removed in their entirety as the excavation approached completion. Such balks were given the numbers of the two adjacent grid squares, e.g., Balk 20/21, having Square 20 to the west of it and 21 to the east.

The 1962 digging had revealed a double oven foundation (#1A, 1B) in the southeast corner of a massive structure which extended at least 54'1" in an east/west direction, and 53'7" north/south, the stone foundations ranging from 1'3" to 4'0" in thickness (Fig. 3). The southeast corner of another interior unit (#2) was found near the western excavated limit of the south wall, and it was believed that this would prove to be situated in the southwest corner of the factory building, more or less a pair to #1A and B. Taking this thinking a step further, I supposed that the plan would be found to follow the layout shown by Diderot in his treatise on "Verrerie à pivette"; a rectangular building with ancillary units in three corners, an entrance in the fourth, and the main working furnance in the middle, ringed by the workers' chairs (Fig. 4). Supporting evidence for such a plan was provided by the discovery in the clay floor of bricks which had probably served as a footing for one of the chairs (Fig. 5). Even more encouraging was the uncovering of a small area of brick flooring more or less in the supposed central area. This was found while making a last minute test hole through the hard-packed metalling of the fleecy Dale Road. Because the site was about to be opened to visitors, it was decided to close the hole again before it came to the attention of any collectors who might be prompted to return and start an excavation of their own.

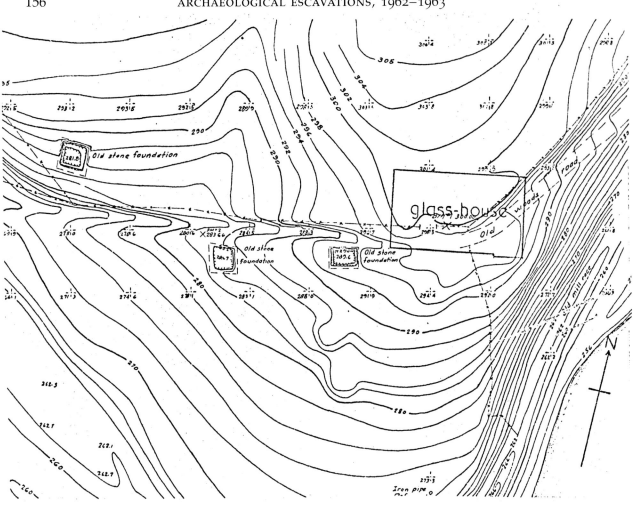

Fig. 2. Detail from Topographic Survey, John Frederick Amelung Glass Works Site, by Thomas B. McNeill, October 1962, with the addition of the excavated glasshouse foundations and the Trench G-H, cutting into the millrace below the escarpment east of the factory site. Scale: 1 inch = 50 feet.

The principal discovery of the 1962 season, the oven unit #1A and B, measured 24'0" × 14'0" with walls averaging 3'0" in thickness (Fig. 6A and 6B). Although built as a single structure, this feature comprised two more or less square oven foundations, each with a stokehole or ash channel extending into its center. These two channels were angled in such a way that they emerged approximately side by side in the center of the north wall and could thus have been operated by a single worker. Only one of the channels was cleaned out; it was found to measure 8'7½" in length, 1'11" in width and was probably about 2'6" to 3'0" in height. To the east and west of the two channels were found the remains of two boxlike structures built from slabs of schist laid on edge. The easterly example was the most intact, measured approximately 3'0" × 1'11", and was lined with roughly laid brickbats. These features were first thought to be foundations for working ledges in front of the oven mouths above them. But as such shelves would have stood some 3'0" above the floor, it was realized that laying the stones on edge would have been a most improbable method of construction. It seemed more likely that the devices were exactly what they appeared to be—simple troughs in front of the furnace mouths to catch something raked from those orifices. The only reasonable explanation was the unit #1A and B was a pair of fritting ovens of an unusually sophisticated form.

Diderot illustrated square fritting ovens with circular chambers measuring from 5'4" to 7'6" in diameter, within walls creating units 8'0" and 9'9" square respectively (Fig. 7). The latter mea-

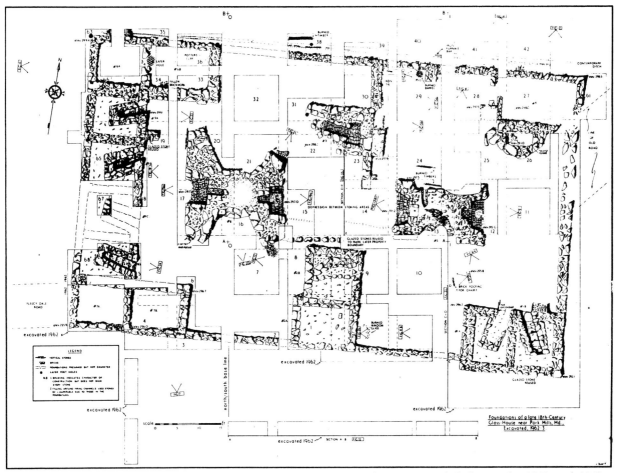

Fig. 3. Archaeological master plan showing areas explored and features revealed during the 1962 and 1963 seasons. Arrowed figure numbers indicate the field of view for photographs illustrating this report, and section lines show the distances embraced by the profile drawings (Figures 32–34). The large isolated numerals identify excavated grid squares and are cross-referenced to the field record Appendix I, while numbers shown thusly, #1, #2, etc., identify structural features discussed in the text and which are tentatively identified as follows:

1A and 1B	Fritting ovens
2A and 2B	Annealing ovens
3	Melting furnace for table glass and flasks
4	Wood-drying room with hearth and chimney foundation
5	Pot arch
6A and 6B	Potting rooms
7A and 7B	Store and packing rooms
8	Melting furnace for bottles with ancillary ovens in each of the four wings
9A	Reheating or annealing oven
9B, C and D	Annealing ovens
10	Small barrel or tub set in floor and containing ground glass

Fig. 5. Laid bricks in the clay floor south of furnace Unit 3, possibly the base for one end of a worker's chair. 62.577 (Corning negative number).

157

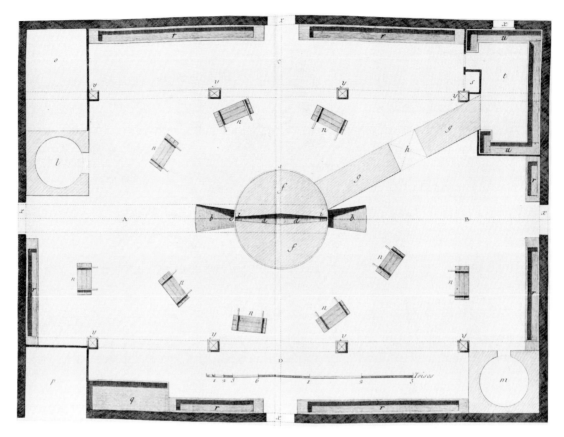

Fig. 4. Floorplan of a small glass factory with ovens. From Diderot, *Encyclopédie,* "Verrerie en bois," Pl. 2, n.d. (after the edition of 1763).

Fig. 6A. Fritting ovens 1A and 1B after the removal of rubble from the latter's firing channel. 62.579.

Fig. 6B. Fritting ovens 1A and 1B showing the two diagonal firing channels. This feature occupied the southwest corner of the excavated glasshouse. 62.586M.

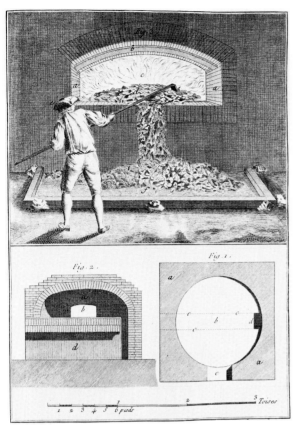

FIG. 7. Furnaceman raking frit from the fritting furnace. Diagram and cross section of the fritting furnace or "calcar." From Diderot, *Encyclopédie,* "Verrerie en Bois," Pl. 15, n.d. (after the edition of 1763).

surements are extremely close to those of the excavated foundations. Diderot's plan differs in that the oven mouth, and its trough below, occur in one face of the structure while the firing chamber emerges at right angles in another. This layout was presumably adopted to prevent the stoker from getting in the way of the frit-extracting process while at the same time keeping the frit-raker's legs away from the heat. However, the clever placing of the firing channels in Amelung's structure to right and left of the oven mouths overcame both problems.

It is not clear from Diderot's drawing exactly how large were the mouths of his fritting ovens. The measured example depicts an oven floor 7'6" in diameter with a mouth measuring 2'0" × 1'3"—proportions which could well have served the Amelung unit. On the other hand, Diderot's picture of fritting in progress shows an opening very much larger, which, if scaled from a 5'0" (?) man in front of it, would measure about 6'0" × 2'6". One can only suppose that fritting ovens came in a variety of sizes.

Firing the fritting ovens would seem to have been merely a matter of laying a log fire in the lower channel, aided by an updraft through the chamber. No provision was made for the ashes to drop into a lower pit, nor was there any evidence of an iron grill being attached to the inside of the channels to raise the logs off the floor. Diderot is similarly unhelpful on this point, and one can only suppose that the temperature required for the secondary processes did not require the extra draft that would have been provided by a grating. It is certainly true of many primitive pottery kilns whose fires were laid on the ground in this way. Although the cleared (eastern) channel exhibited some burning of both stones and bonding clay at its mouth, as well as containing 5" of ash on its stone slab floor, there was surprisingly little evidence of extreme heat.

The areas around the two channels had been packed with the local schist or siltstone to form a bed for the floor of each chamber. A sample of the siltstone was extracted from the fill of oven #1A at a depth of approximately ¾" below the surviving top, i.e., below the floor level of the channel, and at a point close to the northwest corner of the foundation—well away from the source of heat. The thermal history of this sample was studied by Dr. Robert Brill, Research Scientist at The Corning Museum of Glass, who found that one edge of it has been subjected to considerable heat. His conclusions were as follows:

1. Since heating at approximately 850°C did not alter the appearance of the siltstone, it can be concluded that the interior of the stone itself had never been heated to greater than 850°C for a comparable time (greater than two hours).

2. At some time in the past, although not necessarily after the sample became incorporated in Structure #1A, this sample of siltstone has been heated in such a way that one edge reached a temperature of 1180–1190°C for a time of at least forty-five minutes and possible much longer. This estimate depends on the assumption that plane X was the outermost surface exposed to heat. Actually it appears that a piece of the sample broke off during the heating and has been lost. The projecting region Y appears to have been heated to a temperature of about 1230–1260°C. (The heating seems to have continued for some time after the stone fractured).

3. During heating the siltstone was in such a position that one end of the hot edge was heated more strongly than the other edge, and it may have been that the slab was inclined to the horizontal by

about 30° during the heating.

4. Clumps of mortar or clay still adhere to the portion of the stone closest to the heated region. They must have been in contact with the hot edge of the stone while it was heated, since they have become partially 'fused' to the stone.[12]

There seems little doubt that the stone had been heated elsewhere and had been reused in the foundation of oven #1A. The same filling also contained lumps of stone with green glass attached to parts of their surfaces, indicating that they had previously been part of a structure direcly connected with glass-melting. A similar fragment was built into the south wall of oven #1B. In addition fragments of cullet and a quantity of ground quartz were recovered from the fill. There was no doubt that unit #1A and B was erected after glass making had begun on the site or that it was constructed from materials salvaged from a major furnace. The fact that the test siltstone specimen had been heated while lying at an angle of 30° from the horizontal suggests that it may once have been built into the arched firing channel of an ancillary oven similar to that of the structure in which it was re-used. This would readily account for the exposure to high temperature at one end and to less at the other. Furthermore, a temperature of 1180–1190°C would be more than sufficient for any phase of eighteenth-century glassmaking.

In its final resting place the only importance of the tested stone was that it had been re-used from some other furnace structure, as had the previously mentioned glazed stones. Together, as stated above, they proved that unit #1A and B did not belong to the first period of construction on the site. However, the unit was bonded into the walls which extended north and west from it; consequently the feature must have been an integral part of the building—or at least the east end of it.

Pursuing the brick floor found below the Fleecy Dale Road, the 1963 excavations began by uncovering the remains of a melting furnace which proved to have stood north of, and midway between Units #1 and 2—thus supporting the belief that the factory was about to follow the Diderot layout. This furnace, Unit #3, possessed two brick-floored stoke-holes, one to the east and the other at the west, and it had been the former which had been encountered in 1962 (Fig. 8). The furnace had an overall length of 21'0" with a chamber length of no more than 13'6". Small wings projected from each corner

and formed the cheeks of the two stoke-holes, but they were of insufficient area to have contained secondary ovens. The east stoke-hole (Fig. 9) had been almost totally destroyed by the Fleecy Dale Road, but it was doubtless a pair to the one at the west. This last was found to have been deliberately filled with rubble and glass-making refuse. A small, brick-arched channel, 2'3" in length, extended into the furnace from the back of the broad stoking area, and was capped by a massive, carefully worked stone measuring 2'6"×2'5" (Fig. 10). A conical hole passed up through the center of the stone and emerged into what had apparently been a stone-sided box, of which only one fragment remained (Fig. 11). Close to the western edge of the stone was a carefully chiseled slot which almost certainly had served as a seating for a vertical slab which carried the wall up on a line with the mouth of the brick arch. There had been no east wall to the box; instead a slurry of partially fused glass spread from that point away into the main chamber and cascaded over the stones of its foundation. It seemed as though a melting pot had broken and decanted its contents into the furnace. The furnace had had straight parallel walls at north and south, and it was almost certainly into these that the working ports had been built. No traces of the latter were found, but the remains of a narrow brick channel (only one course in surviving height) did pass through the side of the north wall and ran towards the center of the furnace chamber. It is believed that this channel had served as an air duct. However, its location at what had been the working floor level outside the furnace would seem to have been somewhat impractical.

The problem of how the fire was charged has not been explained satisfactorily. Although there was evidence of considerable burning on the brick floor of the stoking area, the bricks of the arch exhibited nothing like the heat damage that one would have expected to find had they been in close proximity to the fire. Similarly, the lining of the tunnel and the inside of the conical aperture which tapered upward through the large stone both exhibited evidence of heat, but not the vitrification and disintegration which would be evident if they had been part of the actual fire chamber.[13] Because the hole through the stone tapered upward it seemed unlikely that its purpose was to carry ashes down into the stoke-hole; besides, the aperture only measured 4½"×3¾". It was suggested that the hole

FIG. 10. Melting furnace, Unit 3, the west stoking area with pierced stone cap over the brick arch. 63.470.

FIG. 8. Melting furnace, Unit 3, showing brick-paved stoking areas at east and west. The covered fritting ovens (1A and 1B) can be seen at top left. 63.484C.

FIG. 11. Detail of stone over the west arch of melting furnace 3, showing remains of walling around the stone, a carefully worked seating in the foreground, also decomposition around the hole which had been cut through the stone into the brick arch below. Note scored mortar spread in background. 63.482.

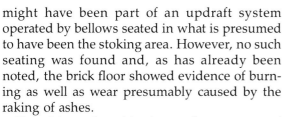

FIG. 9. The east stoking area of melting furnace 3 with the stone cap of the west brick arch in the background. 63.488.

might have been part of an updraft system operated by bellows seated in what is presumed to have been the stoking area. However, no such seating was found and, as has already been noted, the brick floor showed evidence of burning as well as wear presumably caused by the raking of ashes.

Unit #4 was found in the northeast corner of the building and comprised a rectangular room measuring approximately 15′0″ × 10′0″, open into the factory at the west and with an apsidal firebox projecting from it to the south (Fig. 12). The latter was originally equipped with a stone floor, but this had later been replaced by one of brick, thus raising it some five inches. The box contained evidence of heavy burning, but none of it extended into the room to the north. It is believed that Unit #4 was the wood-drying room and that the apsidal foundation belonged to a large chimney which possessed a hearth opening into the room. The floor of the latter was of puddled clay, and this overlay a shallow stone foundation wall which ran north from the southwest corner but terminated before reaching the north wall of the factory. The floor level of the drying room was higher than that of the working floor of the glasshouse and was apparently approached by a clay step retained by a half-brick wall. Fragments of glass and a stratum of burned clay passed beneath the step, indicating that this feature represented secondary construction within the factory building. It is possible, therefore, that the broken foundation beneath the west edge of the drying room's floor had belonged to an earlier unit which had been dismantled. On the other hand it could simply have been a retaining wall to support the filling beneath the raised floor.

Unit #2, the southeast corner of which had been exposed during the 1962 digging, was found to have consisted of two unequal parts, a chamber 10′6″ × 9′6″ (#2A) and another with interior measurements of 8′6″ × 9′4″ (#2B) bonded to the north of it (Fig. 13). A test hole dug into the southwest corner of #2A failed to reach the bottom of the foundation or of a massive rubble fill that covered the entire interior area of the structure. Fragments of glass and other artifacts were found in the fill indicating that this unit did not date from New Bremen's first period of construction. No evidence of the feature's above ground appearance survived. This was not the case with feature #2B where a curved wall was found over the rubble foundation, and within it the remains of another wall line which probably formed part of a firing channel. The stones used in the construction of the channel had been reused from elsewhere, and one was heavily coated with glass. It seems likely that #2A had possessed a similar superstructure but that this had been entirely dismantled when the building was razed. The purpose of features #2A and B was not apparent from their form or from the artifacts which were scattered around them. However, if #1A and B were fritting ovens it might logically be construed that #2A and B were for annealing.

Massive tree roots extended over the northeast corner of feature #2B which made it impossible to determine whether any foundations extended northward from that point. However, it is likely that a short stretch of wall did so and terminated on a line flush with the north edge of

FIG. 12. Aerial view of Unit 4, believed to have been wood-drying room with apsidal chimney and hearth beyond it. The original floor of the firing area has been exposed at the right, but at the left the second raised floor level has been retained. Note northeast corner of the glasshouse in the left foreground, the wall cut through by the Fleecy Dale Road which also destroyed the southwest corner of Unit 4. The brick-walled step or platform abutting the floor at the west can be seen to the right. The west wall has been exposed in a trench, but was originally sealed by the clay floor of the room. 63.484K.

FIG. 13. Oven unit 2B, probably for annealing, with part of 2A to the right and the covered fritting ovens excavated in 1962 in the background. 63.525.

the south wall of the west stoking area of unit #3. A section of stone walling was found to behave in this way west and north of the stoking area. It then continued northward until it reached the remains of another ancillary oven

FIG. 14. View of the northeast area of the glasshouse with the wood-drying room (Unit 4) at left and part of the supposed pot arch (Unit 5) at right. The ditch outside the north wall can be seen in the foreground. The circular hole inside the building to the right represents the remains of a burned barrel (10) seated in the floor. 63.539E.

FIG. 15B. Possible pot arch viewed from the east, showing step or platform foundation in foreground, brick floor partially overlaid by firing channel, and clay "bun" *in situ* (?) at center. 63.481.

FIG. 15A. Aerial view of the western half of the glasshouse, brick-floored pot arch (?) Unit 5 in foreground, the main melting furnace Unit 8 at left, potting rooms at top right, Units 6A and 6B, and probable annealing ovens to left of them, Units 9A and 9B. Note pair of later post holes beyond the pot arch and cutting into the right edge of the exterior ditch. 63.484E.

structure were of different dates. There was some evidence of burning on the bricks, and on removing one of them, burned clay and fragments of glass were found beneath. Thus, Unit #5 could not have belonged to Amelung's first period of construction.

It is tentatively conjectured that Unit #5 was stoked from the west and that the chamber was loaded from the east. Resting on the brick floor in the eastern area was an oval clay "bun" measuring $7'' \times 5''$ with a tapering hole driven down from the top of it. The upper surface exhibited none of the vitrification common to most of the fragments of similar items found elsewhere in the building, suggesting that this one had not been used. It is tentatively believed that such objects were used as temporary supports set up within the ovens (Fig. 15A and 15B).

Unit #5 had a firing channel $2'0''$ wide and approximately $6'0''$ in length, opening into a chamber measuring about $6'0'' \times 3'0''$. I am inclined to identify this structure as a pot arch, though the considerations raised later weigh against this conclusion. On one score there could be no doubt: my contention that the factory followed Diderot's plan for "Verrerie à pivette" was now revealed as incorrect. A wall extended from the northeast corner of Unit #5 and continued to the north wall of the building, thus placing the body of the oven outside the enclosed area. Furthermore, the factory's north wall showed no inclination to end; it continued firmly in a westerly direction.

structure #5 (Fig. 14). This feature was in an extremely mutilated condition, and its form could not be determined with any confidence. The floor was of brick laid on edge in a north/south direction, except for the end course at the west where they formed a border of a single course lying east/west. The remains of a stone firing and stoking channel overlay part of the brick floor, suggesting that it and the super-

FIG. 16. Aerial view of the western section of the glasshouse as seen from the west, potting room 6A and 6B in left foreground, probably annealing ovens 9A and 9B to right with the main melting furnace 8 beyond them. The suggested pot arch 5 can be seen in the background. 63.541C.

FIG. 17. Southeast corner of storage room (?) 7B and showing the south glasshouse wall extending to the right without being bonded into it. 63.540J.

When the north wall was traced to its west corner it was found that the entire length covered a distance of 112'9". Two small rooms were found extending east from that corner (#6A and 6B), the first measuring approximately 10'6"×9'6", and the other 10'9"×9'6" (Fig. 16). In the northeast corner of the latter was found a heap of heavy gray clay of remarkable plasticity which is believed to have been intended for the manufacture of crucibles. More clay of the same type was found in the southeast corner of room #6A, suggesting that both rooms were used either for the storage of clay or for actually making the pots—or perhaps both.[14] Pot clay was usually prepared by treading in shallow wooden bins, a rather primitive process which is still practiced in some glasshouses even today. Because room #6A was approachable only

through room #6B, it is possible that the former was devoted to the treading process and that the pots were actually built in room #6B.

In attempting to identify the use of oven #5, I mentioned that my contention that it had served as a pot furnace was not well supported by the available evidence. If rooms #6A and B were used in the making of pots, it is hardly likely that the vessels would have been carried around oven #5 and inserted from the opposite or east end. The logical arrangement would have been to load the pots into the chamber at the west and to tend the fire in a channel opening at the east.

Corresponding with the rooms at the northwest corner of the factory, two others were found extending from the southwest corner #7A and B (Fig. 17). The most westerly of these (#7A) had been found in 1962 when a test cut was dug across the Fleecy Dale Road. At that time the foundation was believed to have been part of a small free-standing building similar to those whose cellars still survived to the south of the road. Not until the end of the 1963 excavation was it realized that there were two rooms and that, although extending some 3'0" deeper than the overall working floor of the main factory area, they were nevertheless part of it.

FIG. 18. The main melting furnace (Unit 8) with four wings projecting from it, which are believed to have contained small ancillary ovens. The supposed annealing ovens 2A and 2B can be seen in the right background, while melting furnace 3 is visible to the left. Note stone and brick projections extending beyond the main furnace wings in the left foreground and middle distance. These are believed to have been the bottoms of troughs which served to collect frit raked from the ovens above. 63.535F.

Room #7A measured approximately 10'0" × 8'6", while #7B was slightly longer and measured 10'6" × 8'6". It seems possible that the former was a temporary storeroom and that the latter served as a packing room. If this is so, there would have been a large doorway in the west wall opening into a roadway leading to the warehouses and ultimately to the Monocacy. It will be noticed (see Fig. 2) that the two surviving cellars have their north walls on much the same line as the south wall of the factory building. I feel that this was no accident, nor was it a mere coincidence that the Fleecy Dale Road passed directly over the remains of rooms #7A and B. I think it highly likely that the road originally terminated at a door in the southwest corner of the factory, i.e., against the west wall of room #7A.

Occupying much the same position in relation to Units #7A and B and #2A and B, as did furnace Unit #3 to #1A and B and #2A and B, was another, considerably larger melting furnace #8 (Fig. 18). This was oriented on the same east/west line as furnace #3, and they shared a common stokehole trough. Brick-paved stoking areas of similar plan to those of #3 (though missing the tops of the arches and the stone caps) entered the structure from east and west (Fig. 19A and B.) The remains of the fire chamber indicated that the furnace had resembled a truncated egg with a working area at north and south approximately 9'0" in width (Fig. 20). This would have provided room for no more than three ports in each side. Projecting from the corners were four wings having sufficient foundation areas for each to have contained an ancillary oven about 5'0" in diameter. There is no doubt that such ovens did exist, for the remains of brick and stone-floored troughs (like those fronting on Units #1A and B) abutted against three of the four wings—the fourth being in such poor condition that no trace of a trough could have survived even if it had originally existed (Fig. 21). Although it may be argued that nearly all ancillary ovens could have served more than one purpose, the presence of the troughs would suggest that these were primarily intended to be used as fritting ovens, just as units #1A and B provided the frit for furnace #3. A somewhat similar plan from an English glasshouse of 1772 is illustrated in Diderot (Fig. 22); there the proportionately larger wings were used as pot furnaces, while a single fritting oven with its attendant trough was set between two of

FIG. 19A. The east stoking area of the main melting furnace, Unit 8. Note heavy wear on brick floor immediately in front of the arch foundation. 63.521.

FIG. 19B. The west stoking area of the main melting furnace, Unit 8. Note heavy wear on brick floor immediately in front of the arch foundation. 63.533.

them. Because of the small size of the Amelung wings, I do not believe that these could have been used for preheating pots, unless the pots were of very small capacity. It must be admitted, however, that the closer the pot arches were to the working furnace, the more convenient they would be. In passing it may be noted that the wings would not have been used as annealing ovens because the temperature could not have been sufficiently controlled and reduced without interfering with that of the main furnace chamber. Although there were some designs wherein the annealing was achieved in a cham-

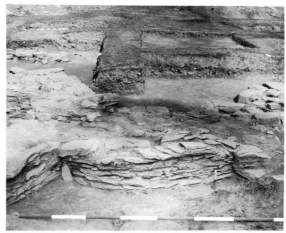

FIG. 20. The south working area of the main melting furnace, Unit 8, with the southwest and southeast wings extending to left and right. 63.523.

FIG. 21. Detail of brick paving or trough bottom in front of the northeast wing of the main melting furnace, Unit 8. Note the large stone and the six bricks curving onto it; these are part of the wing foundation and possibly represent the remains of a semi-circular chamber at floor level. 63.511.

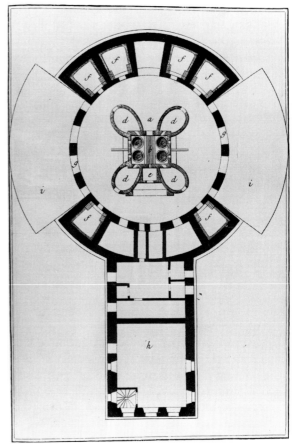

FIG. 22. Plan of an English glasshouse. From Diderot, *Encyclopédie*, "Verrerie Angloise," Pl. 2, edition of 1772.

ber above the working furnace, the heat there was being utilized after it had served its primary purpose. In the Amelung furnace it would have been doing two jobs at the same time.[15] Diderot, of course, shows the annealing oven attached to the side of the furnace, but here again the heat passed into the tunnel above the main furnace chamber and control was achieved by slowly drawing the products away from the source on metal trays. There would have been no room for such movement in the wings of the Amelung furnace.

The method of stoking and providing draft for the main furnace (#8) appears to have been exactly the same as that employed for the smaller working furnace #3—neither is properly understood. The majority of eighteenth-century working furnaces had provision for a draft beneath the fire which sometimes doubled as an ash pit. The fire normally rested on an iron grill, and in a ditch outside the north wall of the factory was found an iron bar which may have served such a purpose. Nevertheless, there was no indication in any of the oven or furnace structures of how or where bars of this type could have been seated.[16]

The main furnace (#8) had been dismantled to within 1'6" of the factory floor level, and the rubble fill inside it is thought to have been nothing more than a plinth on which the superstructure stood. In the center was a fused mass of sand which had turned a bright purple through having been exposed to extreme heat. This sand deposit measured up to eight inches in thickness, and after the purple skin had been broken, it extended down into a fine, clean, white sand which had not reacted to the heat above it. The sand deposit was not removed, but it could be seen that it rested on a bed of silt-stone rubble. There was no indication that any ash pit was sealed beneath it, and not wishing to do further damage to the foundations, neither the sand nor the stones were disturbed. A rather similar situation existed in furnace #3 where the central area of stone fill was partially sealed by a cascade of once molten glass. There was not the slightest indication that an ash pit was concealed beneath it.

The brick-walled channels running into the east and west sides of furnaces #3 and #8 each terminated in a brick back, indicating that they were of the same character as the better preserved westerly example in furnace #3. By no stretch of imagination could they have provided an ash repository beneath an overlying fire chamber.

Filling the west wall space south of the supposed pot rooms (#6A and B) and north of the corresponding pair of storerooms (#7A and B) was found a series of four adjacent ovens (#9A, B, C, and D), each with an angled firing channel similar to those encountered in the southeast pair of fritting ovens (#1A and B). The purpose of the angling was the same—to enable the workmen to approach the chamber without having to stand in front of the firing channel. As was the case with the fritting ovens, the channels in the four western units terminated in the middle of the oven area and seemingly showed that the heat rose into it through a central hole in the floor. The four units were substantially built, and although bonded together, they varied slightly in alignment and size, the average interior measurement being approximately 8'6" × 10'6". The foundations of units #9A and B were well-preserved and readily excavated (Fig. 23); the other two, however, were buried beneath the tree-capped and steeply sloping bank on the north side of the Fleecy Dale Road. The latter were not found until the last day of excavation, as they were not only covered by substantial trees and their roots, but also by the excavators' equipment trailer. After this trailer had been removed, test holes were dug at what were hoped would be the key points needed to plot the angles of the channels and the positions of the dividing walls. Those estimations proved to be reasonably accurate, though it was found that the angles of the firing channels were the opposite of those followed in Units #9A and B, i.e., running northwest/southeast as opposed to southwest/northeast.

Because Units 9C and D were only established through hasty test cuts and not by total excavation, it is possible that certain nuances of construction may not have been found and recorded (Fig. 24). Nevertheless, no doubt exists that all four ovens were of the same type and almost certainly served the same purpose—probably that of annealing. The 1772 factory layout previously illustrated in Fig. 22 possessed

FIG. 23. Detail of annealing or reworking oven (Unit 9A) as seen from the east, showing firing channel in the center and large stones in the foreground exposed after the removal of multiple ash strata; a section through the ash strata is retained to the right of the firing channel. The foundation of a small platform (?) can be seen to the left. 63.532.

FIG. 24. Detail of the firing channel of annealing oven 9D hurriedly exposed on the last day of the excavation. 63.520.

similar independent though abutting annealing ovens. *A History of Technology* also shows a plan of an English bottle house circa 1777 where comparably abutting annealing ovens were ranged along one wall behind the main furnace (Fig. 25).[17]

The problems of identifying any of the oven units relate to the basic question of what the factory was making. There is no doubt that the building was divided into two parts and that both operated independently to the extent that each possessed its melting furnace around which were situated its ancillary ovens. The only unit which seems to have been associated with both parts of the factory was #5; as this may have been used for firing or preheating pots, it might have served both working furnaces.

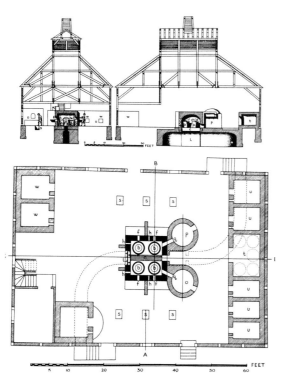

FIG. 25. View and plan of a London bottle-glass works in Gravel Lane, Southwark in 1777–1778, by C. W. Carlberg. The drawing gives sections along the lines A–B and C–D on the plan. The furnace was 9 feet square inside and 6 feet high. The pots (b) were 3 feet high, 3 feet 1½ inches in diameter above, and 2 feet 2 inches below. Note also the grille for burning coals (c), working holes (f), *boccarella* (h), ash chamber (i), fritting-furnace (o), furnace for heating cullet (p), linnet-holes (g), hole in ground for blowing bottles in molds (s), furnace for pre-heating pots (t), annealing-ovens, each of the two largest taking 800 bottles (u,w). From *A History of Technology*, Vol. III, Fig. 149, pp. 222–223.

It was hoped that the glass fragments scattered around the ovens would help to identify their uses. Unfortunately, plentiful though the pieces were, their evidence was inconclusive. Window, bottle, and table glass were littered indiscriminately over the packed clay working floor, some of it undoubtedly cullet, but some of it simply "crack-off" which was left lying where it fell. Large quantities of cullet derived from melted but unshaped glass were found in the filling of the four brick-floored stoking areas of the two working furnaces (#3 and 8). These were the largest assemblages of such cullet found anywhere in the factory, and most of it was of a green hue which could have been intended for either windows or bottles.

Both window and bottle fragments (including spoiled pieces) were plentiful in a massive waste tip against the exterior of the factory's south wall in the vicinity of rooms #7A and B, as well as in the ditch which ran eastward outside the north wall of the building. Immediately east of the presumed annealing oven unit #2A was found a quantity of window glass fragment sealed in a stratum of burned clay. This glass had been brought to melting point *in situ* (Fig. 26), as was evidenced by the fact that the fragments had assumed the contours of the pebbles and clay on which they were lying. To the east of the window glass was encountered a broad scatter of tableware fragments, as well as drips, runs, and crack-off of similar material. This glass was also sealed by the same stratum of burned clay and ash which covered the previously discussed window fragments. The same stratigraphy extended to the west wall of the fritting oven, Unit #1A. Abutting against it, but at a higher level, was a large deposit of crucible chips which suggested that the area had been used for the salvaging of cullet from old pots and also for the breaking down of the pots into chips of suitable size to be ground and used as tempering for the manufacture of new pots. The clay floor in this area presented a highly complex section (see Fig. 33, Section C–D) reminding us that the dirt floors of factory buildings were not necessarily flat, nor were they clean. When swept (or more probably shoveled clear) the dirt would pile up in uneven contours around the footings of the furnaces. (Fig. 27).

The presence of concentrations of table glass fragments and comparable cullet, as well as assemblages of pot chips, might reasonably lead one to conclude that the area between Units #2A and 1A were set aside for the recovery of the waste. It may here be noted that a tool with a hammer at one end and a chisel at the other, which was used in that work, was found in the topsoil (Fig. 46, No. 2). Diderot illustrated bins for cullet and frit around the walls of his buildings, but his pictures of the salvaging processes did not place the workers in any identifiable setting. But even if the cullet was retrieved on the floor of the factory, it would almost certainly have been taken elsewhere to be washed before being placed in the wooden troughs or bins to await re-use. In summation, it must be admitted that the association of window fragments, table glass, and pot chips in the same area of the factory does nothing to indicate the purpose served by the adjacent working furnace.

To the north of furnace #3 and against the north wall of the building were found the remains of a small barrel or bucket (#10) which had been set into the ground and there burned (Fig. 28). The barrel had an internal diameter of 1'10" and the surviving staves extended to a depth of 7" below the clay floor. It was found that the barrel had no bottom and had been thrust into an existing hole whose bottom was already covered by 5" of coarsely ground clear glass. The multitude of small slivers and chips extended up the sides of the hole behind the charred staves, suggesting that they had been drawn up against the damp clay when an earlier barrel lining, had been withdrawn. However, no traces of wood were found below the glass which rested on the natural clay. Therefore it must be presumed that the previous container,

FIG. 27. Interior of the glasshouse and the different processes used in making crown window glass. From Diderot, *Encyclopédie*, "Verrerie en Bois," Pl. 2, n.d. (after the edition of 1763).

FIG. 28. Detail of remains of burned barrel set in floor of the glasshouse. The north wall of the factory and possible buttress foundation are to be seen in the center, while the exterior ditch runs eastward at the left. 63.509.

FIG. 26. Detail of melted window glass lying *in situ* in burned clay between oven Units 1A and 2A. 62.557.

like the burned barrel, possessed no bottom. Unaccountably resting in the top of the clear glass chips were the bases of three tumblers and enough body fragments to reconstruct two of them (Fig. 42), a clear funnel-shaped tube of uncertain purpose, and most of one small drinking glass (Fig. 39, No. 10). These were the most complete objects from the entire excavation, and their presence amid such very small pieces cannot be explained. The latter, however, would seem to have been deliberately ground to be mixed into batches of new first quality glass. The method of achieving this coarse grinding was hinted at by the discovery of a much worn stone ball, 3½" in diameter, which was found in the waste tip outside the south wall of the factory (Fig. 46, No. 3). It is probable that the ball was one of many which were tumbled along with broken glass in a rotating barrel—a grinding technique of considerable antiquity. It is not suggested that the grinding took place in the immediate vicinity of the burned barrel, though that could account for the presence of both ground and unground material in the same container. It is likely, however, that as the supposed storage barrel was set into the ground, it fed an operation conducted in the east section of the factory. Because the deposit contained nothing but colorless (or "white") glass it might be construed that table glass was manufactured in furnace #3.

The foregoing evidence is by no means conclusive, and in rebuttal one must recall the presence of window glass beside oven #2A to the south of the working furnace. Although a number of drinking glass, tumbler, and flask fragments were found on the burned clay floor against the north wall of the furnace and clogging the brick duct which emerged at that side, the actual stoking areas were filled with debris which was liberally mixed with green cullet and bottle fragments. The east stoking area yielded fragments of a molded amber blacking or snuff bottle, while the west contained pieces of pale green rib-molded and plain flasks which had been melted almost out of recognition after having been completed (Fig. 43). It should be noted that the same deposit also yielded most of a wineglass and part of a domed-footed jelly glass, both flattened from unintentional heating after completion. We cannot be sure what accident befell these glasses and bottles, but it is reasonably certain that it happened to both in the same place and at the same time. It is possible that they are the products of an annealing oven whose temperature was allowed to rise too high. If this is the correct explanation, it would place both flasks and table glass in the same oven, an association for which there is ample precedent (Fig. 29). Thus, as it has been established with reasonable certainty that each main furnace (#3 and 8) was provided with all its ancillary ovens, it would follow that bottles and table glass were made together in either the east or west half of the factory. Adding the evidence of the barrel deposit of ground table glass, it must logically be deduced that both products (bottles and table glass) were manufactured in the eastern section, i.e., in working furnace #3.

FIG. 29. View of an annealing oven containing bottles and drinking glasses. Shopmen carrying hampers of bottles and drinking glasses to be packed. From Diderot, *Encyclopédie,* "Verrerie en Bois," Pl. 22, n.d. (after the edition of 1763).

An unidentified "Glass Maker" writing in the *Gazette of the United States* in July of 1789 provided documentary evidence that the glass for both bottles and tableware could be prepared in the same furnace. He also gave a significant description of a New Jersey furnace where fritting, heating, and annealing were carried out in the same structure.

Bottles, black or green, are the most simple of all glass manufacture—the profits in making which depends upon the greatest number of workmen being employed at the smallest expense of fuel. From eight to sixteen blowers can work all at once, at one melting furnace, six feet diameter, which will take six cords of wood every twenty-four hours. The best constructed green glass furnace in this country is in New Jersey—where the whole business of smelting, blowing, and cooling is done with one fire, by the particular construction of the furnace.

White glass may also be made in the same furnace: but it is much more curious in its composition; for to make it white, it must partake of all the colours—for this reason—in smelting the purest materials, they naturally have a greenish and purplish tinge: to dislodge which a blackish fossil substance is made use of upon this principle, that one colour in glass making will destroy another; so that at last a beautiful glass is produced called white; but like the crystalline humor of the eye, it partakes of all the colours, as may be seen in the best English white glass which has a changeableness like soap bubbles; but in the best London crown glass, or mirrors, you will not perceive any of that sparkling, changeable power, because it would distort the object seen through or reflected, on account of the refracting power of such glass; therefore this glass is made of pure salts and sands only and has a native greyish colour, as may be seen by the broken pieces that, like water, they may reflect the objects truly. . . .[18]

Proceeding on the tentative assumption that the east section of the Amelung factory was used for the making of table glass and bottles, there remains the problem of what was made in the west furnace (#8). One might be tempted to suggest that this, too, was a bottle furnace and that only the small molded bottles and flasks were produced in #3. However, among the remelted flask fragments in the filling of the latter's west stoking area was the flattened neck of a larger bottle of plain form which was found in quantity elsewhere on the site. It must therefore be construed that if bottles were made at furnace #3, they were not confined to specialized molded varieties. This does not, of course, rule out the possibility that bottles were also made at the larger, western furnace.

There is no positive evidence to indicate the use of furnace #8, but a process of elimination might suggest at first glance that it was window glass. However, it is unlikely (in spite of the evidence of the previously quoted "Glass Maker") that the smaller east furnace (#3) would have been large enough to handle Amelung's entire table glass and bottle output. If it were not, it would be more reasonable that another furnace in the same building would be devoted to the same ends. This would certainly be more logical than to introduce an entirely different operation into one end of the building while siting the rest of the table glass and bottle production elsewhere. But on the other hand, we still do not know where the excavated factory building ranked in Amelung's operating layout. If this was a secondary structure, then it might

be argued that furnace #3 was not the principal center for the making of quality wares but was merely an additional source of supply, backing up a larger furnace in some other building which was not found. This possibility will be considered a little later.

If furnace #8 was intended to serve the makers of window glass, the four ovens to the east of it (#9A, B, C, and D) should logically have been for flattening rather than for annealing. Before considering the structural requirements for a flattening oven, it may be helpful to summarize once more the processes involved in the manufacture of window glass. This was most succinctly phrased by a spokesman of the venerable James Powell & Sons (Whitefriars) Glasshouse of London, saying:

> The first process in making a 'muff' is to blow a hollow cylinder, leaving a knob at the end furthest from the iron. This knob is knocked off, and in the hole so produced the blower inserts his tool and with it opens out that end to the same diameter as the centre; this end is then fixed to a hot disc of metal, called a 'post,' of the same diameter; the other end is then cracked off from the iron and in its turn is opened out to form a complete cylinder, called a muff from its shape. The muff then has to be spread into a flat sheet; it is split with a diamond from end to end and is then introduced into a well-heated 'spreading' kiln with the split side uppermost. The heat in the kiln is such that the glass gradually melts and the muff collapses. The spreader helps nature by stroking the glass with the end of a long iron rod and flattening it on the bed of the kiln. As soon as the sheet is flat it is pushed into a cooler chamber for annealing and is left there for several days.[19]

The only clue to the facilities for window glass manufacture at New Bremen comes from Amelung's 1795 advertisement which listed, among other structures, "two Glass Houses; two Flattening Houses; Warehouses and Stables . . ." It seems hardly likely that the muffs would have been made in one building and transported to another for flattening and annealing. It might therefore be conjectured that the entire window glass manufacturing process was undertaken in the flattening houses. Even if this was not the case, the annealing must have been done there, as the whole purpose of the process is to bring about a slow cooling of the product. With these factors in mind, we can now look again at furnace #8 and its attendant ovens #9A, B, C, and D.

If furnace #8 was devoted solely to the manufacture of window glass, the four ovens to the west of it are unlikely to have been for flattening as we know that Amelung built separate "Flattening Houses." But then again, if the flattening houses were elsewhere, the four ovens (#9A, B, C, and D) could not have been for annealing window glass. This rather tortuous argument is intended to draw the conclusion that furnace #8 was *not* built for the making of window glass. Instead it is contended that it was part of the bottle-making process and that at least some of the four ancillary ovens were devoted to annealing bottles (Fig. 25).[20]

These four ovens were fired (as already explained) through channels that opened into the center of each chamber. While vessels to be annealed could be pushed on trays around the holes, flattening window glass could only be placed and manipulated in front of the heat source. Consequently at least half the space in the four ovens would have been useless. Owing to the limited time available, the area in front of only one of the ovens (#9A) was entirely excavated. The hard-packed clay floor was found to be covered by a series of thin layers of gray ash and red, burned clay, indicating that the firing channel had seen considerable service. To the south of the channel were found three irregularly shaped stones which may have supported some kind of platform; beside these stones, and slightly north of the wall dividing Units #9A and B, stood a small buttress-like foundation that was not bonded into the main structure (Fig. 23). It is not known whether any more such features flanked the four units, but the presence of even one might raise doubts as to whether all the ovens were for annealing. It is likely that the small foundation (which incorporated one glass-coated and re-used stone) was actually the base for a platform beside the oven port, which acted as a base for a marvering slab or as a rest for the workman's tools. Either explanation fails to jibe with the identification of Unit #9A as an annealing oven. Although no stones from the firing channel of oven #9A were removed for thermal analysis, the presence of such large quantities of ash immediately in front of the orifice (much more than was found before oven #9B) might be construed as evidence that this oven was subject to more stoking and raking than were its companions. In summation, it is suggested that the large melting furnace #8 was built as part of a bottle-making complex, the fritting ovens being

built into the wings of the furnace, and the annealing ovens being ranged behind it to the west.

THE APPEARANCE OF THE FACTORY

Having considered the individual components of the excavated factory building it is now necessary to consider the structure as a whole—under the circumstances an even more difficult task than trying to identify the purpose to which it was put. The first question that is raised is whether or not the entire structure is of the same period. The presence of re-used stones in the foundations of oven units has already been mentioned. The most significant of these stones were those incorporated into the walls and filling of Units #1A and B, for this pair of ovens was bonded into walls running both north and west, and they could not have been rebuilt without tearing down the entire southeast corner of the factory. Because furnaces were generally short-lived and because they were frequently opened to insert new and extract old pots, the presence of re-used materials need not necessarily be of any great significance. It only becomes so when the repairs or changes affect the fabric of the building itself.

Except in the case of the east foundation, the walls of the factory were not nearly as substantially constructed as the individual oven units which were part of the interior. Furthermore, the bonding of the external walls into those of the ovens was not consistent. For example, a comparatively slender wall (1'4" in width) was bonded into the west side of Unit #1A, but it merely abutted against the southeast corner of the solidly built oven Unit #2A. In turn, the wall extending west from the southwest corner of that oven was bonded into it, but it only abutted against the southeast corner of room #7B. It was conjectured that the absence of bonding between certain of the walls might be indicative of different periods of construction, but no sustaining pattern emerged to support such a theory.

In the course of the excavation another possibility acquired some credence, namely that the furnace and oven units had been constructed first and were initially sheltered beneath a roof supported on large posts. This possibility seemed to merit serious consideration because so much of the wall construction was of poor quality and seemingly too light for so large a building. At the northwest corner, for example, the truly excellent stonelaying exhibited by ovens #9A, B, C, and D, was followed by a double line of rubble which showed little evidence of having been bonded into itself. It should be added that this feeble construction was common to the entire north wall of the factory, and in some places it was well nigh impossible to distinguish between the deliberately laid foundation and the mass of stone rubble that was scattered across the factory floor and into the ditch outside it.

No sections of the exterior wall foundations were removed and therefore it could not be stated categorically that no post holes were concealed beneath them. However, the fact that some sections of the foundations were bonded into the various oven units serves to minimize the likelihood that the factory was initially an open assemblage of furnaces protected from the elements by nothing more than a post-supported roof.

Only one short section survived of the walling which had originally stood above grade, and this was found on the east face immediately south of the northeast corner of the building. The stones were carefully selected and laid, and were bonded with puddled and tightly packed yellow clay. The stone used here and throughout the factory was a local schist which has been identified as Harpers phyllite or Bennett Creek Calcareous Phyllite.[21] As has been previously noted, the foundations, of the east wall measured up to 4'0" in thickness at the base, in marked contrast to the average of 1'7" elsewhere. This great thickness at the east was occasioned by the fact that the building stood almost on the edge of the escarpment which dropped dramatically way to Bennett Creek. The east foundation was therefore carried down to a depth of three or more feet below the floor of the factory so as to avoid any possibility of its slipping as a result of erosion.

The location of doorways into the factory building is a problem which has not been solved through the archaeology. Apart from one possible gap in the north wall between Units #4 and 5, the foundations were continuous on all four sides. The one possible break occurred immediately east of a rectangular and well-built buttress-like foundation which was intially thought to have been the base for one jamb of a massive doorway. But when no pair to this feature was found, the theory lost substance. Nevertheless, there was a straight joint through the north wall to the east of the small, offset foundation. Furthermore, the wall between this point and the west edge of Unit #4 was in an extremely fragmentary condition, and there *was* a small abutment springing from it against the western extremity of the raised floor of the supposed wood-drying room (#4). But it must be admitted that the abutment was only one stone in width (approximately 1'7"), about half the thickness of the westerly buttress or jamb foundation. Even with these reservations, the possibility that a large doorway pierced the north wall of the glasshouse between Units #4 and 5 cannot entirely be ignored.

Slightly east of the suggested doorway and partially outside the north wall of Unit #4, the ditch was overlaid and partially filled with stone rubble. Two pieces of stone in this area (and at the bottom of the rubble stratum) projected beneath the north wall and so predated it. The possibility was voiced that all the associated debris was of the same period and therefore the ditch had been abandoned before the glasshouse was built. Ceramic dating evidence from the ditch made such an interpretation highly improbable.[22] Although the line of the ditch does not run exactly parallel with the north wall of the glasshouse, there can be little doubt that it was dug for the express purpose of carrying away water shedding from the building's massive roof.

The filling of the ditch showed considerable evidence of silting from the sides, and it is quite possible that it was cleaned out from time to time. Still unexplained is the fact that the cutting became increasingly shallow as it approached the northwest corner of the glasshouse. This raises the possibility that the ditch was originally created naturally by rainwater and manually enlarged only towards the east.

Reference has already been made to the likelihood that a door existed in the southwest corner of the building, i.e., in the west wall of room #7A and leading to what later became the Fleecy Dale Road. It was suggested that it was through this door that the finished products were carried to the warehouses. The quantity of refuse dumped against the exterior walls of rooms #7A and B, coupled with the fact that most of it was bottle rather than the table glass, points to a doorway in the south wall between those rooms and oven unit #2A. This was probably quite a small door (if it existed at all); the supplies of raw materials and firewood were more likely to have entered through the previously discussed large doorway in the north wall immediately beside the wood-drying room. It must be apparent by now that the excavations left a great many unanswered questions concerning both the nature of the work carried on in the building, and of the appearance of the structure itself. Mr. Kenneth M. Wilson has drawn my attention to an old photograph of the Pitkin Works at Manchester, Connecticut, showing the ruins of a once massive two-storied stone structure—part of a factory building which was contemporary with New Bremen, and which is believed to have specialized in the making of bottles and flasks. A study of the Pitkin ruins makes it clear that to construct such a glasshouse the foundations would have been of much greater width than were those of the Amelung factory. Indeed, so slender were the footings of the latter's north wall that it is extremely unlikely that the stonework would have been carried to a height of more than six or eight feet.

In his *5000 Years of Glass-Making*, Jaroslav Vávra shows a photograph of the Bohemian glasshouse at Breitenstein[23] which possessed comparably low stone walls and similar proportions. The illustrated building has a massive A-roof with descending hips at either end; the smoke emerged through large dormer-like ports along the ridge and through many smaller openings in the slope of the roof. It is my belief that this is a very close parallel for the exterior of the New Bremen factory, and my conjectural reconstruction is based on it (Fig. 1, Lanmon-Schwind section).

The method of supporting so vast a roof span was not revealed by the excavations; no large post holes were found and neither were the bases of piers on which posts might have stood. Nevertheless, there had to be supports beneath the main roof timbers, standing between Units #6B and #4, and #7B and #1A. It is conceivable, however, that much of the weight of the trusses might have been carried by timbers seated in the walls of Units #2A and 2B, and springing from the north/south dividing wall beside Unit #5. Diderot offers precedent for such construction in his section on sheet glass ("Glaces," Pl. II) On the other hand it is quite possible that the supports had stood on piers and that the socketed stones had been salvaged when the remains of the building were stripped.

FIG. 30. Cellar west of the excavated glasshouse, the east end after the removal of overlying rubble. 62.437.

FIG. 31. Cellar west of the excavated glasshouse, north interior corner with test hole cut through to clay floor on which were found artifacts of the third quarter of the nineteenth century. 62.427.

THE SECONDARY STRUCTURES

When the site was first visited in February 1962, the remains of three stone built structures were visible, one lying in a wooded and sharply rising area north of The Fleecy Dale Road and opposite the lower meadow; the others had stood further to the east and on the south side of the road. The program for 1962 included the examination of one or other of the latter structures, both of which consisted only of rubble-filled, stone-walled cellars whose walls had been stripped to ground level. Because it was assumed to stand closest to the main area of industrial activity, the most easterly cellar was chosen for study (Fig. 30).

The building measured 25'10" × 19'0", had walls approximately 1'9" in thickness, and a hard-packed clay floor at a depth of 4'8" below modern grade at the northeast corner. At this point a triangular test hole was dug through the fill of collapsed fieldstone walling to a 1'0" stratum of stones and black dirt which contained wire nails, indicating a date of deposition not earlier than circa 1850 (Fig. 31). Pressed into the clay floor beneath were a small number of cut nails and part of a molded, cylindrical patent medicine bottle of a type which one would attribute to some time in or after the third quarter of the nineteenth century. It was apparent, therefore, that this building had been open and probably in use comparatively recently.

It will be remembered that in 1962, the late Mr. Vernon Yingling (aged 84) recalled having taken shoes to be repaired in one or other of these two buildings when he was a boy.

In clearing around the exterior of the east end of the foundation a layer of bricks was found beneath 8" of topsoil. Some of these appeared to have been roughly laid, perhaps as a gutter to catch water dripping from the eaves. The feature was mutilated toward the northern end of the wall and was there replaced by a stratum of plaster at approximately the same depth. Fragments of window glass were found at this level, and they spilled over the collapsing wall into the interior of the structure. It is likely that the glass came from the window of the building. The only artifact of any possible significance was a crudely made glass stopper, possibly from a cruet, which was found resting on the previously mentioned bricks at the southeast corner of the building. While this object could have been of Amelung manufacture, there is no likelihood that it had remained undisturbed since the eighteenth century.

TEST TRENCH A–B

As stated in the introduction, the 1962 program included the digging of two major test trenches,

each cutting through one of the two mounds which lay south of the Fleecy Dale Road and in the vicinity of the cliff and millrace. It was then supposed that the mound closest to the escarpment concealed Amelung's waste tip and that the other covered an industrial building. Trench A–B, measuring 42'0" × 3'0", was cut through the latter protuberances and it immediately became apparent that no building was hidden there. An examination of the section (Fig. 32) showed that the mound was composed of a series of tipped deposits of glasshouse dross, clay, cullet, fragments of crucible, and quantities of stones, many of which had come from dismantled furnaces and were partially coated with glass. At the bottom of the heap, and overlying natural clay and stones, was a stratum of tamped clay some 4" in thickness.

Principal dating for the waste deposit was provided by a fragment of an English blue-edged pearlware plate which can be attributed to the period 1785–1800. A few pieces of domestic ceramics were scattered through the tip, all of them of types in use in the late eighteenth century. Most interesting among these was the base of a small porcelain cup bearing the factory mark F in cobalt on the underside (Fig. 48, No. 1). This was almost certainly a product of Fürstenburg and was probably among the possessions of one of Amelung's workmen when he arrived from Germany. Unfortunately this object was found at the west end of the trench in ground disturbed by the bulldozing operations of 1948. However, there can be no doubting that the sherd is a relic of the Amelung period.

The supposition that the bulldozing had reached to a depth of about twelve feet made us extremely wary of the stratigraphy at the west end of the trench. But while a piece of modern fence wire was found at a depth of 1'3" below the present surface, the disturbance seemed to have been limited at that point to surface scraping which extended no deeper than 1'6". However, at the extreme west of the cutting a complete lack of stratigraphy indicated that the entire fill had been dug out and thrown back.

Toward the east end of the test trench a stratum of burned clay, stone, crucible, and cullet fragments stretched all the way from the refuse mound to a point south of oven unit #1A—and possibly beyond. It there disappeared beneath a layer of stones which may have formed part of a paved area. Those stones were not removed.

TEST TRENCH G–H (MILLRACE)

The 1962 excavations also included the digging of a test trench across the supposed millrace at a point below the escarpment and southeast of the oven units #1A and B (Fig. 35). The trench measured 20'0" × 3'0" and was intended to locate factory waste believed to have been thrown into it from the refuse deposits above, which, as it turned out, did not exist. The cutting was oriented at a right angle to the east/west base line and therefore crossed the millrace at a tangent. It was carried to a depth of 5'3" in its midsection, cutting through an upper deposit of clay silt and beneath it through a complexity of glasshouse refuse including pot and cullet fragments. An outcrop of natural rock from the escarpment prevented the trench from being dug through to the natural subsoil, and at 5'3" (where digging stopped through lack of space) glass fragments were still being recovered. Although the unfortunate angle of the trench and the shortage of time combined to prevent a complete section through the millrace from being drawn, the cutting did reveal a considerable quantity of factory waste; in it were the largest number of blue fragments found at any point in that year's digging. No signs of the expected water-washed clay were found running through the section, except at the top, and this would be dismissed as erosion from the escarpment rather than the product of the millrace. The relationship of the factory waste to the water channel remained obscure when the trench was abandoned and backfilled. It was then expected that another would be dug in 1963. However, owing to the unexpected size of the factory remains, there was to be no time or labor available to dig this or any other test trench in 1963.

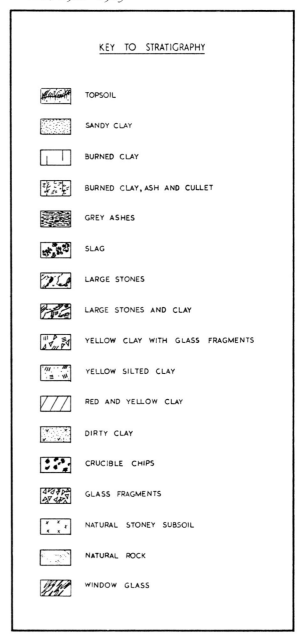

KEY TO STRATIGRAPHY

TOPSOIL

SANDY CLAY

BURNED CLAY

BURNED CLAY, ASH AND CULLET

GREY ASHES

SLAG

LARGE STONES

LARGE STONES AND CLAY

YELLOW CLAY WITH GLASS FRAGMENTS

YELLOW SILTED CLAY

RED AND YELLOW CLAY

DIRTY CLAY

CRUCIBLE CHIPS

GLASS FRAGMENTS

NATURAL STONEY SUBSOIL

NATURAL ROCK

WINDOW GLASS

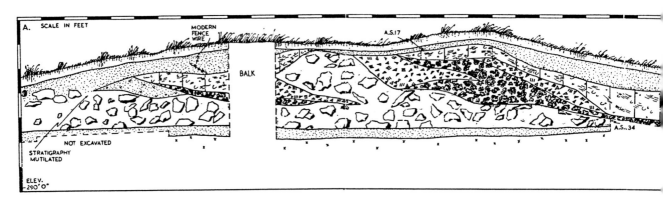

FIG. 32. 1962 test trench, profile A-B, south of glass factory. See plan Figure 3.

DATING EVIDENCE FOR THE EXCAVATED GLASSHOUSE

The role of the archaeologist is generally to study the material remains of successive ages and cultures and, on the evidence of surviving artifacts, to arrive at a reasonably accurate chronology. In the field of pre-history that "reasonable accuracy" may be achieved within a span of centuries, even thousands of years. But once the archaeologist brings his techniques into the historic period he must do immeasurably better if he is to be of any help to the historian.

In the last ten years the study of American historical archaeology has made great strides, and the excavator is now frequently able to provide the historians with a wealth of confirmatory and supplementary information. The Amelung excavations have revealed more about New Bremen's manufacturing processes and products than anyone dared hope. The operative life of the venture was about eleven years, and having found a factory building, the archaeologist can assert without fear of contradiction that it was in operation between 1785 and 1795. But that is hardly all that is required of him.

The re-use of glass-surfaced stones in various parts of the excavated factory building leaves no doubt that this was not the first structure in which glass was produced at New Bremen. In addition, the presence of glass waste underneath some of the oven units, coupled with the apparent redesigning of Unit #5, indicated that significant changes occurred within the building in the course of its life. Then again, no evidence was found to suggest that the factory had served any other purpose (e.g., as a barn or stable) after glassmaking ceased. On the contrary, there were indications that it had been destroyed by fire while still used as a glass manufactory. Thus, if the archaeologist is really to win his spurs, glass historians will expect to learn where this building fitted within the eleven year history of the site.

Unhappily, the spurs may escape us. We can only be sure that this building was not standing when the first glass was blown, and we can suspect that it had ceased to exist by the time the

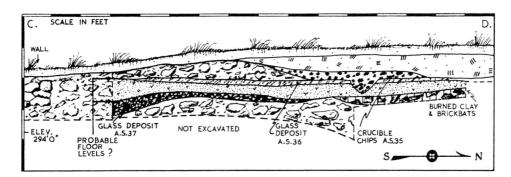

FIG. 33. Section C-D west of Unit #1A, showing rough, working floors and accumulated glasshouse refuse. See plan Figure 3.

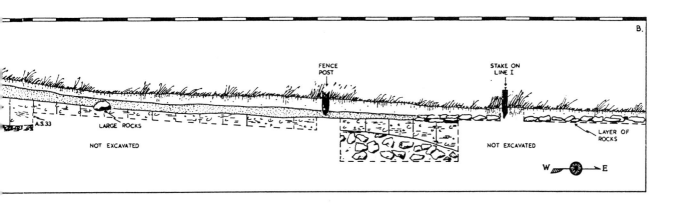

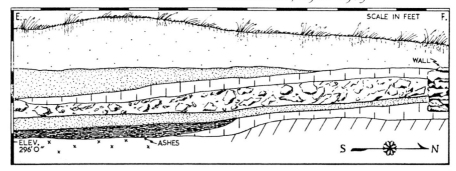

FIG. 34. Section E-F, west of squares ¹⁴⁄₂₃, showing ash-filled depression between furnaces #3 and #8. See plan Figure 3.

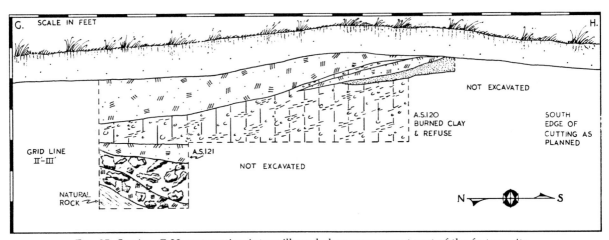

FIG. 35. Section G-H; test cutting into millrace below escarpment east of the factory site.

last iron was laid aside.

It is almost entirely on the archaeological evidence that one is led to believe that the excavated factory was built after New Bremen was in production. However, there is a vague support to be drawn from Amelung's *Remarks* wherein he noted that in 1786 (?) he was ". . . now building another glass oven. . . ."[24] Later, in his longhand notes, Amelung recalled that by 1790 he had acquired another thousand acres and had erected another glasshouse, though it is hardly likely that that had any bearing on the problem; but it is conceivable that the earlier reference was to the glasshouse whose foundations have now been found.

One of the difficulties of interpreting the documentary evidence is that of deciding what Amelung meant when he wrote "glass oven" and "Glass House." Did the former simply describe a single furnace unit, or did it include all of the furnace's ancillary ovens, plus the building in which they stood? As for the "Glass House," did that refer only to one building or was it a collective term used to encompass an entire glassmaking complex? The latter would seem to have been what George Repold meant when he told his wife to go to "die Glass Hütte zu Amlunge."[25] But when Amelung advertised his manufactory for sale he was more specific, offering ". . . two Glass Houses; two Flattening Houses; Warehouses and Stables. . ."[26] But was he always that precise?

It might be tempting to claim that Amelung's reference to additional construction in 1786 was actually to the building of the factory found in 1962–1963. But the building contained two melting furnaces and there was no indication that both were not built at the same time. Whatever Amelung's usage, it is most unlikely that he would have written "glass oven" to describe a structure of these proportions and containing at least two melting units. In short, the documentation is more tantalizing than helpful.

The newspapers document that a "Manufactory and Magazine" were destroyed by fire on May 6, 1790. The evidence of the excavated factory was that it was destroyed by fire and that it was used only for glassmaking. As discussed in the Lanmon/Schwind section, a factory which existed in this area in the early nineteenth century had been a glassworks, but it was being used as a wool factory. It seems logical to conclude that the excavated factory was the one which burned in 1790, and that a new glasshouse was built nearby, not on the old foundations. Rebuilding an entire glasshouse of the size of the one found in the excavations would have been a time-consuming and costly undertaking. If the building was, as suggested, similar to the one at Breitenstein, a fire breaking out in the huge roof would cause the destruction of the entire building.

Already mentioned is the absence of evidence regarding the method of supporting the glasshouse roof (p. 170), but no matter how it was carried inside the building, there can be no doubt that tie beams would have anchored into the tops of the low stone walls. If the roof burned and the timbers collapsed, there is every likelihood that they would have pulled large sections of the walling in with them.

It is almost trite to note that glasshouses were particularly vulnerable to fire. Every time the melting furnace was opened to receive a new pot the danger was considerable. This operation comprised opening the pot oven and extracting the new pot (which may have been up to 3'0" in diameter) while it was red hot, carrying or trolleying it across to the main furnace and levering it into place before it had a chance to cool. At the same time the equally hot old pot (probably in fragments) was pulled or raked out onto the factory floor. It is true that there would have been very little that was combustible lying on the floor, and even if the pot was dropped, the damage would have been more to the personnel than to the fabric of the building. A much greater danger lay in the fact that the furnaces had a comparatively short life and would tend to crack as they became old. When large sections of the side were pulled out to replace the pots on the siege, there was a temporary weakening of the entire unit. Thus, if the furnace was almost ready to be scrapped and rebuilt, there was always the possibility that opening the side might cause the whole structure to collapse, and if this happened a great shaft of flame and sparks could be discharged into the roof.

The archaeological evidence points to considerable burning of the floor over the entire factory area. But this could have been occasioned by the fact that the dirt floor was built up from the debris of glassmaking, much of it consisting of reddened clay removed from the furnaces when they were being opened or rebuilt. However, the burning of the barrel (feature #10) in situ strongly points to the burning of the building around it. On the other hand, this was one of the very few items of burned wood which was found. A single 8"×4" timber (6'0"+ in length) was found lying beyond the ditch outside the north wall, and two others, 5" in width, were encountered immediately north of the smaller working furnace (#3), the latter having a few 2½" nails in them. Nails were scattered all over the factory area, the two greatest concentrations being in the top filling of the barrel (#10) and alongside the west wall of oven Unit #1A. The majority of nails from both these groups had been exposed to considerable heat and were found to have resisted the corrosion which affected those through the rest of the factory. So slender is this evidence that it must be concluded that if the roof did burn, no traces of it remained after the building had been dismantled and the stones re-used.

There is not the slightest doubt that the factory was dismantled and its stones carried away for use elsewhere. The question is merely the date at which it was done. Local tradition has it that stones from the Amelung factory were carried away and used in buildings erected at Park Mills. This may well be so—though it is possible that the materials came from the Kohlenberg Factory rather than from the Amelung home meadow site. Support for that possibility was provided by Mr. Richard Muzzrole of the Smithsonian Institution who undertook minor excavation work on the site of the mid-nineteenth-century Bear Branch School which stood in the narrow valley between Park Mills and the Kohlenberg site. Re-used in the doorway of the school house was a partially glass-covered stone which undoubtedly came from the latter factory site. Nevertheless, there can be no doubt that the stones from the furnaces and walls of the excavated Amelung factory had been deliberately removed.

Four post holes were found cutting into the factory remains toward the northwest of the building; one pierced the northwest exterior corner, another disturbed the north wall at the northeast corner of room #6B, yet another cut into the north side of the ditch further to the east, and the fourth was found inside the glasshouse beside the west foundation of the pot arch. This last hole seemed to make a pair with the one cutting through the ditch, and it contained four fragments of blowing irons which had been shoveled back with the fill around the post. Together, the four holes may indicate the corner of a fenced area constructed soon after the glasshouse was removed.

A few of the stones from one of the furnaces were laid along the north side of the Fleecy Dale Road as the base for either a stone wall or an earth bank—the latter being the more probable. In either case this was clearly intended to make a property boundary, and it passed over the southeast wing of the main furnace. Because the stones rested directly on the old foundations it was deduced that the line was established almost immediately after the building was destroyed. The stones had been disturbed here and there by subsequent post holes and in some case the remains of posts survived. The same line was followed by the modern fence between the Smith and Yingling properties. Furthermore, the locating of the "Home Place" and the "210 Acre Mill and Factory Site" on the nineteenth-century Brown land plat would suggest that the Fleecy Dale Road then served as the division between the two parcels. It will be remembered, too, that some such division existed between the house and the factory tract when the Amelung lands were auctioned in 1798. It might therefore be suggested that the Fleecy Dale Road even then marked the dividing line between the two parcels, in which case it might further be construed that the excavated factory had ceased to exist and that the stone boundary line had already succeeded it.

Unfortunately, the historical archaeologist is very rarely able to draw lines within a ten-year period unless somewhere within it he has one or more documented anchors. Such things as tools, cutlery, buttons, buckles, and ceramics did not, as a rule, evolve or decline in popularity abruptly enough for their presence or absence to enable the archaeologist to arrive at specific dates.[27] Amelung's glass may have changed in one way or another during the eleven years of the factory's operation; new molds may have been acquired and others abandoned; certain forms or colors may have been favored in one period and not in another; seals may have been attached to bottles for one customer only—all

these factors might be dating clues. But if they are, we have been unable to make use of them. In the absence of any consistent stratigraphy laid down during the life of the building one could only say that the glass on and in the uneven floors was deposited in the operative period and that all the material from the overlying strata was dumped over the area at some date late in the eighteenth or early in the nineteenth century. So obvious a conclusion contributes nothing.

Because the factory site was not disturbed by subsequent occupation, very few artifacts were found which did not belong to the Amelung period. The principal exception was provided by the fenceline between the Smith and Yingling fields and the gateway through it. Numerous horseshoes had been hung on the fence and gate posts through the years, and had eventually fallen to the ground. Thus the ridge of the fencelines contained a considerable quantity of horseshoes—also recent beer bottles, wire nails, pieces of fence wire, and other irrelevant odds and ends. A few similar items were found in the often ploughed topsoil in the Yingling field as well as pressed into the surface of the Fleecy Dale Road. However, no intrusive items penetrated into the Amelung stratum and we can safely accept it as being undisturbed.

Ceramics found on the clay floors of the factory consisted largely of creamwares (including one almost complete saucer); coarse, local, lead-glazed earthenwares, and German porcelains, often rib-molded and decorated in underglaze blue. In addition, a few very small pieces of transfer-printed pearlware were found, but these were in the overlying layers. Pewter and brass shoe buckles were among the small finds, plus a great many tinned brass buttons, and several table knives, and clasp knives. All of these items were of eighteenth-century origin and there was no evidence that any (except, perhaps, the pearlware sherds) dated any later than 1790. From the ash fill stratum of the west stoking area of furnace #3 came a tin-plated brass knee buckle and an English halfpenny of George II (old head, 1741–1754). The latter was in too worn a condition for the date to be read, but it would have been of no significance even if it had been legible.

In summation, it may be said that no evidence has been found to indicate a *terminus post quem* for the construction of the excavated factory building except, of course, that which shows that the structure incorporated stones which had previously been used in another furnace. At the other end of the story, the archaeological evidence suggests that the factory had ceased to exist by 1795. As none of the datable objects need have been manufactured after 1790, it is conceivable that the building was the one destroyed on May sixth of that year. It may have been the sight of these ruins that caused a member of Amelung's household to be "Thinking" on May 7, 1790,[28] and it may have been this same loss which caused Amelung himself to petition Congress for funds on May 26, and again on June 29, asking in part for a grant to ". . . enable him to repair his heavy well known Loss by Fire. . . ."

CONCLUSIONS

Although a great deal of work has been put into the Corning-Smithsonian excavations at New Bremen, and although a spectacularly large and well-equipped factory structure was uncovered, few firm conclusions can be drawn. It is very tempting to be dogmatic and claim for facts what are really suppositions. But as the entire site has not been excavated and because a great many loose ends dangle from the documentary file, all our conclusions must remain tentative. I have attempted to show the various pieces of evidence and to weigh them against both the known facts and the possibilities which might become facts if and when the entire site is excavated.

The date range of the factory, as shown above, appears to lie within both extremities of Amelung's venture, with a possible termination date of 1790. If the dating is right, it must follow that the foundations did not belong to either of the "Glass Houses" offered for sale in 1795. At the same time, because of the re-used materials in the outer walls, neither may they have been part of the units constructed in the winter and spring of 1784–1785. If both contentions are correct, there is clearly a great deal still to be uncovered at New Bremen.

Following the 1948 incursions into the site with a bulldozer the Baltimore *Sun* stated that the excavator had ". . . hit the site of the initial Amelung factory, one that had burned and was rebuilt at a different spot." The bulldozer work is understood to have begun immediately south of the excavated factory building and to have proceeded in a southerly direction down the meadow. Although the 1962 east/west test trench ran into the edge of the bulldozed area,

no structural remains were found. The trench did cut through a deep and tightly packed mound of glassmaking waste which included stones that had been coated with glass while in use in a furnace. Similar deposits of waste were found along much of the exterior of the excavated building's south wall. Owing to the limitations of time and labor, no further test trenches were dug in the meadow other than the series of negative test holes cut immediately south of the Fleecy Dale Road in 1962. However, in that meadow, there are two large mounds of stone over which trees have grown as well as traces of foundations in the side of a bank where the land drops down to the flood plain of Bennett Creek. It is quite possible that the main factory complex stood in this meadow, south, east, and west of the two surviving stone-walled basements. It will be noted that it was in that area that the nineteenth-century surveyor wrote the word "Factory" on the Brown plat. Until these disturbing possibilities have been proved or disproved, the archaeological history of New Bremen cannot be written.

The total number of structures now located is but four out of a documented thirty-six or more—one excavated factory building (probably not documented) and three still visible basements. It is possible that the dwelling houses were not all grouped together and that if they were, the assemblage stood at some distance from the factory area. Consequently, the search for them could be costly and time-consuming without adding much to our knowledge of the actual manufactory. But even if the factory is confined to the lower meadow, the task of excavating it would be very considerable, particularly if, as Mrs. Milford has stated, the remains are much deeper than were those explored in 1962 and 1963. Although neither Corning nor the Smithsonian has any plans to continue the excavations in the immediate future, the possibility that only a small portion of the manufactory has yet been found serves to emphasize the need to protect the site from mutilation. While the excavations have demonstrated the historical importance of the area, the fact that the work is generally assumed to have been completed might promote the belief that the ground has yielded all the information that can be extracted from it. It might therefore be assumed that the site is of little further archaeological significance. Nothing could be further from the truth; the excavations have shown only that those Maryland antiquaries and historians who believed in the importance of New Bremen as an archaeological site were entirely vindicated.

Thanks to the enthusiastic interest of Congressman Charles McC. Mathias, Jr., the first step has been taken towards designating the site as a national historic landmark. On October 29, 1963, Mr. Mathias introduced the following bill in Congress:

Be it enacted by the Senate and House of Representatives of the United States of America in Congress assembled, That the Secretary of the Interior is authorized and directed to designate as a registered national historic landmark the site of the Amelung Glassworks, Frederick County, Maryland, which was one of the earliest industrial operations in the United States and at which was carried on a quality and quantity of glass production unequaled in America in the eighteenth century.

The bill was referred to the Committee on Interior and Insular Affairs.[29]

Even if the principal conclusion must be that a deal more work is necessary before the full archaeological story of New Bremen can be told, much positive information has been acquired. The size of the excavated glasshouse building was as large as any of its type in England or France, and considerably more impressive than any American glass factory of its period that had previously been excavated. In addition, the great quantities of glass retrieved can now make possible a thorough artistic and chemical study of Amelung's product which, when completed, will add immeasurably to our knowledge of early American glass and glass technology.

IV. THE EVIDENCE
OF THE ARTIFACTS

IT IS NOT THE PURPOSE of this report to provide a detailed analysis of the excavated glass. That is a task for students with a wider knowledge of the products of other American glasshouses, and it is also for someone with ready access to all the pertinent comparative material. The report will summarize what was found and examine the findings in the light of the archaeological and documentary evidence. It is hoped that a thorough chemical analysis of the salient pieces will ultimately be made, along with an equally thorough study of the raw materials found in the building and the local natural resources which would have been available for use at New Bremen.

The distribution of the glass and its possible relevance in identifying the various oven units have already been explored and need not be repeated. The various tools have also been discussed, but these *do* have something to tell us with regard to the technique of manufacture, and repetition is therefore necessary.

TOOLS AND RELATED METAL ITEMS

The most prevalent item to be recovered, and the only one directly associated with the shaping of glass, was the blowing iron. Many end pieces of such irons were found, four of them in a small hole in the clay floor at the west end of the supposed pot arch.[30] Of all the metal tools used by the glassmaker, the blowing iron wore out the most quickly. The gather ends of the irons became weakened by frequent insertion into the white hot crucibles of molten glass; they also became clogged with both glass and oxida-

tion. From the pieces recovered, it would appear that when this happened the end was cut off and the iron continued to be used a while longer. Such shortened irons were not very satisfactory because the original length, coupled with a thickening at the gather end of the tube, provided the correct balance for swinging and manipulation. The best example of the iron's true end shape is to be seen in Fig. 48, No. 27. Another fragment (Fig. 47, No. 3) is flattened at one end and had been partially cut preparatory to breaking the tube from the spatula-like terminal. The significance of this piece has not been determined.

A heavy cast iron rake-like fragment was one of the more important discoveries, for this is believed to have been used in the stirring of frit components spread on the floor of the oven. The object has a series of diamond-sectioned prongs or standards (some now missing) which were set in groups in such a way that nothing through which it was pushed could pass in a straight line. When pushed through sand, the prongs move the grains in a snake-like pattern. Thus, two or three different ingredients would be cleverly mixed together merely by pulling this rake through them. The weight of the cast iron back is sufficient to ensure that the prongs pass *through* the sand rather than sliding over the top of it.[31]

A rectangular iron slug weighing 13 lbs. 15 oz., was also among the finds. This is thought to have been a counterweight suspended by a now-missing ring at the top. Unfortunately, this interesting object was found in the topsoil beside the bank between the Smith and Yingling properties and it may therefore have come from a gate—though its length would make it rather impracticable. If it does date from the Amelung period, it could very well have been used as an aid to opening and closing an oven port, or perhaps a none-too-accessible air duct.

From the waste deposit immediately outside the south wall came a much-worn stone ball which may indicate the method used for grinding cullet or silica—by tumbling it in a barrel containing large numbers of these balls. Although no documentary evidence has been found to substantiate this theory, it may be noted that rotating barrels filled with corn husks were used in Venice for the polishing of beads.

The only other tools recovered obviously were not related to glassmaking, though their prevalence suggests that they were used in some associated capacity; these items were simply knives—ordinary table knives and pocket clasp knives of various sizes. In addition, the blade of one double-edged dagger or hunting knife was found. All save the table knives could have been used for whittling wood and so might have served for trimming the burned surfaces from wooden tongs, blocks, lippers, and battledores. The table knives were too long and unwieldy for such uses, but they may have been used in shaping glass.[32] The absence of forks and spoons (though the bowls of two teaspoons were found) seems to indicate that the knives were not used for cutting food.

The most readily identifiable tool recovered was the head of a heavy hammer-chisel combination (Fig. 46, No. 2), which was used to break up old crucibles prior to grinding them into grog for potmaking and also to chip glass from the insides of the pots for use as cullet. Examples of such tools in use are well illustrated by Diderot (Fig. 36).[33] Also identifiable—but not necessarily as a specific glassmaking item, were fragments of two shovel blades with hollow sockets for attachment to wooden handles. The shape was very similar to that of modern coal shovels and represents a form which had not previously been encountered in eighteenth-century contexts. The first was recovered from the top of the waste deposit south of the factory; it was dismissed as being of recent date. Later, the second was found in an undoubted eighteenth-century layer.[34] Shovels of one sort or another were necessarily used for a variety of glasshouse tasks from throwing frit into the melting pots to

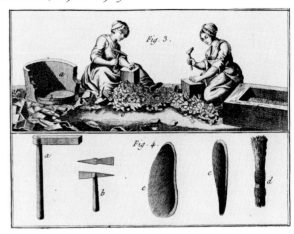

FIG. 36. Burned out crucibles are broken. In this engraving from Diderot women tediously salvage glass from the sherds using hammering-chisels (4b) similar to the excavated example (Fig. 46, No. 2). From Diderot, *Encyclopédie,* "Verrerie en Bois," Pl. 7, n.d. (after the edition of 1763).

removing ashes from stokeholes. Four broken tines from large forks were also recovered, and these might have been used in the preparation of raw materials.

The crucibles themselves must be included among the tools of the craft. Many fragments of these were found, most of them in quite small pieces—apparently relics of the first step in grog preparation. The largest single piece was found against the inside of the east foundation of the factory building at a point well below the working floor, indicating that it had found its way into that position while the glasshouse was being constructed. The fragment (Fig. 45, No. 1) came from a cylindrical pot 2'9" to 3'0" in diameter. Other pot fragments were flat-sided and possibly octagonal or hexagonal in form. Unfortunately the pieces were all too small for any reconstructions to be attempted. The bodies of all these pieces were coated with a thin surface of glass both inside and out. Because this surface was more or less uniform in thickness and did not, as a rule, vary in color from inside to out, it seems possible that it represents a vitrification achieved in the heat of the furnace rather than a deposition of the crucible's contents.

In addition to the tight-grained gray ware of the crucibles, other less highly fired fragments of earthenwares were found, all with their yellow clay bodies well-mixed with a very coarse grog. The objects made from this material varied considerably in form from the rings of furnace ports to oval clay "buns" of the kind found on the brick floor of Unit #5 (see Fig. 44, No. 6). Most of the sherds had been shaped against boards and the grain of the wood had been transferred to the clay. In some cases the objects were vertical pots apparently shaped in tubs or wooden forms bound with iron hoops which could be released to remove the finished object. On these earthenwares the marks of the individual staves of the form can readily be seen. It has been estimated that the vessels were fired to a temperature of about 1600°F, and the size of the grog makes it obvious that even if they had been fired to stoneware temperature they never would have achieved the appearance or consistency of the crucibles.[35] On the other hand, the majority of the "buns" and ring fragments are covered on one side with a thin, green vitreous coating, and in a few instances the "buns" are actually covered with fabricated glass.[36]

It had been hoped—though without much conviction—that the excavations would have yielded examples of molds, intact irons, and other glasshouse equipment. But with the possible exception of the hammer, all the items recovered were fragmentary, worn out, and were of no further use to their owners. Had the factory been destroyed by fire and immediately abandoned, it is probable that all sorts of tools and other paraphernalia would have been found. If this factory did burn, it is very clear that someone came back afterward to salvage anything and everything that could possibly be of any further use.

MISCELLANEOUS SMALL FINDS

Surprisingly plentiful were fragments of brass and pewter shoe buckles. None of them was complete and most had broken more or less in half. The only reasonable explanation for their presence seems to be that they caught on projections from the chairs or walls of the glasshouse and were snapped from the shoes of hurrying workmen. One of the larger pewter buckles had a clean break on one side, but obviously had been deliberately twisted off at the other. Buttons of various types were also fairly plentiful, but in a period in which a coat alone might carry up to a couple dozen buttons, their presence is not unexpected. The only other dress item was a small oval knee buckle of tinned brass which was found along with buttons and an English halfpenny of George II in a gray ash stratum of

the fill within the east working furnace's west stoking area (#3).[37]

Although they were not part of the Corning collection of excavated material, it is worth recalling that Mrs. Exel Yingling had previously picked up one of a pair of oval sleeve-links while walking down the Fleecy Dale Road. The link and its two buttons were of tinned brass and decorated with molded hatching around a central oval. They were of a type common in the second half of the eighteenth century and were surprisingly well preserved.[38]

An unexpectedly small number of tobacco pipe fragments was recovered, but unexpected only because one has grown so accustomed to finding literally hundreds of pieces on domestic sites. Pipe smoking was a leisurely pursuit to be enjoyed while seated and conversing with one's friends. It was also a somewhat clumsy operation: the long-stemmed pipes of the eighteenth century had to be held and balanced in the hand and not gripped between the teeth as were the short pipes of the nineteenth century. Of course the stems could be broken and the pipe drastically shortened; such doctored examples are found from time to time. Nevertheless, the eighteenth century was not a period in which smoking had become the obsession that it has today, and pipes did not dangle from every workman's lip like the modern cigarette. Besides, a glasshouse was not a leisurely place; the gaffers had something better to do with their lungs, while the servitors and "takers-in" were kept too busy fetching and carrying to have time for pipe smoking. Thus, when one stops to consider the matter, it would have been odd if many pipe fragments had been found.

THE CERAMICS

The collection of pottery and porcelain was quite small and only one item, a creamware saucer, was anywhere near complete. This was found on the burned clay floor west of the barrel (#10) and, like the tobacco pipes, it is curious that it was found there at all. Domestic pottery, particularly pieces of quality, would seem to have had very little to do with glassmaking. Another piece of a creamware saucer was recovered from the gray ash on the floor of the firing channel of the southeast fritting oven (#1B). Creamware was by far the most prevalent single ware represented and the sherds ranged from pitchers to plates in the "Royal" pattern.

In the evolution of English pottery, creamware was succeeded by a whitened variation known as pearlware which possessed a blue tinted glaze rather than the greenish-yellow of its predecessor. This ware was most common in the period 1790 to 1815, but there is a growing evidence that it was in production at least as early as 1780. A dozen or so sherds were recovered from the factory site; with the exception of those from the topsoil, all the pieces were found in or over the ditch outside the north wall. Because pearlware was not common in the early eighties, it provides strong evidence to suggest that the ditch was open at least until the demise of the glasshouse, thus casting doubt on the previously discussed possibility that the ditch might have ceased to exist before the building was erected (see p. 169).

Next to the creamwares, fragments of coarse lead-glazed earthenware kitchen pots were the most abundant; in this category also were sherds of polychrome slipwares which were probably produced in Pennsylvania. Pieces of a few brown stoneware jars and one jug, the former almost certainly American, were also encountered. Of more importance was the discovery of numerous fragments of porcelain tea wares, most of them of German origin. The most informative single item was the base of a small teacup decorated in under-glaze blue and marked on the bottom with a script capital "F." This was a product of Fürstenberg and dated from the latter years of the eighteenth century, or post 1770.[39]

THE GLASS

As previously stated, there has been insufficient comparative work devoted to the glass to assess its significance within the panoply of American glass history. One can only compare the excavated pieces with the statements made by Amelung and the inventories listed in his advertisements. The latter have already been considered at some length in an earlier section of this study. Therefore, the full texts need not be repeated here. It is enough to recall that in February 1785 Amelung announced that he intended to produce ". . . all kinds of Glass-Wares, viz: Window Glass, from the lowest to the finest sorts, white and green Bottles, Wine and other Drinking-Glasses, as also Optical Glasses and Looking-Glasses, finished compleat . . ."[40] Three years later he advertised that he had for sale "½ gill to quart tumblers, ½ to 1 quart Decanters (exact measure), Wines, Goblets, Glass Cans with

Handles, different sizes. Phials, assorted, Green bottles, pt. to gal. Useful glass ware Suitable for the assortment."[41] Fragments fitting all these descriptions (except, perhaps, for mirror plate) were found in the excavations, along with a number of other forms which figured in none of the advertisements.

Generalizations always demand qualifications, and even with them they tend to be dangerous. Nevertheless, it would seem from the fragments recovered that the most popular items produced in the excavated glasshouse were plain tumblers and drawn-stemmed wines with folded feet. Having said this, one must immediately add that the stems and bases of those pieces are readily identifiable, but the fragments of larger objects are less so. Furthermore, the popularity of an item is not automatically gauged by the number that were dropped or otherwise failed to make it to the warehouse. But the prevalence of tumblers and wineglasses, coupled with the placing of these items so high in Amelung's 1788 list of products, does suggest that they were manufactured in quantity.

Tumblers were found in a great variety of base sizes—sizes which might well run the Amelung gamut from half gill to quart. Although plain examples were by far the most common, some were rib-molded, diamond-molded, decorated with horizontally tooled ribbing, and with horizontal spirals of trailed threads. Two small pieces were rather crudely wheel-engraved, one with a wavy line below the rim and another with inverted swags filled with hatching. It is extremely unlikely that these engraved pieces were ornamented in the factory building. It is probable that they were broken in an engraving shop elsewhere and brought back for use as cullet.

The bases of tumblers may have been indistinguishable from those of Amelung's cans. A number of handle pieces was recovered which shows (as Amelung advertised) that they came in a variety of sizes. Of great interest was one colorless fragment with a splendidly rich blue handle attached to it. A colorless rim piece (thinner than most of the others) may have come from a beaker rather than a tavern can, and this was decorated with a blue trail at the edge.[42] Fragments of what must have been quart cans in both blue and amethyst were also found, though large handle pieces were confined to those of amethyst.[43]

It is important to note that two repairable,

plain, colorless tumblers were found amid the ground glass below the bottom of the burned barrel (#10) with the base of another of much larger capacity. Also of significance was a single base fragment from a tumbler with its sides ground and polished into straight vertical facets.

Three pieces of cut stems were among the wineglass fragments. All three were lead glass and were probably cullet rather than products of the factory. A shoulder fragment from a facet-cut perfume phial retrieved from an unstratified context is also lead glass. Another perfume flask had been found in a burned stratum of the 1962 test trench A–B. This flask, ground and polished at the corners to give the oval phial an octagonal section, was of non-lead glass.

It is known that Amelung did produce engraved glass, but we also know that he had difficulties with his "Looking glass" and may never have brought it to perfection. One wonders, therefore, just how far Amelung succeeded with his cut glass. The art of "cutting" and particularly the marriage of cutting and engraving to embellish a single piece was brought to breathtaking artistic heights in Silesia in the first half of the eighteenth century. It would be reasonable to suppose that German craftsmen would expect to include cutting among their normal decorative devices. However, the English (and perhaps the American) taste in cut glass favored the clean, light-reflecting qualities of facet cutting alone—without the addition of complicated engraving. But this facet cutting, generally in large diamonds, was best accomplished using a lead glass which not only adapts itself well to the grinding wheel, but also has the ice-like quality considered so desirable. The Amelung excavations yielded two styles of cutting: diamond and lozenge faceting on wineglass stems and on a perfume (?) phial, and straight paneling on a tumbler and on another perfume flask; all, except one perfume phial, were lead glass.

Did Amelung prepare special batches of lead glass for wineglasses which were to be cut? On the other hand, was Amelung's cutting confined to non-lead glass which would benefit from panel grinding, but which, when cut into diamond and lozenge patterns, would compare unfavorably with the imported English and Irish products?

No pieces ornamented with air or enamel twists have been found attributed to Amelung, but examples of both were found in the excavations, and both were unfinished or distorted. The air twist evidence rests largely on a curved colorless rod fragment through which run a pair of primary and two secondary spiral twists (Fig. 44, No. 4). Another twisted rod of slightly greenish glass contains a thin spiral of amber up the middle. This might be dismissed as fortuitous were it not for the presence of the air twist fragment and also an elaborate but somewhat burned non-lead object which contains a six-thread enamel twist (Fig. 39, No. 19). Together, these pieces suggest that twists of one sort or another were attempted at the Amelung glasshouse. This does not, of course, rule out the ever-present question of whether these unusual pieces may not be cullet brought in for remelting. One cannot forget that no fragments of white rods were found.

Nine-tenths of the wineglasses recovered possessed simple drawn stems without any deliberate tears and, as previously noted, the only example with such a tear proved to be a glass of lead. On the other hand, the heavy knop base of a dessert glass exhibited very carefully inserted and stationed blows, i.e., round tears.[44] The vast majority of the drawn-stemmed glasses possessed slightly rising folded feet. A much smaller number of plain feet of similar shape was found, and an even smaller number of rather thick feet was encountered, the latter probably part of goblets or water glasses. Two miniature glasses were also found, both with balustroid stems, and one with a small and most impracticable solid foot. It is possible that both were mere friggers (Fig. 39, No. 7 and Fig. 44, No. 1).

Bowl fragments from two and perhaps three extremely unusual goblets were found. Their bowls had been shaped in a mold; all three were of colorless glass and reasonable quality. One piece exhibited molded bands below the rim and another possessed radiating ribbing spreading from its junction with the missing stem.[45]

Collectors will be disappointed to learn that no goblets of the form usually associated with Amelung in the 1790's were among the discoveries nor, indeed, were any of the broadtopped inverted baluster stems. On the other hand we note that one badly burned inverted baluster with a heavy knop above it was found[46] which closely paralleled the style of that used in the stem of the Bremen goblet. If the excavated glasshouse had ceased to exist in 1790, we may wonder whether the Bremen goblet was made in that building, and that all the later specimens (e.g., the Schley, Mifflin, Repold, Mauerhoff, and Trisler goblets) were made in the building which, presumably, replaced it. An additional negative piece of evidence may be provided by the absence from the excavations of any examples of the rather curiously domed feet characteristic of so many of the large goblets. The Bremen goblet, it will be remembered, possesses a plain foot with only a very slight dome; one of the Trisler goblets is steeply conical. Domed feet (all folded) for wineglasses were recovered, and one of them was decorated with a trailed spiral thread.[47] But even these were quite unlike the style used for the Schley goblet.

A small number of lid fragments was found, and the more shallow examples could have come from glasses of the goblet form. The more bulbous and everted specimens were likely to have been made for large tumblers. No examples of the baluster knobs which occur on all the covered goblets and tumblers were among the excavated terminals. Ball and button knobs, which may have been finials, were found, but as none was actually attached to identifiable lids one cannot assume that they belonged to any specific type.

Next in this brief summary of the table glass we come to the colored pieces, with the sugar bowls the most interesting and recognizable. It must be admitted, nevertheless, that some of the foot fragments so identified may have come from small pitchers or footed cans. Such feet occurred in amethyst, blue, and green, while handles of sugar-bowl type (with rigaree or crimped ornament) were found in colorless glass, colorless with pale blue ornament, and in amethyst.

Amethyst glass was also used for large domed and folded-footed goblets, for large cans or cylindrical bowls, and also for small molded flasks and for tall case bottles or straight-walled decanters.[48] Blue was less common and, as mentioned earlier, in addition to its use for sugar bowls, small bottles, and cans, it was also used for ornamenting otherwise colorless pieces. Amber seems to have been used only for coarse wares such as flasks, case and snuff bottles, and for dishes or bowls. The deliberate use of green in tablewares occurred only as a foot for creamer, salt, or small sugar bowl.[49]

At the tail end of the table glass, mention must be made of various fragments of doubt-fully identified jelly glasses, shot or firing glasses, and cruet bottles, the last ornamented with molded wrythen expanded ornament. All these pieces were of colorless glass and good quality.

The use of expanded molded ornament was common on numerous flask fragments found in the glasshouse, but the majority of the pieces did not possess a full circumference and therefore the numbers of ribs could not be counted.[50] Such molds were used for decorating (both colorless and green) flasks. One colorless fragment of the diamond-daisy pattern was found, and two pieces (colorless and green) exhibited lozenge or diamond molding, the so-called "checkered-diamond."[51] Pieces of crack-off exhibiting rib molding were also recovered, one of them markedly twisted and doubtless having come from a wrythen flask. Undecorated flasks were probably more common than molded, though the smallness of some of the fragments, coupled with the fact that molding is often absent from the base pieces, could be misleading.[52]

Bottles were almost entirely of a pale to emerald green, round or oval in section, with weak shoulders extending upward into the characteristic chestnut bottle neck topped by a heavy trailed string-rim which doubled as a lip. Such bottles varied widely in size, but insufficient fragments of any one example were found to enable any measurements to be obtained. Nevertheless, if Amelung claimed to produce bottles ranging from pint to gallon, the fragments supported his claim.

A few body fragments of colorless bottles were found, but these probably came from decanters. Square-bodied, molded bottles and jars were apparently produced, as were the smaller octagonal snuff or blacking bottles in green or amber. One colorless, square bottle base was found, but it was of lead glass. Pharmaceutical bottles and phials were also represented by small fragments, but they were not plentiful. Some colorless ones were of lead glass. Wine bottles, too, were found, but these were all of the so-called "black" varieties and there is no evidence that they were manufactured at the excavated glasshouse. Not only was the glass different, but so too were the string-rims which included examples of both English and French styles. Just as a potter is identified by his handles, so a glassmaker can be known by his string-rims, and those on the wine bottles were quite unlike the styles on the excavated Amelung bottles.

There was no evidence of any really fanciful work being conducted in the glasshouse, such as chicken finials, tobacco pipes, rolling pins, hats, boots, and other glassmakers' oddities. But the excavation of one glasshouse does not, by any means, give us a fair picture of the entire enterprise. It is perfectly possible that all manner of products may have been made elsewhere at New Bremen without any evidence reaching the comparatively small area which has now been investigated. This, of course, brings us back to the oft repeated conclusion that with so much of the story still untold, it is extremely dangerous to attempt to draw final conclusions on the basis of what has been accomplished by the Corning-Smithsonian excavations of 1962–1963.

1. I.N.H. to P.P., February 1962.

2. The most important of these was an agreement drawn up and signed between Charles Smith and Corning on September 1, 1962, enabling the latter to enjoy sole archaeological rights on the Smith property for a period of five years and to become permanent custodian of all glass and other artifacts which might be found thereon.

3. It had not then been determined whether the millrace was contemporary with or later than the Amelung factory.

4. Even wider distribution of the waste was noted by Mrs. Exel Yingling who had found pieces of both cullet and product on the high ground north of the Amelung mansion.

5. Ivor Noël Hume, *Preliminary Report on Archaeological Excavations at the Site of John Frederick Amelung's New Bremen Glass Factory near Frederick, Maryland,* Corning Museum microfilmed ms. 1963.

6. D. Diderot and J. Le R. D'Alembert, *Encyclopédie ou dictionnaire raisonné des sciences, des arts et des métiers,* Paris, 1765, vol. 17, article "Verrerie," vol. 10 (plates) "Verrerie en Bois," Pl. 2., "Plan Géometral d'une Halle de petite Verrerie à pivette avec son Four au centre et les dépendances."

7. The original of this plat is owned by Mr. H. D. Shankle of Bukeystown, Maryland, through whose courtesy it is illustrated here.

8. Virginia Yerby McNeill, "There's Glass in Them Thar Hills," *The Sun,* Baltimore, October 16, 1949, magazine section, p. 15.

9. Harriet N. Milford, "Amelung and His New Bremen Glass Wares," *Maryland Historical Magazine,* 47, March 1, 1952, p. 7.

10. McNeill, p. 12.

11. Donald Hubbard, Lillie B. Jenkins and Elizabeth M. Krumrine, "Amelung Glass Compared with Some Modern Commercial Glasses," *The Scientific Monthly,* Dec. 1952, p. 329. The extract was softened by the following perfectly valid footnote:

> Although the archaeologist and the anthropologist, who do so much of their excavation of delicate specimens with tiny trowel, brush, and toothpick may be horrified at this bulldozer technique, nevertheless it has resulted in an attractive, instructive, and easily examined exhibit presented by Mrs. W. R. Milford to the Maryland Historical Society, of Baltimore, which displays all the types (colors) of glasses produced at the New Bremen works. No student of antique American glass can afford to overlook this mounted collection of Amelung cullet.

12. Robert H. Brill, *Thermal History of Siltstone Sample from Structure B at the Amelung Site,* Corning Museum ms. research report, June 1963, pp. 5–6. It should be noted that the identification of the excavated structures was changed in 1963 when their relationships were more fully understood.

13. From the stoking area in front of the tunnel came the only example of brick furnace construction found on the site. It was not *in situ,* but it is possible that it had been thrown into the hole when furnace #3 was dismantled. The bricks were unevenly coated with glass as well as being vitrified as a result of exposure to extreme heat; they varied widely in color and most of them had cracked and fused together again at distorted angles. No laid bricks found in any of the oven foundations exhibited these temperature-producing characteristics. It may be noted that Mr. James E. Maloney, owner of the Williamsburg pottery in Williamsburg, Virginia, has stated that bricks used in his saltglaze kilns and fired at temperatures around 2600°F will dissolve into shapeless masses after being heated between fifteen and twenty times.

14. Samples of the clay were carefully washed free of the ashes which had covered them and were then thrown into pots by Mr. Maloney and fired along with his white saltglazed stonewares at a temperature of 2300°F. Mr. Maloney stated that the clay was of splendid tough quality. It failed to dissolve in water, and although difficult to throw, it could produce a thinly potted ware of fine texture. But to produce vessels of any size it would be necessary to mix in considerable quantities of grog (i.e., old pots ground down). Such a binding agent is clearly visible in most of the refractory fragments from the New Bremen site. A tall cylindrical pot made by Mr. Maloney from the Amelung clay cracked while cooling, indicating that the temperature had been brought down too quickly for this particular clay. (The rest of the pottery in the kiln was cooled at the same rate without any mishap). The broken pieces showed that while the body was tight and grained and very hard, it was still slightly porous to the taste. The clay, therefore, would well withstand temperatures higher than that reached in the Williamsburg pottery kiln. It should be noted that no grog was added to the test sample.

15. This supposes that the orifices would have been on a level at which they could be reached for the working of frit. Were it not for the presence of the presumed frit troughs, it might be argued that the secondary ovens were higher and drew their heat from channels projecting from points close to the top of the furnace arch.

16. If what was found represented only the ash and raking channels below the fires, then in most cases the bars would have been located higher than the surviving tops of the foundations.

17. *A History of Technology,* ed. Charles Singer, E. J. Holmyard, A. R. Hall, and Trevor I. Williams, London, 1957, Vol. III, Fig. 149, pp. 222–223. This was drawn by a Swede, C. W. Carlberg, and shows a London bottle house in Gravel Lane, Southwark in 1777–1778. There the annealing ovens measured 7′6″ × 4′9″ and 7′6″ × 6′0″ and were each supposed to have a capacity of 800 bottles. It may be noted that this factory had a single pot-making room measuring 14′ × 10′6″ in one of its four corners.

18. *Gazette of the United States,* July 25, 1789. Source used, Gottesman, *The Arts and Crafts of New York 1777–1779,* p. 298.

19. "Design in Relation to the Problem" (no author) rpt. from *Commercial Art & Industry,* Aug. 1932, London, rpt. pp. 10–11.

20. See Note 17, Fig. 149.

21. For a thorough study of the local geology, see David M. Scotford, *A Structural Study of the Sugarloaf Mountain Area, Maryland, as a Key to the Piedmont Stratigraphy,* (Ph.D. thesis, John Hopkins University) Baltimore, 1950. The schist is here identified as Harpers phyllite, p. 32 ff. See also Byron K. Thomas, *Structural Geology and Stratigraphy of Sugarloaf Anticlinorium and Adjacent Piedmont Area, Maryland,* (Ph.D. thesis, Johns Hopkins University) Baltimore, 1952, no pagination. This work provides an excellent description of what the writer describes as "Bennett Creek Calcareous Phyllite." He notes that in stretches east of Park Mills, "The rock typically weathers reddish, becomes soft and crumbly, and gives the appearance of an unmetamorphosed siltstone sequence." It may be added that these characteristics might easily be confused with reddening caused by fire.

22. The presence of fragments of English pearlware in and above the ditch fill did not support such a contention. Although the ware was being produced in England earlier, it would be most surprising to find it in America before c. 1790.

23. Jaroslav R. Vávra, *5000 Years of Glass-Making: The History of Glass,* Prague, 1954, Fig. 17.

24. John Frederick Amelung, *Remarks on Manufactures, Principally on the New Established Glass-House near Frederick-Town in the State of Maryland,* printed for the author [in Frederick?], 1787, p. 12.

25. Translated for Mrs. Hunt by John G. Frank, American University, Washington, D.C., May 29, 1961.

26. *The Federal Intelligencer and Baltimore Daily Gazette,* March 23, 1795.

27. There are some *termini post quem* which are provided by documented developments in design and composition in the field of glassware, ceramics, etc. *Termini ante quem* are much more difficult to establish on strictly archaeological evidence.

28. James W. Foster, *Amelung Glass,* 1952, Maryland Historical Society Catalogue of its exhibition of Amelung glass in Baltimore, March 11–June 9, 1952, p. 16, No. 86, H. 10″, W. 8 ¹⁵⁄₁₆″. The pane loaned by Mr. Marshall Etchison.

29. The 88th Congress, first Session, H.R. 8953,

Congressional Record, vol. 109, No. 173, Washington, Oct. 29, 1963, pp. 19395–6.

30. A.S. 162A. This was almost certainly the bottom of a post hole dug after the building was destroyed and associated with another cutting into the north side of the ditch in Square 38 (See Fig. 15A). The blowing iron fragments were on end, suggesting that they had been used as wedges around the post. This might suggest that the post hole was dug soon after the building ceased to exist and possibly while glassmaking was still going on in the vicinity.

31. This identification was presented by Mr. Paul Perrot. Although no published parallels have been found, experiments have shown that the tool would have served the suggested purpose extremely well (see Fig. 46, No. 10).

32. Even today common table knives are to be found in the tool boxes of glassblowers. They are often used to sharpen angles between knops and mereses.

33. D. Diderot and J. le R. D'Alembert, *Encyclopédie ou dictionnaire raisonné des sciences, des arts et des métiers,* Paris, 1765, vol. 17, article "Verrerie en bois, l'Operation de briser les vieux pots . . . pour les mêler avec la Terre glaise . . ." Pl. 7, Fig. 4b.

34. A.S. 165B.

35. A test sample of this body was fired in a stoneware kiln at the Williamsburg Pottery. Placed close to the firebox and raised to a sustained temperature of 2600°F (12 hrs.), the fragment developed cracks around the major particles of grog, clearly showing that this mixture was not used for the making of crucibles.

36. It may be significant that the almost complete "bun" found on the floor of the suggested pot arch (#5) exhibited no vitrification, possibly supporting the belief that this oven was not used for glassmaking.

37. A.S. 131C.

38. The sleeve link was cleaned by Colonial Williamsburg and returned to Mrs. Yingling.

39. A.S. 15B, see Fig. 48, No. 1.

40. *Maryland Journal and Baltimore Advertiser,* Feb. 11, 1785.

41. *Maryland Journal and Baltimore Advertiser,* March 14, 1788.

42. The materials and wall thicknesses of both fragments tempt one to suggest that they are parts of the same handled can. See Fig. 38, Nos. 9 and 15.

43. Even these were so small as to leave open the possibility that they were waste rather than parts of handles.

44. A.S. 152.A.

45. A.S. 134C, 152D, 188, Fig. 44, No. 2.

46. A.S. 174A, Fig. 39, No. 13.

47. A.S. 27. Fig. 39, No. 14.

48. A.S. 142A.

49. A.S. 163A. Fig. 38, No. 4.

50. A colorless neck, another from a green flask, and a clear knop were all decorated in 18 rib molds (Fig. 40, Nos. 17, 19 and 20).

51. A.S. 153A and A.S. 134B. Fig. 40, No. 6 and 7.

52. Fragments of one flask with half-post (?) rib molding were found (Fig. 44, No. 5), but it is not certain that this flask was made at the excavated glasshouse.

THE ILLUSTRATED ARTIFACTS

The fragments of glass, ceramics, glasshouse furniture and miscellaneous small finds illustrated in Figures 37–48 are merely a representative selection from the many thousands of items recovered in the 1962 and 1963 excavations.

Because the glass has not been fully studied, identifications are not as full as one might wish. Measurements are only given when the visual scale in the photographs cannot be used. Most of these measurements relate to diameters projected from small or distorted fragments and they are quoted in increments of .25 cm, except in measuring thicknesses of less than a centimeter when millimeters are used. Each item is followed by its field number (e.g., A.S. 131) which identifies the area and stratum whence it came. That information can be obtained by checking the number and its archaeological data in Appendix II.

FIGURE 37

1) Neck of green bottle, the mouth slightly expanded and the rim thickened, with a well-marvered and down-tooled applied collar creating the string-rim. A.S. 52.

2) Mouth and string-rim of bottle similar to the above, but the trail less carefully marvered; pinched at three points to ensure that it adhered to the neck. A.S. 124.

3) Base of oval bottle, slightly deeper green than the foregoing examples, shallow conical kick. A.S. 94.

4) Neck from thin flask, glass a very pale green; mouth very irregular and not fire-polished but possibly complete without addition of string-rim. A.S. 105.

5) Neck and shoulder fragment from square molded bottle for blackening or snuff; the mouth thick and only slightly everted, possibly unfinished; the metal green to bluish. A.S. 105.

6) Neck and shoulder fragment from square molded bottle for blackening or snuff, amber glass; thin-walled. Base and body fragments of bottles of the same type were found in association with this neck. A.S. 105.

7) Neck fragment, probably from oval-bodied flask, the glass a rich green similar to that of No. 3. A.S. 71.

8) Bottle seal, poorly formed and the device illegible; green glass similar to that of No. 1. A.S. 71.

9) Base fragment of square bottle (probably case bottle), with molded cross in relief on the base and beneath the rough pontil mark; the glass as No. 1; width approximately 7.25 cm. A.S. 118.

10) Neck and everted lip and upper body of small pharmaceutical phial, the walls extremely thin and of the color of Amelung window glass. A.S. 18.

11) Crack-off, example of compounded gathers from the end of a blowing iron, the glass colorless and of good quality. A.S. 94.

12) Wall and rim fragment from shallow cylindrical bowl, the glass a rich olive-green and much bubbled; height approximately 7.5 cm. and diameter 17.5 cm. A.S. 102.

13) Folded rim from object of uncertain form, possibly the edge of a small bell jar, conical lid or, if inverted, the rim of a bowl, the glass a pale green. Diameter about 23 cm. A.S. 59.

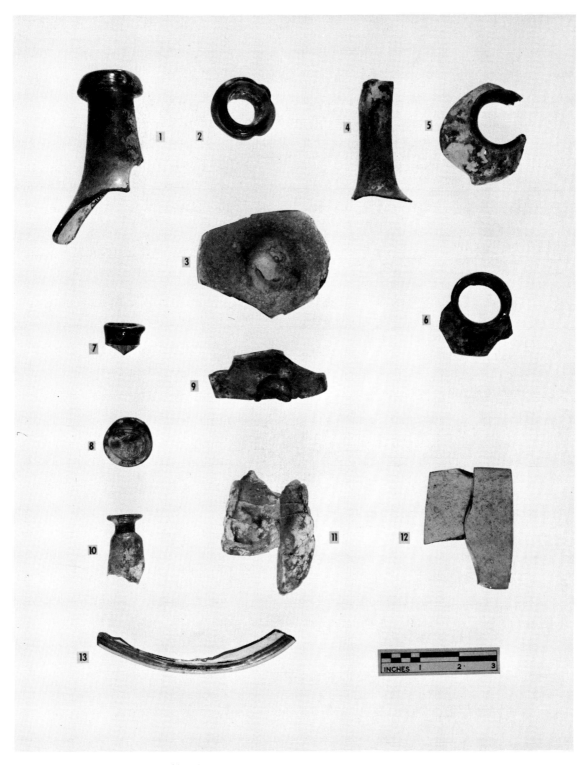

FIG. 37. Examples of bottle and glass waste recovered in the course of 1962 excavations.

FIGURE 38

1) Foot fragment from small vessel of uncertain form, pale poorly mixed amethyst glass, the foot applied as a pad to the base of the bowl; rough pontil scar on the slightly concave base, diameter of foot approximately 5.6 cm. This is considerably smaller than the foot of the "Mis C.G." sugar bowl at the Henry Francis du Pont Winterthur Museum (7.7 cm), though it is close to that of a small pitcher or creamer in the same collection (5.4 cm). A.S. 143A.

2) Handle and rim fragment, probably from a sugar bowl, a deep amethyst glass of good quantity; the body bulbous with a trailed cordon or seating for a lid 1.5 cm below the lip, the handle attached after the cordon and tooled up against it before being brought down to touch the wall and subsequently looped back on itself, the bottom of the loop finally being tooled down onto the folded terminal. Rim diameter approximately 12 cm. This bowl was probably of similar proportions to the Winterthur example discussed above. A.S. 200.

3) Sugar bowl lid fragment, a deep amethyst glass, rim and finial missing. A.S. 142A.

4) Foot fragment similar to No. 1, but fashioned from green bottle glass. Foot diameter 5 cm. A.S. 163A.

5) Bowl and foot fragment from a vessel of uncertain form, a deep amethyst glass somewhat marred by salts in the batch. Unlike the bases of Nos. 1 and 4, the foot is created by the addition of simple trail to the base of the bowl, diameter of foot approximately 6 cm. A.S. 153B.

6) Foot fragment, possibly from small bowl, poorly mixed blue glass, the footring roughly applied by the use of a trail around the flattened base of the bowl, a large and rough pontil scar in the center, foot diameter approximately 6 cm. A.S. 144A.

7) Rib-molded and expanded flask, oval section, pale amethyst glass of poor quality, shoulder and upper wall fragment only. Probable height about 7.5 cm. A.S. 94.

8) Folded and domed foot from large goblet, vase or candlestick, deep amethyst glass of fine quality, diameter approximately 10.5 cm. A.S. 163A.

9) Beaker or handled can rim fragment, thin colorless wall with a thicker blue trail tooled onto the top of it. Rim diameter approximately 10 cm. A.S. 125A. (See also No. 14).

10) Body fragment from expansion-molded ribbed flask, pale blue glass marred by salts in the batch. A.S. 200.

11) Sugar bowl (?) rim fragment with down-tooled trailed cordon 1.5 cm below the lip, pale blue glass. Rim diameter approximately 10 cm. A.S. 91.

12) Rim fragment from straight-sided bowl, large tumbler or can, pale blue glass, the 1.5 mm wall thickening to 4 mm below the lip. Rim diameter approximately 14 cm. A.S. 134A.

13) Foot, thick pale blue glass, possibly from a salt. Rim diameter 5.5 cm A.S. 64.

14) Can, thin colorless glass with the upper attachment from a blue handle, the latter much bubbled and with a tool mark pressing it to the colorless wall before the handle was drawn outward. This fragment could well have been part of the same can as No. 9. A.S. 94.

15) Pincered fragment drawn from the end of a blue handle of splendid quality and color. A.S. 125A.

16) Lower wall and base fragment, probably from a large oval-sectioned flask of chestnut form, a rich amber glass of good quality. A.S. 131.

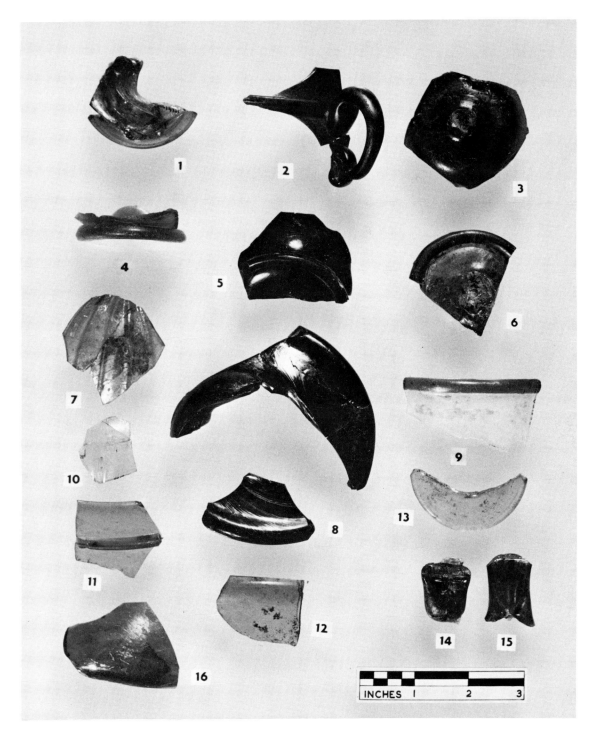

Fig. 38. Examples of amethyst, green, blue, and amber vessels; among them sugar bowl, goblet, flask, and can fragments.

FIGURE 39

1) Wineglass, tall drawn stem and trumpet bowl, large tear at the top of the stem and a corresponding raised nipple in the base of the bowl, the foot thin, markedly conical and poorly attached to the base of the stem, non-lead glass much crizzled and reduced to a sugar-like purple consistency at the fractures. Possibly French. A.S. 153B.

2) Wineglass, drawn stem fragment tapering too steeply to have been completed, a large shallow nipple at the base of the bowl, an unusual feature among supposedly Amelung glasses from the site; clear glass slightly purple in transmitted light. A.S. 133.

3) Wineglass, short drawn stem and plain slightly conical foot, clear lead glass of good quality. Foot diameter approximately 6 cm. A.S. 134. Analysis No. 569.

4) Wineglass, drawn stem and gently conical folded foot, colorless glass much bubbled and slightly gray tinted in transmitted light. Foot diameter approximately 7 cm. A.S. 153B.

5) Wineglass, fragment of drawn stem marred in manufacture, colorless glass with few bubbles. A.S. 133.

6) Two wineglasses fused, drawn stems, colorless glass, probably originally of good quality. A.S. 125B.

7) Miniature wineglass (?) fragment, balustroid stem and remains of slightly domed foot, colorless glass, crizzled, slightly purple in transmitted light. A.S. 135.

8) Fragment of multiple-knopped stem with part of large tear extending down through the two upper knops, colorless glass somewhat bubbled. A.S. 200.

9) Domed and folded foot which apparently broke from its stem in the course of manufacture, colorless glass slightly gray in transmitted light, somewhat bubbled. Rim diameter approximately 6.5 cm. A.S. 182.

10) Ogee-bowled glass with short stem and remains of domed foot, short poorly formed stem, colorless glass somewhat gray in transmitted light. found with the tumblers shown in Fig. 42 amid ground clear glass in the burned barrel (#10). Bowl diameter 5.5 cm. A.S. 134D.

11) Foot, plain and flat, probably from drawn-stemmed wineglass, rough pontil scar on the base, also considerable evidence of wear suggesting that this was not a manufacturing reject, colorless though slightly green-tinted glass. Diameter approximately 6.5 cm. A.S. 142.

12) Foot, probably from goblet; a solid, stepped cone; colorless lead glass. Diameter approximately 7.0 cm. A.S. 185. CMG 4283.*

13) Baluster stem with hollow knop above, colorless glass, badly damaged by fire, possibly from goblet with stem of comparable form to that of the Bremen Goblet. A.S. 174A.

14) Foot from small champagne or sweetmeat glass, steeply domed but the edge flat and folded with trailed thread ornament above, colorless glass. Diameter approximately 6 cm. A.S. 27.

15) Firing glass (?) straight drawn stem and massive plain foot, large and rough pontil scar on the base, colorless glass with slight gray cast, very few bubbles. Foot diameter approximately 6.5 cm. A.S. 153B. CMG 570.

16) Stem fragment, probably from English wineglass, colorless lead glass cut into pointed-ended lozenge facets. (See E. Barrington Haynes, *Glass Through the Ages*, Revised Edition, London, 1959, Fig. 91f.) circa 1765–1780. A.S. 152A.

17) Wineglass drawn stem with elongated tear well placed, colorless lead glass cut into six flat panels. circa 1790. A.S. 155A.

18) Perfume flask, oval in section and cut to create octagonal form, colorless non-lead glass. A.S. 116.

19) Ovoid, flattened rod containing six-thread opaque white spiral twist, colorless non-lead glass with slightly gray cast. A.S. 131D.

20) Curved, spiral-ribbed rod, colorless non-lead (?) glass with slightly green cast in reflected light. A.S. 133.

21) Stopper, oval pad terminal rather crudely fashioned, the plug unground, colorless glass, gray in reflected light. A.S. 153A.

22) Stopper (?) with large hollow knop and solid button terminal above and with hollow, open-ended shaft below; colorless glass. This piece had not been annealed, and when blown into by the excavator to extract loose dirt from within, the hollow knop burst. A.S. 125C. CMG 571.

23) Stopper, similar to No. 21 but the pad terminal more round. Note the weak shoulders on the plug which seem to be characteristic of this class of stopper. A.S. 163A. CMG 4281.

24) Stopper, pad terminal only, slightly more slender than No. 21, the glass having a slightly green cast in reflected light. A.S. 24.

25) Stopper terminal flat-sided and more or less square, probably from perfume bottle, glass as No. 24. A.S. 163.

26) Rigaree ornament perhaps from the base of an ornamental finial, colorless lead (?) glass. A.S. 139.

27) Handle, probably from a sugar bowl, part of the collar below the rim remains attached to the top of the handle, colorless glass with many small bubbles. A.S. 146.

28) Handle fragment, a plain strap with another attached to the back of it and pinched up into a series of small ornamental pads, possibly from a small sugar bowl; colorless glass. A.S. 135. CMG 4282.

29) Handle, miniature, from vessel of uncertain form, a colorless rod backed with a pale blue strip pinched out as No. 28. A.S. 139.

30) Handle, a drawn rod backed with an ornamental strip roughly crimped, both colorless glass with few bubbles, probably from a sugar bowl. A.S. 18.

31) Handle fragment, a plain strap backed with another drawn out into short ornamental pad, both colorless glass slightly gray in transmitted light, perhaps from a larger sugar bowl than the foregoing or possibly from a lid. A.S. 125B.

*"CMG" *numbers refer to samples analyzed by The Corning Museum of Glass. They are listed in the Sample Descriptions of Dr. Bill's section of this* Journal. *The analyses are reported in the same section.*

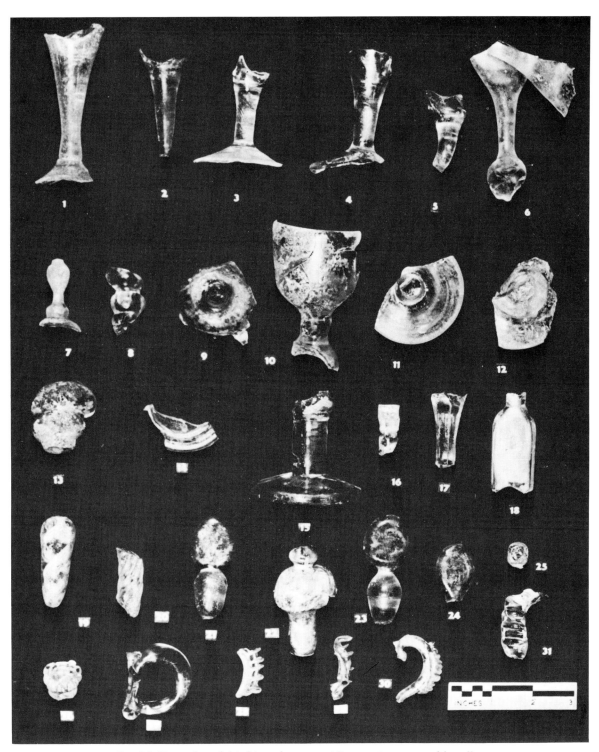

Fɪɢ. 39. Examples of drinking glasses, cut items, stoppers and handles.

FIGURE 40

1) Lid fragment, colorless glass of good quality, slightly bulbous above the trailed collar, rim diameter approximately 11.25 cm. A.S. 153B.

2) Lid fragment, of large size, the wall slightly concave above the rim and the collar overhanging, the colorless glass heavier than that of No. 1, and somewhat gray in reflected light. A.S. 175.

3) Bowl (?) fragment, badly flattened and distorted, colorless glass decorated with trailed threads. A.S. 200.

4) Tumbler base, cut vertical panels with an average width of 1.5 cm at the bottom, the base polished flat and the pontil mark ground away, colorless non-lead glass of above average quality. Base diameter approximately 6.5 cm. A.S. 171.

5) Tumbler base, ornamented with molded vertical ribbing (approximately 32 ribs), the pontil mark partially ground but not polished, the colorless glass slightly straw colored in reflected light. Base diameter approximately 5 cm. A.S. 153A.

6) "Diamond-daisy" pattern (twelve petals around an oval center) molded on wall fragment from vessel of uncertain form, perhaps a flask, colorless glass, its surface heavily crazed. A.S. 153A.

7) Diamond molding on wall fragment probably from tumbler (See No. 8), colorless glass somewhat bubbled. A.S. 134B.

8) Tumbler base fragment with diamond molding above pointed flutes at the base, similar to that of No. 7, and colorless glass of the same quality. Base diameter approximately 5 cm. A.S. 171.

9) Wheel-engraved rim fragment, probably from large tumbler, running scroll pattern over a curving line enclosing a zone of cross-hatching. See George S. and Helen McKearin, *American Glass*, 14th edition, New York, 1962, Pl. 43, Nos. 2 and 3. A.S. 125A.

10) Tumbler, lower body fragment decorated with trailed threads, the glass colorless but gray in reflected light. A.S. 32.

11) Waste fragment, colorless glass of fine quality, marked with a square-ended pair of pincers used to impart the hatched grip to one face of stopper terminals. (See No. 12) A.S. 130D.

12) Stopper terminal of pad form, pincered hatching on one face similar to that of No. 11. A.S. 41.

13) Tumbler base, mold-decorated with vertical ribbing (17 ribs) which extends beneath the large and rough pontil scar; colorless glass with many small bubbles; base diameter, 5 cm. A.S. 125C.

14) Tumbler base, larger but with similar ornament to No. 13, colorless glass, slightly purple, diameter 6 cm. A.S. 127. CMG 4284.

15) Neck (?) fragment with heavy ribbed molding (approximately 16 ribs), perhaps from a carafe, no grinding on the inside of the mouth, the glass much crazed and slightly straw colored. Diameter approximately 4 cm. A.S. 18.

16) Loop finial (?) fashioned from a solid twisted rod of clear glass, perhaps from a lid. A.S. 107.

17) Neck with fire-polished rim, possibly from flask, colorless glass shaped in an 18-rib mold. Diameter 2 cm. A.S. 152A.

18) Waste material, pale green bottle glass bearing the marks of a pair of pointed-nosed tweezers. A.S. 142A.

19) Knop, solid colorless glass much bubbled, decorated in an 18-rib mold. A.S. 125C.

20) Neck fragment from oval-sectioned flask, blue-green glass, decorated in an 18-rib mold. A.S. 144A.

21) Handle, heavy tapering strap, probably from a mug or can, colorless glass slightly green tinted, few bubbles. A.S. 134A.

22) Terminal from handle of form similar to No. 21, pale green glass, the base of the handle pressed against the wall of the can, then drawn out and pressed back on itself. A.S. 139.

23) Pitcher handle (?) a wide strap decorated with pronounced reeding, colorless glass of good quality appearing slightly purple in reflected light; this piece never applied to a vessel. A.E. 135. CMG 572.

24) Spiral-ribbed rod, perhaps preparatory to making an ornamental handle, green bottle glass. A.S. 144A.

25) Handle and rim fragment, possibly from small pitcher, the handle oval-sectioned and ornamented with a single vertical groove, colorless glass of good quality. A.S. 139.

26) Crack-off impressed with molded ribbing, colorless, slightly straw-colored non-lead glass. A.S. 134D.

27) Crack-off impressed with molded ribbing, blue-green glass similar to that of No. 20 and containing unintentional triangular-shaped bubbles. A.S. 179. CMG 573.

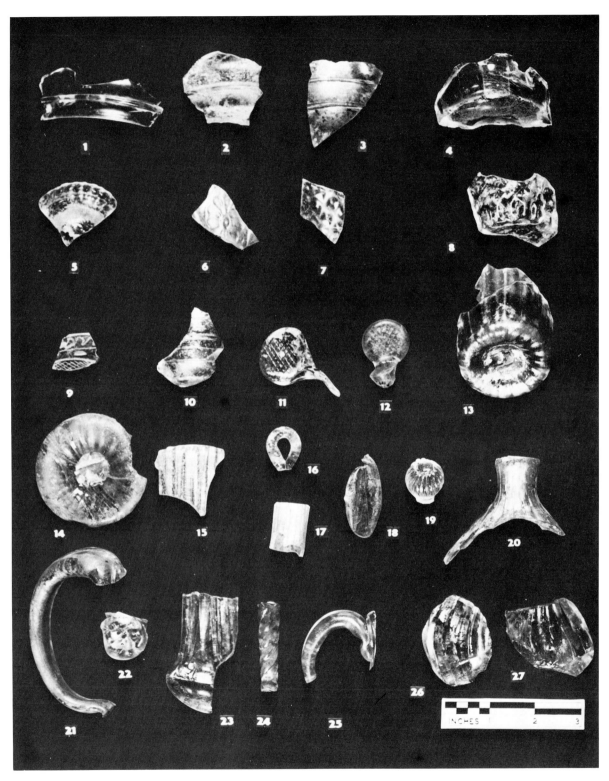

FIG. 40. Examples of lids and various ornamental techniques, including engraving, trailing, expansion, and pattern molding.

FIGURE 41

1) Bottle seal, the motif possibly a script capital "A" with a mullet at upper left and lower right, or "JP." Both the engraving of the die and the quality of the imprint are poor, and in these respects they have much in common with the seal found in 1962 (See Fig. 37, No. 8) the glass an emerald green; probably from the shoulder of a bottle similar to that of No. 8. A.S. 157.

2) Foot fragment, possibly from vase or bowl, a folded form created by flattening the base of the bubble, spreading it, and then pushing it up into itself; pale green glass. A.S. 146A.

3) Cylinder fragment, thinning and everted at the lower edge possibly prior to spreading outwards and up to create an open-centered jelly mold or poultry feeder, the glass a pale blue-green, diameter about 16 cm. A.S. 156A.

4) Flask, oval-sectioned, slightly rising base, no molded ornament, the glass colorless with a slight purple cast and with many small bubbles. Height 15.5 cm, maximum width approximately 11 cm. A.S. 163A.

5) Case bottle, base, shoulder and mouth fragments, olive-amber glass, original height uncertain. There is no proof that this bottle was manufactured at the excavated glasshouse. A.S. 128A.

6) Bottle or flask neck, the mouth thickened with a heavy trail, the glass a pale blue-green and retaining a brilliance rare among bottle fragments from the site. A.S. 144A.

7) Bottle, round-sectioned base and lower wall fragments, gently domed and with a rough pontil scar, typical Amelung bottle, green glass of good quality. A.S. 171.

8) Bottle neck of large size, possibly from vessel of gallon capacity, the lip thickened with a heavy marvered trail and tooled slightly outwards, the glass as No. 7 though with more bubbles. A.S. 197B.

9) Bottle base and lower wall fragment, slightly oval, the base gently conical and with a rough pontil scar, the glass a rich olive-green with more brilliance and more bubbles than No. 7. A.S. 128A.

10) Bowl, everted and folded rim fragment, pale green glass, approximate diameter, 16.5 cm. A.S. 128A.

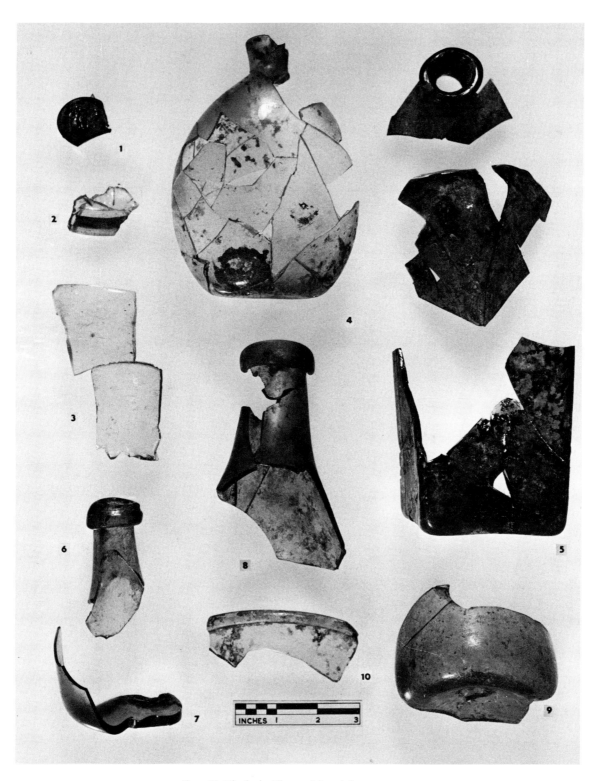

FIG. 41. Flask, bottle, and bowl fragments.

FIGURE 42

Tumblers found together in a deposit of ground glass at the bottom of a burned barrel seated in the floor against the north wall of the factory. The pieces are here seen prior to the removal of surface incrustation; the colorless glass appears gray in reflected and slightly green in transmitted light. Both are of reasonable quality, and bubbling is largely confined to the thick bases, the bottoms of which still retain their pontil scars. Left: Height (H): 10.5 cm, Diameter (D) (rim): 8.25 cm, D (base): 6.5 cm. Right H: 9.5 cm, D (rim): 7.5 cm, D (base): 6.25 cm. A.S. 134D.

Fig. 42. Tumblers found in the burned barrel (#10) against the north wall of the glasshouse.

FIGURE 43

All the items in this figure had collapsed from excessive heat and were found together in the filling of the west stoking area of the east melting furnace, Unit 3.

1) Flask, oval-sectioned, possibly ornamented with molded vertical ribbing, colorless glass with a slightly purple cast. A.S. 131E.

2) Base from oval-sectioned flask, the glass colorless but pale green in reflected light. A.S. 131E.

3) Flask neck similar to No. 1, though somewhat tapered above the shoulder with clearly visible rib-molding surviving on one side. A.S. 131E.

4) Flask neck of similar form to No. 1, rib molding clearly visible, the colorless glass pale green in reflected light. A.S. 131E.

5) Flask neck of similar form to No. 3, slight traces of rib molding surviving, colorless glass with slightly purple cast in reflected light. A.S. 131E.

6) Wineglass bowl trumpet form, probably with stem as No. 7, colorless glass with slightly green cast. A.S. 131E.

7) Wineglass foot, drawn stem and base of bowl, the foot folded, colorless glass with slightly purple cast. A.S. 131E.

8) Tumbler, colorless glass with pale green cast, base diameter approximately 6.5 cm. A.S. 131 E.

9) Tumbler, colorless glass with pale green cast, base diameter approximately 7 cm. A.S. 131E.

10) Jelly glass foot, stem and lower bowl, the foot folded and domed with a rough pontil scar beneath; the stem a solid cushion knop; colorless glass with a pale green cast; foot diameter approximately 6.5 cm. A.S. 131E.

11) Bottle neck of similar form but slightly smaller than the example shown in Figure 41, No. 8; green bottle glass of uncertain hue. A.E. 131E.

FIG. 43. Fragments of badly burned flasks, wineglasses, tumblers, and a bottle, found together in the filling of the west stoking area of the east melting furnace, Unit 3.

FIGURE 44

1) Miniature wineglass (?), perhaps a toy, plain slightly rising foot with full-size pontil scar, the stem a rudimentary inverted baluster above a large knop, the bowl of uncertain form with a large nipple filling the base; a three-piece glass; colorless non-lead glass, crizzled, somewhat gray in reflected light. Foot diameter approximately 4 cm. A.S. 188.

2) Goblet (?) bowl fragment, pattern-molded with radiating ribbing extending from the junction with the stem and stopping at a ridge running around the base of the wall, colorless non-lead glass, crizzled, slightly gray, with many small bubbles. A.S. 188.

3) Wide-mouthed neck from small pill bottle, of a type often used in medicine chests, brilliant colorless lead glass. Rim diameter 4.0 cm. A.S. 171B.

4) Handle (?) fragment, round-sectioned with four-spiral air twists (two main tubes and two secondary), perhaps from a pitcher or possibly the bent stem from a wineglass, colorless non-lead glass, the surface uncoated. A.S. 185.

5) Flask, oval section chestnut form, decorated with half-post (?) expansion-molded, ribbing slightly swirled, the glass a brilliant emerald green much bubbled. This is the only example of molded half-post technique from the site and caution must be exercised in claiming it as a product of the excavated glasshouse. A.S. 179.

6) Clay "bun" from the brick floor of the suggested pot arch (Unit 5), flat on the underside and bearing the marks of grained wood on which it was shaped, maximum height 3.5 cm, and with a hole pressed into the top. This hole does not go all the way through, and it would appear to have been made with a woman's finger as the mark of what appears to be a narrow finger nail can be seen at one side. The clay is well mixed with grog and has been fired at low temperature, perhaps no more than 500–600°F. There is none of the vitrification which is present on most of the fragments of these still unidentified objects. A.S. 143A.

7) Rim fragment of clay vessel which has been shaped in a wooden staved mold. The marks of the wood stop 6 cm below the rim, but it is possible that a horizontal matrix rim extended for a distance of another 1.25 cm above it. A small round hole passes almost through the pot wall towards the interior immediately above the horizontal band. The rim of the vessel is slightly incurved above the top of the matrix, and shows evidence of hand smoothing on the inside. The body is only lightly fired and heavily tempered with grog derived from ground crucibles, brick, and small particles of glass. Interior rim diameter approximately 25.5 cm; wall thickness at lowest point 1 cm. (For the rim form see *Diderot*, "Verrerie en bois . . . Verrerie en Plat" (Pl. 5, Fig. 4, and for the shaping of pots in frames, "Glaces, Attelier des Mouleurs" Pl. 5). A.S. 163A.

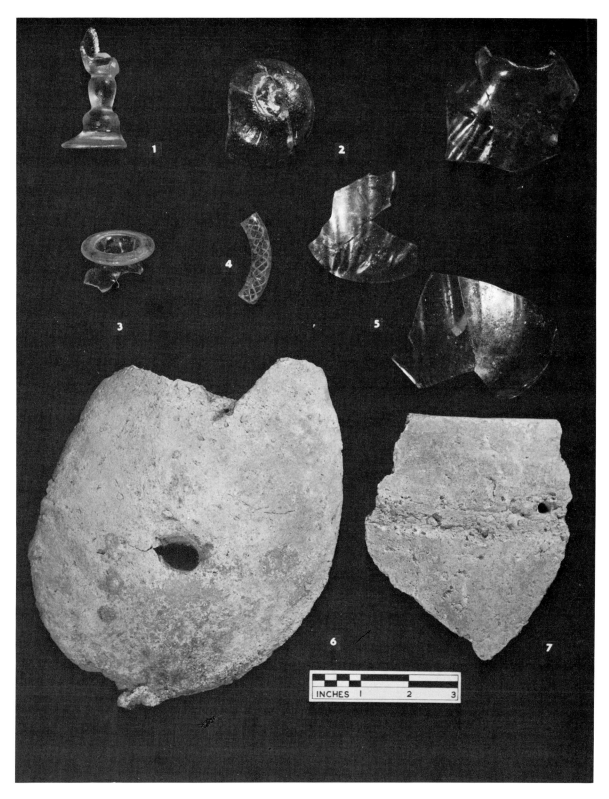

FIG. 44. A miniature drinking glass, molded goblet, bowl, half-post decorated green flask, and other fragments; also the clay "bun" from Unit 5, and part of a fireclay pot found in the supposed potting room, Unit 6B.

FIGURE 45

1) Rim fragment of crucible, not exhibiting excessive use; thickness 3.25–3.75 cm, approximate diameter of vessel 2'9" to 3'0". An important fragment found against the west face of the east wall of the main complex. A.S. 60.

2) Body fragment of crucible with a thin skin of clear glass adhering to the interior and with multicolored streaks running down the exterior: thickness 2.25 cm. A.S. 18.

3) Rim fragment of crucible coated with virtually clear glass both inside and out, with occasional streaks and spots of amber, this apparently caused by elements leaching from the pot. It should be noted that the pot has become porous and cellular at one corner, an effect that may have caused the vessel's destruction; thickness 1.75 cm. A.S. 18.

4) Possible body fragment of crucible, never used in the furnace, bearing impressions of a coarsely woven textile that had been used in shaping it; thickness 3.25 cm A.S. 44A.

5) Fragment of furnace port ring, shaped by hand on a board and the clay containing a high proportion of ground pot (?) temper. The flat back of the fragment is not highly fired and retains the marks of the grain of the board on which it was shaped, but the face of the orifice is burned to stoneware. It seems possible that this ring was never used in the working furnace, but achieved its appearance while being fired in the pot arch. If the opening exhibited by this fragment were circular, it would measure only about 15 cm in diameter, much too small for the average port, although it might be used as a special small port or "glory hole" for the reheating of such things as bottle necks before applying the string-rims. However, it is more probable that the clay objects merely formed the arches of furnace ports and were set into the tops of openings that were otherwise straight-sided A.S. 18.

6) As No. 5, but the lower edge a shaped end and not an unintentional fracture, thus supporting the supposition put forward above. A.S. 18.

7) Bun-shaped object of clay with hole driven through the middle before firing; the clay tempered with ground pot (?) and laid upon a wide-grained board during shaping; thickness at center 5 cm, approximate diameter 18.5 cm (if circular). Perhaps a furnace port plug. A.S. 33.

8) Bun-like object of clay, similar to No. 7, but not circular and unevenly glazed on the curved surface and into the central (?) hole; great thickness 5 cm. (See also Fig. 44, No. 6). A.S. 18.

9) Fragment of bun-like object of clay, roughly hand-shaped as are the others, the upper surface pierced, presumably to prevent cracking in firing. It should be noted that this feature is not present on the other fragments. The uneven placing of the holes suggests that they were not inserted with a carefully-made tool. They have the appearance of being made with nails, and as they are not all of the same size, it is possible that a piece of wood with a number of nails driven through it was used to create them. A.S. 15B.

10) Fragment of bun-like object of clay with large central hole, but other features similar to the objects discussed above. This fragment is coated with glass on the upper curved surface and in the central hole; glass also presented to a thickness of 3 mm on parts of the back. The glass would appear to be that used in the making of window glass. Greatest thickness 5.5 cm. A.S. 15B.

11) Fragment of shaped clay of uncertain purpose, the back surface illustrated, showing an apparently folded rim. The clay is heavily tempered with ground pot (?) and has been pierced twice with the other side, presumably to prevent cracking. Greatest thickness at rim 3 cm. A.S. 18. Other fragments of this same composition appeared to have been pressed against wood and straw and have been paddled or brushed on their exposed surface.

FIG. 45. Fragments of crucibles and clay oven furniture found during the 1962 excavations.

FIGURE 46

1) Tie, iron, slightly wider at the ends than in the midsection, the latter 1 cm in thickness and tapering to 3 mm at one end and 5 mm at the other. Four countersunk nail holes in each section, one oval and strangely off-center. Possibly for reinforcing the junction of two structural timbers. A.S. 199.

2) Hammer-chisel, iron, with traces of the wooden handle in the socket, probably used to break up old pots for grog and to chip out re-usable cullet. Thickness: 3.1 cm; weight: 2 lbs. 12 oz. A.S. 200.

3) Stone ball, hard purple sandstone, slightly flattened on two sides, diameter: 5.5 cm; weight: 8 oz. This may have been used as a tumbler in a rotating barrel for grinding quartz or cullet. A.S. 128A.

4) Counterweight (?) cast-iron, spade-shaped, a narrow projection broken from the top, thickness: 1.75 cm; weight: 13 lbs. 15 oz. It is believed that this object originally possessed a loop at the top for suspension, and that it may have been a counterweight to help raise a heavy furnace port or to open an inaccessible louver in the roof. A.S. 147.

5) Weight, iron, with four holes impressed into the slightly concave upper surface, thickness: 2 cm; weight: 1 lb. 3 oz. or probably 1 lb. Troy with slight loss due to decay. A.S. 145.

6) Latch, iron, roughly square-sectioned, possibly to hold open a casement window or shutter. A.S. 142A.

7) Scraper (?), iron, the entire tool shaped from a single strip, the handle rolled into a half circle to provide the grip. The blade is not sufficiently strong at the curve for the tool to be used in woodworking, and it is therefore likely that it was employed in the pot rooms for shaping crucibles or oven furniture. A.S. 158C.

8) Bar, iron, probably from the grill of a furnace firing channel, square sectioned, length: 1'9". A.S. 126.

9) Blade and tang from double-edged hunting knife or dagger, iron, the blade tip broken and the tang split at the terminal probably to retain a washer or pommel at the top of the hilt A.S. 146C.

10) Rake (?), cast-iron with diamond-sectioned teeth 2.2 cm in length (some now missing) arranged in diagonal patterns; the fragment represents less than half the width of the original object. Its great weight (4 lbs. 8 oz.) was probably to hold the teeth down when pushed and pulled horizontally on a long handle. It is believed that this tool served to mix the materials in the fritting ovens. A.S. 201A.

11) Wedge or cold chisel, iron, weight 12.5 oz. A.S. 153C.

12) Shovel, iron, round wrought socket and fragment of blade only, handle diameter approximately 4.5 cm and held in place by a single nail, original width of shovel about 10". A.S. 128.

13) Hoe, iron, with oval wrought socket and shallow cast spine, no maker's mark, the blade oval but possibly originally larger and now badly worn. The edge suggests heavy use in unyielding material. This condition could easily be achieved through agricultural work in the stony soil in the vicinity of the factory, and it need not be supposed that the tool was used in glassmaking, though it could have been used for raking frit from the ovens into the adjacent troughs. A.S. 152C.

FIG. 46. Examples of glasshouse tools and fittings.

FIGURE 47

1) Blowing iron fragment, apparently with remains of nail stuck in the tapering, fractured end. A.S. 149.

2) Blowing iron fragment illustrating the thickening and expansion of the gather end; thickness at the orifice: 6 mm, hole diameter: 8 mm. A.S. 144A.

3) Blowing iron fragment flattened into a spatula-like terminal at the upper end and with no evidence of hole, though it is present at the lower end. The iron has been grooved below the spread area, seemingly prior to being freed from this terminal. The fragment appears to be part of an iron in the course of manufacture. A.S. 204.

4) Saucer, English creamware, ornamental beaded circle around the center, of good quality, circa 1770–1785. Found on the floor beside the burned barrel (#10). A.S. 134B.

5) Shoe buckle, brass, originally covered with ornamental pewter, a most unusual combination. Second half of eighteenth century. A.S. 152B.

6) Shoe buckle fragment, brass, with classical revival type ornament. Late eighteenth century. A.S. 209.

7) Shoe buckle fragment, pewter, with beaded edges and two small molded flowers at each side, one end deliberately broken by twisting. Second half of eighteenth century. A.S. 154A.

8) Padlock, iron back-plate and wards, with brass guide below the key pintle. Late eighteenth or nineteenth-century. A.S. 127.

9) Teaspoon bowl, brass, probably originally tin-plated. Late eighteenth or early nineteenth century. A.S. 142.

10) Tobacco pipe bowl, small size, possibly American manufacture, spur broken, stem hole diameter: 5/64". Late eighteenth or early nineteenth century. A.S. 133.

11) Blade of straight, folding knife, iron. A.S. 162.

12) Clasp knife, pistol-grip type handle originally with short bone plates over iron. Eighteenth century. A.S. 146C.

13) Clasp knife, closed, iron with pistol-grip type handle originally bone plated. Eighteenth century. A.S. 134A.

14) Clasp or pen knife, medium size, the blade missing, iron pistol-grip (?) handle originally bone or wood plated. Probably eighteenth century. A.S. 144A.

15) Table knife blade, iron, incomplete, solid shoulders, and originally with bone-plated handle. Second half of eighteenth century. A.S. 183B.

16) Table knife, iron, pistol-grip handle with bone plates decorated with stained scroll ornament, the blade end originally bulbous, the shoulders small and cordoned. Late eighteenth century. A.S. 125D.

17) Table knife, iron, in an advanced stage of decay, the blade originally bulbous at the end, solid shoulders similar to No. 15, the handle originally bone plated. A.S. 153B.

18) Rim fragment of small iron pot, small cordon below the slightly everted lip, rim diameter approximately 12.75 cm. Eighteenth or nineteenth century. A.S. 143.

19) File, iron, wood-working, triangular with very short tang with stamped maker's mark "I" at the shoulder. The type is well paralleled by examples found in excavations at the Anthony Hay Cabinet Shop in Williamsburg, Vriginia, in contexts of circa 1770–1780. A.S. 153A.

20) Pintle (?), iron, or perhaps tang for attaching a handle to a wooden paddle, two countersunk nail or screw holes pass through the flat blade-like end; the shank or pivot round-sectioned. A.S. 205.

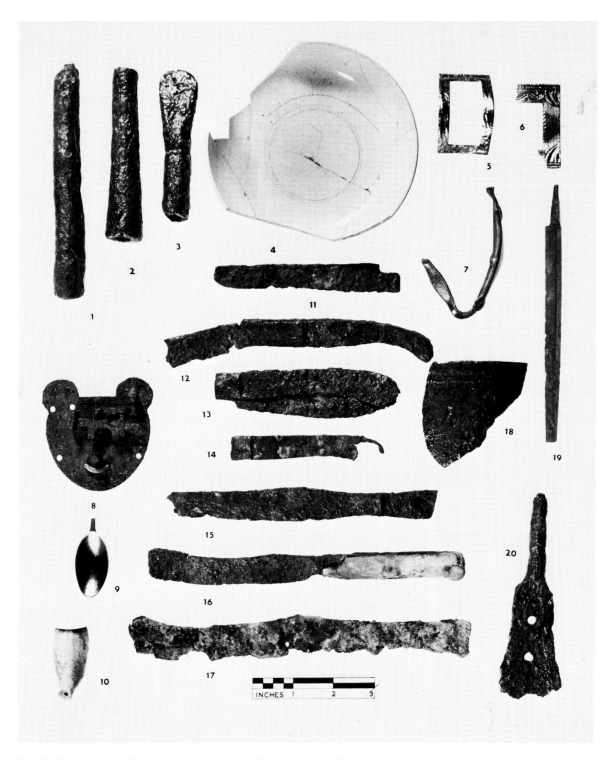

FIG. 47. Fragments of blowing irons and miscellaneous small finds including a creamware saucer, shoe buckles, clasp knives, and table knives.

FIGURE 48

1) Base fragment of porcelain cup, basket-molded on the interior, and decorated with poorly executed floral devices in underglaze blue both inside and out; hard paste body, V-shaped foot ring, script capital F on the underside of the base; Fürstenberg, after 1770. Cf. George Savage, *Porcelain through the Ages*, Penguin, Hammondsworth, England, 1954, p. 161, and Reginald G. Haggar, *The Concise Encyclopedia of Continental Pottery and Porcelain*, New York, 1960, p. 202. A.S. 15B.

2) Body sherd from bowl, English porcelain, decorated in underglaze blue with transfer-print of rural scene. The glaze is finely crazed and according to Savage (*op. cit.*, p. 255), this precludes it from being a Worcester piece. It may therefore be suggested that it emanated from Liverpool, in the period 1765–1785. A.S. 40.

3) Rim sherd from mug or pitcher, English porcelain, brownish orange in transmitted light, decorated on inside and out with similar floral motifs; probably Bow, circa 1760–1776. A.S. 12.

4) Rim sherd of plate of cream-colored earthenware, in the Royal pattern, English, 1770–1790. A.S. 18.

5) Rim sherd of saucer, burned, but apparently cream-colored earthenware, English, 1770–1790. A.S. 18.

6) Rim sherd of saucer, pale cream-colored earthenware. English, 1785–1800. This piece was found on the floor of the east firing channel of oven Unit 1B. A.S. 61.

7) Rim sherd of cooking pot or storage jar, coarse lead-glazed red earthenware, the rim rolled and trimmed beneath, the body close grained; probably of local manufacture. Date uncertain. A.S. 96.

8) Base fragment of vessel as above, similar body, lead-glazed on the inside. Fragments of this ware were found in widely scattered parts of the site. A.S. 120.

9) Rim sherd of lead-glazed red earthenware bowl decorated on the inside with white slipped concentric rings, the rim folded and shaped with the finger to create a collar. This treatment is found on Flemish and Wanfried slipware as early as the sixteenth century and suggests that the bowl was made by Pennsylvania Germans. Probably second half of eighteenth century. A.S. 15C.

10) Rim sherd of lead-glazed red earthenware plate with slipped decoration of white and manganese concentric rings, the rim folded. Pennsylvania German, second half of eighteenth century. This sherd found by Mrs. Milford in 1948 while bulldozing immediately west of Trench A–B. A.S. 100.

11) Rim sherd of lead-glazed red earthenware bowl, slipped decoration of white and manganese concentric rings and swags of the latter, the rim hammer-shaped in the Wanfried manner. Pennsylvania German, second half of eighteenth century. A.S. 18.

12) Body and handle sherd of bottle or jug, brown stoneware, the body a pale brown, the handle thumbed at the base and possibly reeded. Perhaps American, second to third quarter of eighteenth century. A.S. 51.

13) Copper shoe buckle with molded, reed and beaded ornament. Second half of eighteenth century. A.S. 99.

14) Copper shoe buckle with elaborately cast rope and lozenge ornament, maker's initials BB raised on the back. Second to third quarter of eighteenth century. A.S. 4A.

15) Fragment of brass buckle, shoe (?), simple tooling at the edge. Eighteenth century. A.S. 107.

16) Fragment of elaborately cast oval pewter shoe buckle, rope and filigree ornament. A fragment of a larger buckle of similar design was found on the foreshore of the river Thames at London in 1952. It is probable, therefore, that the Amelung buckle is of English manufacture. Probably third quarter of eighteenth century. A.S. 20.

17) Copper back from two-piece button, the lost front possibly pewter, but if so, this is an extremely unusual specimen; eye braised to back without shrank. Second half of eighteenth century. A.S. 71.

18) Small brass button, plain front, slightly concave back with central trunk-like seating for wire shank and eye. This mounting is unusual, and the button is unlikely to be English. Probably second half of eighteenth century. A.S. 12.

19) Small button, copper front and pewter or lead back with two small holes in center to seat wire eye. This is an unusual method of manufacture and is unlikely to be English. Eighteenth century (?). A.S. 12.

20) Drawer pull fragment, brass, hand-trimmed; insufficient material survives for the form to be determined. Probably second half of eighteenth or early-nineteenth century. A.S. 10.

21) Part of small horseshoe, iron, the small number of nail holes suggest an eighteenth-century date. Note absence of fullering. A.S. 1B.

22) Part of horseshoe, iron, very crudely fashioned, only two nail holes visible, no fullering. Stratigraphy indicates its eighteenth-century date. A.S. 26.

23) Linch-pin, or ratchet of uncertain purpose, iron, hand-wrought, date not known. A.S. 15.

24) Short iron spike with roughly square head 1½" in width, hand-wrought, A.S. 15A.

25) Short iron spike or nail, rectangular rose head ⅞" in length, the shaft clenched at the end and the tip missing, hand-wrought. A.S. 1A.

26) Tine from agricultural fork or rake, iron, hand-wrought. A.S. 44.

27) End of blowing iron with green glass adhering to the inside of the orifice, the fragment 5¾" in length, thickening towards the end from ⅕" to 1", and the somewhat encrusted hole having a diameter of approximately ⁷⁄₁₆". A.S. 94.

28) Clasp knife, iron, handle of pistol-grip form originally with bone or wooden plates held by rivets to half its length. Eighteenth or nineteenth century. A.S. 11.

FIG. 48. A selection of ceramics and small finds recovered during the 1962 excavations.

V. APPENDICES

APPENDIX I

TABLE OF EXCAVATION AREAS AND THEIR FIELD NUMBERS

The 1963 excavations were laid out in a formal 10'0" grid, each square possessing a number (in Arabic figures), but because the 1962 program developed from test trenches no formal pattern was established, though the Field Number Series (A.S.) was carried through both years. The 1962 areas are therefore described in relation to the structural remains, while the 1963 squares are designated by number. N.B. secondary A.S. numbers (e.g., A.S.2a) are included in the listing as they relate to the same areas, features, and squares as their parent figures.

Trench A–B. 1, 4, 10, 15, 17–21, 33, 34, 57, 69–72, 101, 112, 114, 116, 117

Trench E–F. 90–92, 103, 120, 121

First Basement West of Glasshouse on the Fleecy Dale Road. 5–9.

Test Trench across Rooms #7A and 7B. 11–13

Units #1A and 1B. 22–30, 32, 35–46, 61, 63–67, 107, 111, 113

Floor Area North of Units #1A and 1B. 52–54, 62

Areas Southeast of Unit #3. 31, 93, 104–106

Area between Units #1A and 2A. 55, 56, 94–99, 110

East Wall of Glasshouse. 58–60

Test Holes in Yingling Field. 47–51, 68, 73

Test Holes to Southwest of Glasshouse in Smith Field. 74–89, 115

Square	A.S. Number
1	137
2	136
3	118, 128
4	149
6	187
7	184
8	147
9	132, 148
10	129
12	130
13	131
14	138, 161
15	127, 201A
16	160
17	183
19	178
20	158
21	179
22	145
23	143
24	139
25	135
26	173
27	182
27/42	152
28	125
29	133

Balk	A.S. Number
8/15	156
9 south	175
12/13	141
12/25	207
13/24	163
14/23	189
15/16	196
16/17	170
16/21	204
20/33	193

Balk	A.S. Number
21/32	159
22/31	206
23/24	188
23/30	155
25/28	174
25/36	180
26/27	181
27/28	191
28/29	199
28/41	154
29/40	202
30/39	172, 202

Square	A.S. Number
30	146
31	157, 159, 162
32	185
33	169
34	194
35	168
36	144
38	142
39	171
40	126, 134
41	153
42/27	152
61	140
63	165
65	117
66	186
67	209
68	203

Balk	Square
1/8	164, 176
6/17	208
7/8/15	205
7/16	192
8/9	151
8/9/14/15	150

APPENDIX II

Description of Field Numbers

N.B. All numbers are prefixed by the letters A.S., i.e., Amelung Site.

1962

1. Trench 1 (A–B), topsoil.

1a. Trench 1 (A–B), mid-section, burned clay at 10″–1′3″ sloping east to 1′2″–1′6″.

1b. Trench 1 (A–B), ash and stony fill below 1a, extending to depth of 2′7″+.

2. Trench 2, topsoil, west end, crossing structure #1A and 1B.

2a. Trench 2, burned soil with brick dust, down to mortar spread 9″–1′1″. Note presence of burned wood and much clear vessel glass.

3. Trench 2, topsoil, central section. Note presence of 1864 penny.

3a. Trench 2, central section, 4″ burned clay under topsoil and over Units #1A and 1B.

3b. Trench 2, mixed rubble fill between west firing channel and dividing wall between Units #1A and 1B.

4. Trench A–B, east extension, east of N/S fenceline, topsoil.

4a. Trench A–B, burned clay and brick mixed with stone, extending to depth of 2′0″ and resting on burned clay level.

5. Cellar west of factory, loose fill inside N.E. corner, recovered in initial clearance. Note stone roofing slab with two peg holes.

5a. Cellar west of factory, dark fill in N.E. corner 1′0″ thick; note wire nails. Stratum terminating on clay floor at 4′8″ below surviving top of wall.

5b. Cellar west of factory, finds found rammed into clay floor below 5a; note cut nails.

6. Cellar west of factory, disturbed topsoil outside N.E. corner.

7. Cellar west of factory, outside S.E. corner, topsoil over brick rubble of gutter(?). Note presence of glass stopper at 8″ below top of corner.

8. Cellar west of factory, N.E. corner, surface finds.

9. Cellar west of factory, finds from washed fill overlying east wall.

10. Trench A–B, topsoil, east end, 4′0″ west from fence.

11. Trench 3, cutting across junction of glasshouse rooms #7A and 7B. 10′0″ section at south end, topsoil to depth of 9″.

11a. Trench 3, mixed burned fill of clay and bricks, terminating at 1′9½″ below modern grade, 1′1½″ in thickness. Large piece of glazed rock in this stratum.

12. Trench 3, 10′0″ central section, topsoil to burned stratum, 9½″ at south, 9″ at north, 5″ in middle stretch.

13. Trench 3, 22′0″ north section, topsoil across wall between rooms #7A and 7B.

14. Units #1A and 1B. Topsoil finds from outside west wall of #1A.

15. Trench A–B, west section, topsoil.

15a. Trench A–B, west section, burned rubble at 2″, apparently part of bulldozer disturbance.

15b. Trench A–B, as above, but deeper. All stratigraphy ruined by bulldozer or other earlier digging.

15c. Trench A–B, brick rubble from 2′0″ to 3′0″. All disturbed.

16. Trench 2, outside east wall of factory, topsoil.

17. Trench A–B, central section, burned stratum below topsoil.

18. Trench A–B, central section, yellow clay over rubble and beneath clinker layer at 2′2″, containing much glass. Note presence of furnace port fragment, mold-decorated neck and sugar bowl handle.

19. Trench A–B, east of central section, clinker and sandiver stratum over packed clay.

20. Trench A–B, east end, east of fence, on burned clay level (See 4a).

21. Trench A–B, extension to east end of cutting, topsoil over stone paved (?) area.

22. Unit #1B, burned fill overlying remains of rubble packing around firing channel.

23. Unit #1B, mortar sample from exterior of south wall at 1′1″ below the surface top.

24. Unit #1A and 1B, topsoil removed while cutting northward from trench 2.

25. Unit #1A, west of west wall of structure and south of trench 2.

26. Unit #1A, dirty yellow clay abutting against the exterior of the south wall.

27. Unit #1B, over firing channel remains at southeast corner.

27a. Unit #1B, as above, from burned debris inside corner.

28. Unit #1A, from rubble fill around firing channel south of trench 2.

29. Unit #1A, topsoil outside west wall north of trench 2.

30. Unit #1B, slope east of oven and exterior factory wall, topsoil.

31. Unit #3, east melting furnace, finds overlying remains of southeast cheek, topsoil.

32. Unit #1B, topsoil overlying northeast corner.

33. Trench A–B, section west of north/south fence, burned layer under topsoil. Note presence of wine-glass stem.

34. Trench A–B, central section, base of porcelain cup from beneath slag and clinker level.

35. Unit #1A, outside west wall north of trench 2. Stratum of crucible and stone chips above window glass layer resting on burned clay, immediately below topsoil.

36. Unit #1A, as above, window glass layer.

37. Unit #1A, as above, burned clay and brick stratum dipping against west wall under A.S. 36 and overlying thick mortar layer. Much vessel glass, very distorted, from the bottom of the burn and mixed into the mortar beneath.

38. Unit #1A, mortar layer under topsoil and over A.S. 36 at northwest corner.

39. Unit #1A, burned clay inside top of rubble-filled foundation at northwest corner.

40. Unit #1B, topsoil scree sloping to cliff east of oven and factory exterior wall. (See also A.S. 4a.)

41. Unit #1B, topsoil immediately north of northeast corner of oven foundation.

42. Unit #1B, from yellow clay over brick rubble (frit trough?) immediately east of the entrance to the firing channel.

43. Unit #1B, on top of 5″ rubble and clay layer over floor of firing channel.

44. Unit #3, finds from Fleecy Dale Road surface immediately south of the southeast cheek of the furnace.

44a. Unit #3, as above, dirty clay of road on hard-packed burned floor.

45. Unit #3, as above, find in the hard-packed burned floor.

46. Unit #1B, burned fill toward back of the firing channel. Note presence of shaped brick.

47. Test hole at A' of 50'0″ grid, 2'6″×2'6″, glass in topsoil at 5–6″ below present grade.

47a. As above, burned stratum 3″ in thickness.

48. Test hole at CI', 2'9″×2'9″, topsoil. Gravel at 5″.

49. Test hole 19'5″ east of BI', 3'0″×3'0″, topsoil. Gravel at 7″.

50. Test hole at BI', 2'8″×3'0″, topsoil. Stopped in gravel at 8″.

51. Test hole 26'8″ south of BI', 2'8″×3'0″, topsoil. Stopped at 1'1″ in gravel.

52. Unit #1A, trench 2, mortar level below burned layer (A.S. 37) west of west wall of oven.

53. Area between Unit #1A and #3, topsoil.

54. As above, burned floor north of Units #1A and 1B, finds immediately overlying burn.

55. Area excavation over and immediately north of the glasshouse wall linking Units #1A and 2A. Topsoil over wall.

56. As above, from top of burned clay with mortar spreading north from the wall.

57. Trench A–B, east extension east of N/S fenceline; from rubble under burned fill (A.S. 20).

58. East wall of factory, north of Unit #1B, topsoil.

59. East wall of factory, as above, burned clay and rubble over wall and under topsoil.

60. East wall of factory, fragment of crucible from west face of wall at elevation 292.4. (See Fig. 45, No. 1).

61. Unit #1B, burned clay and rubble, 5″ in depth, overlying stone floor of firing channel. Note presence of creamware saucer sherd (Fig. 48, No. 6).

62. Floor area north of Unit #1B and southeast of Unit #3 topsoil.

63. Unit #1B, rubble fill sealing lower mouth of firing channel, as A.S. 61.

64. Unit #1A, topsoil over firing channel.

65. Unit #1A, rubble construction fill west of firing channel.

66. Unit #1A, topsoil over northwest corner of structure.

67. Unit #1A. As A.S. 65, from bottom construction fill at level of offset, elevation 292.5.

68. Area between Units #1A and 2A, topsoil over brick rubble spread west of N/S fence.

69. Trench A–B, west end, undisturbed burned stratum under bulldozer spread.

70. Trench A–B, central section, bottom of mixed rubble over primary clay.

71. Trench A–B, west end, rubble under A.S. 69.

72. Trench A–B, central section, on natural under A.S. 70.

73. Test hole at CII, 2'0″×2'8″, topsoil to depth of 4″.

74. Test hole at CIII, 2'2″×3'4″, topsoil to depth of 5″.

75. Test hole at CIV, 3'2″×2'4″, topsoil to depth of 3″.

76. Test hole at OI, 3'0″×3'0″, topsoil to gravel at 4″.

77. Test hole at OII, 3'0″×3'0″, topsoil to depth of 4″.

78. Test hole at OIII, 3'0″×3'0″, topsoil into gravel at 5″.

79. Test hole at OIV, 3'0″×3'0″, topsoil into gravel at 4″.

80. Test hole at OV (west), 3'0″×3'0″, topsoil into gravel at 4″.

81. Test hole OVI (East), 3'0″×3'0″, topsoil into gravel at 4″.

82. Test hole at OVII, 3'0″×3'0″, topsoil into gravel at 4″.

83. Test hole at OVIII, 3'0″×3'0″, topsoil into gravel at 4″.

84. Test hole at OIX, 3'0″×3'0″, disturbed topsoil and gravel to 9″.

85. Test hole at VIII (south), 3'0″×3'0″, topsoil with plaster and gravel to 5″.

86. Test hole at AVII, 3'0″×3'0″, topsoil into gravel at 8″.

87. Test hole at AVI, 3'0″×3'0″, topsoil into gravel at 4″.

88. Test hole at AV, 3'0″×3'0″, topsoil into gravelly clay at 3″.

89. Test hole at AIV, 3'4″×2'3″, topsoil to gravelly clay at 4″.

90. Trench E–F (trench 5) on O base line 29'0″ west of coordinate III'. Topsoil.

91. Trench E–F, reddish clay beneath yellow clay wash and sloping downward to the north to a depth of 3'7″.

92. Trench E–F, mixed stone chips under clean clay dividing this stratum from A.S. 91.

93. Area east of Unit #3, topsoil overlying northern section of the factory's east wall, beneath Fleecy Dale Road.

94. Floor area west of Unit #1A, stratum of burned glass 4″ in thickness at 11″ below modern grade.

95. Floor area west of Unit #1A, extension of clearance to N/S fenceline. Topsoil.

96. Floor area west of Unit #1A, rubble stone and brick layer under A.S. 95.

97. Area south of south wall of factory east of Unit #2A, topsoil to first 1'0″.

98. Between Units #1A and 1B, various locations west of N/S fenceline; all topsoil.

99. Between Units #1A and 1B heavily burned stratum west of N/S fencelines under 8″ of topsoil and 6″ of rubble. Note burned window glass pressed into burned clay "floor." (Fig. 26).

100. Slipware fragment presented by Mrs. Harriet Milford, apparently founded in bulldozing west of Trench A–B in 1948.

101. Trench A–B finds recovered from spoil heap.

102. Trench E–F, mixed fill of silting below red clay (A.S. 91) to depth of 5'0″ below modern grade.

103. Trench E–F, mixed clay and rock to 5'7″.

104. Unit #3, test to brick floor of east stoking area

4'0" north of coordinate line A'. Topsoil.

105. Unit #3, test hole as above, ash stratum 4-1/2" below the surface of the Fleecy Dale Road, extending to depth of 7" at the eastern edge of the cut.

106. As A.S. 93, topsoil over east wall of factory.

107. as A.S. 36, N/S trench west of Unit #1A.

108. As A.S. 98.

109. As A.S. 96.

110. Unit #2A, from bottom of junction of factory south wall and southeast corner of Unit, interior. Note presence of clinker similar to those found in Trench A–B. (See A.S. 19.)

111. Unit #1A, post hole (?) to west of northwest corner, filled with stone chips and cutting into clay stratum under window glass deposit, and burned when both hole and clay were exposed. (See section, Fig. 46.)

112. Trench A–B, east end (west of N/S fenceline), burned clay over clinker and sandiver.

113. Unit #1A, from rubble outside southwest corner.

114. Trench A–B, unstratified.

115. Test hole at AIII, 3'0"×3'0", topsoil to 5" with pieces of cullet and crucible present. This hole inadvertently back-filled before its stratigraphy could be examined. This may warrant further investigation.

116. Trench A–B, east end, burned stratum. (As A.S. 112.)

117. Trench A–B, west end on bottom at 2'11" below modern grade. Note presence of complete brick: 8¼×4¼×2⅛×, rich salmon.

118. Square 3, test hole on south wall line of factory, 3'4" west of base line OA. Topsoil.

119. Trench A–B, unstratified.

120. Trench E–F, burned clay stratum. (As A.S. 91.)

121. Trench E–F, layer of clay under the above and overlying rubble stratum, A.S. 103. (See section, Fig. 34.)

122. Miscellaneous spoil heaps.

123. Area of supposed mill south of race. Topsoil.

124. Not used.

End of 1962 Season

125. Square 28, topsoil.

125A. Square 28, 6" below humus, brown stony soil continuing to 1'7" below modern grade.

125B. Square 28, on flat rubble layer in doorway (?) at 1'1". The doorway theory was not substantiated.

126. Square 40, no topsoil finds. From stony fill of ditch, much glass and iron furnace bar at the bottom. (Fig. 46, No. 8.)

127. Square 15, topsoil.

127A. Square 15, stone with hole for iron support (?) from burn under yellow clay at 3'2" below modern grade.

127B. Square 15, rubble beside stone boundary foundation post dating factory.

128. Square 3, topsoil.

128A. Square 3, outside south wall of factory, burned clay to depth of 1'6" below modern grade at southwest corner.

128B. Square 3, clinker and sandiver at 2'2" below modern grade, under small rubble; location as A.S. 128A.

129. Square 10, topsoil, 6".

129A. Square 10, glass over yellow clay layer, possibly working floor.

130. Square 12, topsoil.

130A. Square 12, red burned clay lapping over rubble of west face of Unit #3 east stoking area and extending down to ash at 1'2" below the surviving top of the wall.

130B. Square 12, ash under 130A. (See also A.S. 105.)

131. Square 13, topsoil.

131A. Square 13, burned clay overlying Unit #3, varying thickness, under topsoil.

131B. Square 13, finds overlying brick flue and part of northwest wing.

131C. Square 13, ash stratum in lower filling of west stoking area. Note presence of small finds including halfpenny of George II.

131D. Square 13, cullet layer sloping to floor at south side of west stoking area.

131E. Square 13, burned clay and ash overlying A.S. 131C at north side of stoking area. Note presence of much burned glass, mostly flasks, tumblers and wines. (Fig. 43.)

131F. Square 13, interior of brick arch, mostly lumps of green cullet, but also one table knife.

132. Square 9, topsoil. (See also A.S. 148.)

133. Square 29, topsoil and destruction debris south of factory north wall.

133A. Square 29, location as above, off burned clay floor.

134. Square 40, topsoil, west section. (See also A.S. 126.)

134A. Square 40, ditch filling immediately west of A.S. 126.

134B. Square 29, burned layer south of factory north wall, over red and yellow clay spread at northwest corner of area. Note presence of ground quartz.

134C. Square 29, top of burned barrel set in clay floor, Feature #10, first 7". Note presence of numerous burned but well-preserved nails.

134D. Square 29, bottom of burned barrel below level of wooden staves, packed with ground glass and a few large pieces including fragments of one ogee glass and three tumblers (Fig. 42.)

135. Square 25, topsoil to 2'2" below modern grade, to dirty yellow clay and large stones.

136. Square 2, topsoil, south 5'0" section, over south wall of factory.

137. Square 1, topsoil to 1'7", yellow sandy clay beneath, barren to top of wall at 1'6" below modern grade.

137A. Square 1, burned wood and rubble in foundation fill at southwest interior corner of Unit #2A.

137B. Square 1, ash outside south factory wall; probably part of refuse dump cut through by Trench A–B.

138. Square 14, topsoil. (See also A.S. 161.)

139. Square 24, topsoil to dirty clay at 1'6" below modern grade.

139A. Square 24, rubble under topsoil and over burned clay.

139B. Square 24, burned clay layer.

139C. Square 24, packed clay working floor (?) under A.S. 139B.

140. Square 61, northeast corner of factory, topsoil

and scree over wall.

141. Balk 12/13, topsoil over rubble of the east melting furnace #3.

142. Square 38, topsoil, 9".

142A. Square 38, rubble outside north wall of factory, to 1'0" below modern grade.

142B. Square 38, post hole fill, the hole cutting into the north slope of the ditch.

143. Square 23, topsoil.

143A. Square 23, on burned clay beside foundation; also clay bun resting on floor of the supposed pot arch, Unit #5, northwest corner of area.

143B. Square 23, rubble layer southeast of foundation of Unit #5.

143C. Square 23, burned clay south of south wall of Unit #5 and abutting against its foundation.

144. Square 36, topsoil immediately over foundation of east wall of the supposed potting room #6B.

144A. Square 36, dark gray soil at 1'0" outside fallen wall.

144B. Square 36, from shallow trough of ditch as it sloped up towards the west of the area.

145. Square 22, topsoil, northern 5'0" area excavated.

146. Square 30, topsoil to burned clay.

146A. Square 30, topsoil over rubble in northeast corner.

146B. Square 30, from rubble wall north of Unit #5.

146C. Square 30, under rubble, in ash east of wall.

147. Square 8, topsoil.

147A. Square 8, burned clay to stone foundation of west wall of Unit #2B.

148. Square 9, topsoil (As A.S. 132.)

148A. Square 9, scrapings from packed clay floor, largely very fine clinker and glass, east of Unit #2B.

149. Square 4, topsoil; note presence of blowing iron fragment and bottle bottom.

149A. Square 4, slag and sandiver deposit outside south wall of room #7B.

150. Junction of Square 8, 9, 14, and 15. Balk topsoil.

151. Balk 8/9, topsoil.

151A. Balk 8/9 burned clay under topsoil.

152. Square 27/42, topsoil. This area relocated to avoid balk between Squares 27 and 42 and to uncover north wall of factory which passed beneath that balk.

152A. Square 27/42, rubble under topsoil.

152B. Square 27/42, rubble outside wall and extending over ditch.

152C. Square 27/42, rubble fill of ditch.

152D. Square 27/42, silt under rubble in ditch.

153. Square 41, topsoil.

153A. Square 41, fine rubble over ditch and natural. Cut nail at approximately 8" below modern grade.

153B. Square 41, ditch filling.

153C. Square 41, concavity outside wall and south of ditch.

154. Balk 28/41, topsoil.

154A. Balk 28/41, as A.S. 153A.

155. Balk 23/30, topsoil.

155A. Balk 23/30, burned clay on brick sill (?) of Unit #5.

155B. Balk 23/30, post hole (?) at east edge of sill bricks.

156. Balk 8/15, topsoil.

156A. Balk 8/15, burned clay over foundation and around stones of later boundary wall foundation.

157. Square 31, topsoil. (See also A.S. 159 and 162 series.)

158. Square 20, topsoil over northwest wing of west of west melting furnace, Unit #8.

158A. Square 20, burned clay west of foundation.

158B. Square 20, on flagstone floor of trough (?) north of the ancillary oven foundation.

158C. Square 20, burned clay east of oven foundation.

159. Balk 21/32, scrap of porcelain from brick floor of Unit #5.

160. Square 16, topsoil.

160A. Square 16, burned clay over furnace Unit #8.

160B. Square 16, rubble over southeast wing of furnace Unit #8.

161. Square 14, cullet layer sloping to floor at south of long stoking trough between Units #3 and #8. (See also A.S. 138 for topsoil.)

161A. Square 14, ash on clay and edge of brick floor to north of the stoking and raking trough.

162. Square 31, burned clay on gray ash to south of north wall of Unit #5. (See also A.S. 157 and 159.)

162A. Square 31, post hole (?) at southeast corner of the above wall, containing fragments of blowing irons.

163. Balk 13/24, topsoil.

163A. Balk 13/24 rubble under topsoil and over northwest wing of Unit #3. Note presence of broken flasks actually merging into A.S. 163B.

163B. Balk 13/24, in burned clay in entrance to brick air duct (?). Finds similar to A.S. 163A. (See also A.S. 131B.)

164. Balk 1/18, topsoil. (As A.S. 176.)

165. Square 63, topsoil 6'0" × 4'0" cut.

165A. Square 63, ash and burned clay outside northwest corner of factory, i.e., beyond room #6A.

165B. Square 63, from very slender traces of ditch line north of north factory wall.

166. Unit #1B, stone sample extracted from west wall at 1'6" below the surviving top. (Interior)

167. Unit #1B, stone sample extracted from east wall at 1'6" below the surviving top. (Interior)

168. Square 35, topsoil cutting confined to trench over N/S wall between rooms #6A and 6B.

169. Square 33, topsoil.

169A. Square 33, rubble layer over disturbed foundation of southeast corner of room #6B.

170. Square 17 and Balk 16/17, topsoil. (As A.S. 183.)

170A. Square 17 and Balk 16/17, burned clay outside south face of Unit #8 east of southwest wing.

171. Square 39, topsoil, south 5'0" section only.

171A. Square 39, number not used.

171B. Square 39, cont. brown soil over natural outside north factory wall and south of ditch.

171C. Square 39, ditch filling.

172. Balk 30/39 topsoil. (As A.S. 202.)

173. Square 26 and Balk 26/27, topsoil. (As A.S. 181.)

173A. Square 26 and Balk 26/27, in burn over stone floor of firebox, Unit #4.

174. Balk 25/28, topsoil.

174A. Balk 25/28, in gray ash under stone rubble and over brick step or platform west of Unit #4.

175. Square 9, balk south of, topsoil.

176. Balk 1/8, topsoil. (As A.S. 164.)

177. Square 65, topsoil.

178. Square 19, topsoil 3′0″ trench across north of square, over foundation of wall dividing Units #9A and 9B.

178A. Square 19, ash under rubble at 2′0″ below modern grade, at northeast corner and east of oven foundation.

179. Square 21, topsoil.

179A. Square 21, burned clay and rubble over foundation of northeast wing and trough of melting furnace, Unit #8.

179B. Square 21, on natural (?) under rubble north of foundation.

180. Balk 25/36, topsoil.

181. Balk 27/27, topsoil. (As A.S. 173.)

182. Square 27, topsoil, southern half of square only.

182A. Square 27, from packed clay floor of Unit #4.

183. Square 17, topsoil. (As A.S. 170.)

183A. Square 17, burned fill of brick-floored west stoking area of furnace Unit #8.

183B. Square 17, from filling of firing channel (?)

184. Square 7, topsoil.

185. Square 32, topsoil.

186. Square 66, topsoil.

187. Square 6, topsoil.

187A. Square 6, cont. beneath topsoil over floor (?)

188. Balk 23/24, under rubble at working floor level.

189. Balk 14/23, in ash on floor of stoking area west of furnace Unit #3. (As A.S. 161A.)

190. Balk 27/61, topsoil over working floor.

191. Balk 27/28, topsoil.

191A. Balk 27/28, under working floor.

192. Balk 7/16, topsoil.

193. Balk 20/33, topsoil.

194. Square 34, topsoil.

194A. Square 34, in burned clay and brickbats in southwest corner of room #6B.

194B. Square 34, bottom to topsoil over the above.

195. Square 17 and Balk 6/17, topsoil. (See also A.S. 170 and 183.)

196. Balk 15/16, filling of east stoking area of furnace Unit #8, burned clay, stone rubble and much green cullet. (See A.S. 201 for topsoil finds.)

197. Square 34, top of burned fill at entrance to firing channel of Unit #9A.

197A. Square 34, gray ash below A.S. 197.

197B. Square 34, burned fill and ash inside firing channel of Unit #9A.

198. Balk 34/35, topsoil, cut over wall between room #6A and 6B. (See also A.S. 168.)

198A. Balk 34/35, in ash and clay over foundation and under topsoil.

198B. Balk 34/35, from ash filling of hole through foundation.

199. Balk 28/29, burned clay over working floor, iron tie. (Fig. 42, No. 1.)

200. Unstratified finds from soil heaps and from Smithsonian backfilling, also subsequent surface finds picked up after winter rains.

201. Balk 15/16, topsoil. (See also A.S. 196.)

201A. Square 16, burned clay and ash on floor of east firing channel (?) of furnace Unit #8. (See also A.S. 160.)

202. Balks between Squares 29/40 and 30/39. Topsoil.

203. Square 68, rim of Pennsylvania slipware dish from floor of firing channel of Unit 9D.

204. Balk 16/21, topsoil.

205. Balk 7/8/15, disturbed soil under roots of tree and over rubble boundary wall.

206. Balk 22/21, topsoil to burned layer beside foundation of northeast wing of furnace Unit 8.

207. Balk 12/25, topsoil around roots of tree on boundary line over northeast wing of furnace Unit 3.

208. Balk 6/17, topsoil and rubble over southeast corner of southwest wing of furnace Unit 8.

209. Square 67, topsoil and root disturbance in test hole to locate northwest corner of firing channel of Unit 9C. Shoe buckle fragment only. (Fig. 43, No. 6.)

APPENDIX III

TABLE OF EXCAVATED BRICK DIMENSIONS

Filling of cellar southwest of the excavated glasshouse.	8 × 3-3/4 × 2-1/4″ deep salmon 8-1/4 × 4 × 2-1/4″ deep salmon
From guttering (?) at southeast corner of the above structure.	8-1/4 × 4-1/4 × 2-1/4″ deep salmon 8-1/4 × 4 × 2-1/4″ deep salmon

Unit 1A, from construction fill around firing channel and beneath oven floor.
8 × 4-1/4 × 2-1/4″ pale salmon
8 × 3-3/4 × 2-1/4″ pale salmon

Unit 2A, rubble construction (?) fill at southwest interior corner.	8-1/4 × 4 × 2-1/8″ salmon 8-1/4 × 4-1/8 × 2-1/4″ salmon (one end rounded)
Unit 3, floor of east stoking area.	8-1/4 × 4 × ? color changed by burning.
Unit 3, from side of air duct (?) through north wall.	8-1/4 × 4 × 1-7/8″ salmon
Square 3, from rubble outside south wall of excavated glasshouse.	8-5/8 × 4-1/4 × 2-1/4″ rich red

Unit 4, brick retaining wall around clay step or platform.
8-3/8 × 4-1/8 × 2-3/16″ salmon

Room 6B, southwest corner A.S. 194A.	8-1/4 × 3-3/4 × 2-1/16″ rich red, very sandy clay. (pinkish mortar attached containing ground brick.)

CHEMICAL ANALYSES OF AMELUNG GLASSES
Robert H. Brill, Victor F. Hanson

I. INTRODUCTION
Robert H. Brill

CHEMICAL ANALYSES and laboratory studies of glasses from the ancient and medieval worlds have provided a great deal of useful information for archaeologists, curators, and historians,[1] but until now, few such studies have been carried out on glasses from more recent periods. One reason is that in more recent times, from about the seventeenth century onwards, sources of raw materials have become more numerous and commercial trade in these materials has grown more competitive and farther-reaching. Therefore, it has been expected that there might have been as much variation in chemical composition within the production of a given factory as there was variation among different factories. If that were true, the chances of characterizing the products of a given factory on the basis of chemical composition would be poorer than when dealing with glass manufactured in earlier times.

To some extent, then, the analytical study of Amelung glass reported here is opening a new field, and as it is with most new fields of research, one must proceed with caution when interpreting the results. Because so few analyses have been made of glasses of this period, either American or European, there is as yet little information available in the way of comparative data.[2]

This study was initiated as a part of the excavation of the New Bremen factory site, but it quickly broadened with the development of analytical techniques which made possible the nondestructive analysis of complete glass objects. Through this development, it became possible to compare the compositions of excavated fragments with known—and suspected—Amelung objects. The result was a cooperative analytical program between The Corning Museum of Glass and The Henry Francis du Pont Winterthur Museum, a program which has been most fruitful. It will become apparent to the reader that the analysis of American glass is indeed a very promising field of research, a finding which seems especially appropriate in the nation's bicentennial year.

The investigation consists of five parts, each of which was directed towards specific goals. The five parts are described briefly below, and results from the two major parts are presented in the sections which follow. Several important aspects of this research are still in progress, and it can be expected that our knowledge of Amelung's glass and its overall place in the history of glass will be expanded even further in the future.

1) CHEMICAL ANALYSES OF AMELUNG OBJECTS
Because of the great historical importance of Amelung objects, they can only be analyzed by completely nondestructive, nonsampling methods, and the only method currently available for analyzing glass within this restriction is the Energy-Dispersive X-ray Fluorescence Analyzer. During the past three years, a large group of Amelung glasses and related glasses has been analyzed by Mr. Victor F. Hanson and his colleagues on this instrument in the Analytical Laboratory of the Winterthur Museum. This marks the first time that such an extensive study

222

of museum glass objects has been conducted. To date, more than a hundred objects have been analyzed.

The objective of this part of the study was to determine if any specific chemical compositions or peculiarities could be associated with the products of Amelung's factories. Therefore, the most important part of the study was the analysis of pieces with unquestioned attributions. An ancillary objective was the strengthening or weakening of attributions for objects whose origins are less certain. A critical point in the logic behind this study was to determine not only whether the known Amelung glasses resemble one another, but also whether they differ as a group from glasses from other factories.

2) Chemical Analyses of Fragments Excavated at the Amelung Factory Site

During the course of digging at the site of the New Bremen factory, thousands of fragments of glass were uncovered. From among these, thirty pieces were selected for chemical analysis. Some of the pieces came from recognizable glass forms, while others were pieces of cullet or waste glass. Because the pieces are fragments, it was permissible to sacrifice samples large enough for full quantitative chemical analysis. These analyses were carried out as part of the scientific research program of The Corning Museum of Glass. The objective of this part of the study was to characterize the chemical compositions of the glass made at the factory and to use the findings to learn as much as possible about how the factory operated.

3) Fluorescence of Amelung Glasses

When examined under ultraviolet light, most glasses will fluoresce, that is, they emit visible light. The color of the light and its intensity vary depending primarily upon the chemical composition of the glasses examined. Thus, fluorescence is often a useful clue to chemical composition and, more importantly, is useful for identifying glasses which might have been made in the same factory.

Most of the Amelung objects mentioned throughout Mr. Lanmon's and Mrs. Schwind's contribution and all of the fragments used for chemical analysis have been examined under both long-wave and short-wave ultraviolet lamps. Several different types of fluorescence were observed, which serve as an additional basis for classifying the objects. These observations were of a subjective and qualitative nature

only, because it was experimentally impossible to determine actual fluorescence spectra on large pieces of glass. For this reason comparisons between groups of objects were especially important. The human eye is a remarkably sensitive instrument for detecting small differences when comparing colors, but it is relatively poor at remembering colors.

Excavated fragments representative of the various types of fluorescence found among the glasses have been analyzed chemically so as to determine what compositional features are associated with fluorescence colors observed in the objects. This research is still in progress, and the results will be reported in the future.

4) Other Studies

Viscosity-temperature curves were estimated for Amelung glasses. These curves were extrapolated from data obtained from simple pull tests carried on small fragments of the glasses. The resulting curves allow one to estimate the minimum temperatures required for forming various types of objects and thus tell something about the furnace capabilities. A gradient-furnace experiment was carried out on a sample of mudstone removed from the furnace. This also yielded some information on the temperatures achieved in the furnaces. Several experiments have been planned for various other materials excavated at the site, including crucible fragments, bricks, and possible raw materials. However, these experiments have not yet been completed.

5) Activation Analyses of the Glasses

Very small samples of pontil glass have been removed from several Amelung objects. Although these samples were too small to be analyzed by the x-ray fluoresence method or wet-chemical methods, they were large enough for analysis by activation methods. The samples were removed only from those objects where a convenient protrusion of pontil glass was found. In no case were samples removed from objects where there was any danger of breakage. The sacrifice of a tiny piece of glass from a pontil mark is justified on the basis that the information to be gained by its chemical analysis is potentially more valuable than a few milligrams of glass itself. Samples have been submitted to Dr. Phillip Lafleur at the National Bureau of Standards for analysis by his group.

The question arises whether pontil glass is necessarily the same as glass from which the body of an object itself was made. In most cases, they obviously should be the same, but one cannot be certain that this is always true. The ultraviolet fluorescence colors of the pontil glass samples were compared to the bodies of the parent glasses, and in all but one instance the fluorescence was identical to that of the parent glass. It is, therefore, reasonable to assume that for the glasses analyzed here (other than the one with the non-matching fluorescence), the pontil samples do truly represent the compositions of the objects. These analyses have not yet been completed.

NOTES

1. For general information on the scientific investigation of early glasses see: R. H. Brill, "The Scientific Investigation of Ancient Glass," *Proceedings of the VIIIth International Congress on Glass, London,* Sheffield, England: The Society of Glass Technology, 1968, pp. 47–68.

2. A few analyses are scattered among the literature, and at The Corning Museum of Glass there are as yet unpublished analyses of some American and European glasses of the eighteenth and nineteenth centuries. Some analyses of surface finds at the New Bremen site were published earlier. *See:* Donald B. Hubbard, Lillie B. Jenkins, and Elizabeth M. Krumrine, "Amelung Glasses Compared with Some Modern Commercial Glasses," *The Scientific Monthly,* LXXV, No. 6, Dec. 1952, pp. 327–338.

II. CHEMICAL ANALYSES
OF GLASSES ATTRIBUTED
TO JOHN FREDERICK AMELUNG
Victor F. Hanson

In 1969 the Henry Francis du Pont Winterthur Museum established a research laboratory to develop methods for characterizing the objects in its collection on the basis of chemical compositions. The analytical programs at the laboratory center around a new instrument, the Energy-Dispersive X-ray Fluorescence Analyzer.[1] The most remarkable feature of this instrument—a unique feature for the chemical analysis of certain types of materials—is that it employs a method which is completely nondestructive and nonsampling. The instrument enables the analyst to identify all the chemical elements above element 19 (potassium) in the periodic table without removing a sample or defacing an object in any way. The X-ray Analyzer has been used for numerous analyses of metallic and ceramic objects and plays a key role in the glass-analysis program at Winterthur.

In 1973 the Winterthur Museum and The Corning Museum of Glass undertook a cooperative venture in which the X-ray Analyzer was used to analyze Amelung glasses in connection with Corning's bicentennial exhibition and the publication of the archaeological excavations of the Amelung site. Since the beginning of this project, just over a hundred objects have been analyzed. The key pieces in the study are 10 signed or documented Amelung objects and about 15 others with strong Amelung attributions. The balance consists of some objects with looser Amelung associations along with an assortment of glasses from other American factories or of European origin.

The study has so far included about 80 glasses from the Winterthur and Corning collections and more than 20 glasses lent for chemical analysis by other institutions and private collectors. (A list of the objects analyzed appears below.) After the analyses were completed, the objects were returned to the shelves of the owners perfectly intact and in exactly the same condition as when they had left.

A detailed description of the analytical procedures and a complete compilation of the data will appear elsewhere in the near future, because the full exposition of these subjects on a rigorous scientific basis goes beyond the scope of this publication. The objective here is to outline a few analytical aspects of the work and to summarize some of the more important findings.

The Energy-Dispersive X-ray Fluorescence Analyzer brings together radioactive x-ray-emitting isotopes, solid state x-ray detectors, minicomputers, and compact data storage devices. In simplest terms, the object to be analyzed is positioned above a radioactive source. X-rays from the source excite atoms within the material being analyzed, causing them to emit a pattern of secondary x-rays. The pattern emitted is uniquely characteristic of the types and numbers of atoms within the material. The secondary x-rays are collected and counted and ultimately lead to the identification of the chemical elements within the object and to the measurement of their concentrations. About twenty minutes is required to irradiate the sample and obtain a teletype readout of weight percentages of thirty elements.

In order to adapt this method to the analysis of glasses, a procedure was worked out which makes use of separate sequential irradiations by three radioactive isotopes, Fe^{55}, Cd^{109}, and Am^{241}. This procedure provides the potential for quantitative determinations of 25 chemical elements in the glasses analyzed. The method makes use of a series of several reference glasses of known chemical compositions, some of which were especially prepared so as to simulate the compositions anticipated for the Amelung glasses.[2]

One limitation of the method in its present stage of development at Winterthur is that the analyses do not provide information on low-atomic-number elements, and it is known that such data are useful for classifying glasses. This was recognized at the outset. But in view of the fact that the X-ray Analyzer is the only method of analysis which is truly nonsampling and nondestructive for glasses, it is also therefore the only method by which the Amelung objects may now be analyzed. Instrumental improvements planned for the future should allow for analyses of some of the light elements as well. It should also be noted that this method, unlike wave-length dispersive x-ray fluorescence, does not pose any hazard of discoloration of the glass.

Several special problems had to be solved first involving the geometry of the objects; that is, the effects of thickness of the glass, distance from the source, and shape of the object. These factors were all taken into account and compensated for before the objects were analyzed.

It often happens that problems of handling and interpreting large bodies of analytical data can be as difficult and time-consuming as the processes which go into acquiring the data. That would certainly have been true in this instance were it not for the computerized techniques of data handling built into the instrument. Even so, this does not entirely relieve the investigators of the responsibility for deciding what parts of the data are most significant for the ultimate interpretation relative to the objects themselves.

In this study it was decided that the analyses of the 10 signed or documented Amelung pieces was the place to start the interpretation. The first important observation is that all are potash-lime-silica glasses, and although several contain traces of lead, none are high-lead compositions. Beyond that it appears that these glasses have in common the compositional features listed below. It was also discovered that several additional glasses having strong Amelung attributions, and a few of less certain attributions, share these same compositional features, which are:

1) The mean potassium:calcium ratio is 16:10.
2) The average ratios Rb:Sr:Y:Zr are 7:10:2:6.
3) The antimony content is 0.1–0.2 percent.
4) The barium content is 0.02–0.08 percent.

A most important feature of Amelung glasses is the presence of significant amounts of antimony. Based on present studies, it is evident that objects having compositional features matching those of Amelung glass, except for antimony, were made in another factory.

The analytical results for the ten signed or documented objects are shown in Table 1. The chemical similarities and variability can be judged from the table. For comparison, analyses of seven Lauenstein objects are presented in Table 2. There are differences in the concentration of two major ingredients, potassium oxide and calcium oxide, and in six trace elements: titanium, manganese, rubidium, lead, antimony, and barium.[3] The ratios of rubidium, strontium, yttrium, and zirconium are distinctly different from those of Amelung glass. There is, however, overlapping among some of these elements. In Table 3 are given analyses of some fragments excavated at the New Bremen factory. These were reported from among a total of nineteen fragments analyzed, because they were also analyzed by The Corning Museum.

The data in Table 1 also contain an intriguing hint of possible systematic differences between the first five objects dated up through 1789 and those dating from 1791 and 1792. The distinction shows up especially in the lead contents. The difference could mark a distinction between the glasses made before the fire of 1790 and those made afterward. About half of the signed objects contain no titanium, whereas half have titanium in concentrations from 0.003 to 0.03 percent. Titanium occurs widely in the earth's crust as ilmenite, the black magnetic particles frequently found in sand. It appears that either the source of sand was changed during the fabrication of this group of signed pieces or that a method was found to remove the ilmenite from the sand. The iron in ilmenite produces an objectionable greenish color in the glass which was often offset by adding manganese. While the arsenic contents vary considerably and arsenic does not yet appear to qualify as a characterizing feature, it may prove significant in future studies.[4]

After the chemical features of the documented Amelung objects had been established, the analyses of the remaining glasses were considered. These were classified solely on the basis of chemical similarities, grouping together those which have the most chemical features in common. Three other major chemical groups were defined, and the large majority of all the glasses analyzed (79) fit into the four categories. The categories are built up around 13 chemical elements. The first group, the A group, contains 38 objects, all but five of which have some Amelung association. The group also includes a patty of glass made by melting together crushed cullet from the excavation. Three objects attributed to Stiegel and two with European attributions also fell in this group. Further studies of the data will be required to explain the chemical differences among the groups in terms of glass technology, but at least part of the variation is related to the color chemistry.

Beyond the four major groups, eleven other chemical types appeared, but for the moment some of these are only "splinter groups," and none contains more than three glasses. This is significant and encouraging, however, in that these groups imply a diversity of compositions among glasses of this period. It is expected, therefore, that as this project continues, compositional categories matching particular factories, regions, or periods will eventually emerge.

ACKNOWLEDGEMENTS
The success of this project was due in large part to the cooperation of those institutions and individuals who lent objects for chemical analysis. The author thanks them and also Arlene Palmer Schwind and Dwight P. Lanmon who delivered the objects to the Winterthur Laboratory for analysis. Special thanks are expressed to the author's associates at the Winterthur Museum, especially those listed below: Karen Anderson, Janice Carlson, Charles Hummel, Justine M. Mataleno, Karen M. Papouchado, George J. Reilly, and Helen F. Szczecinski. Special thanks are also expressed to P. H. Gaither of Winterthur's Scientific Advisory Committee for his valuable contribution to the computer programing used in this study.

OBJECTS IN THE CATALOGUE ANALYZED IN THIS STUDY

Amelung vessels analyzed at The Henry Francis du Pont Winterthur Museum, Winterthur, Delaware.

CAT. NO.

1. "Bremen" goblet and cover
2. "Tobias and the Angel" tumbler and cover
3. "Ghequiere" tumbler and cover
4. "J.F.C.H." tumbler
5. "B. Johnson" case bottles
   (four examples)
   The Corning Museum of Glass
   The Maryland Historical Society
   The Smithsonian Institution
   The Henry Francis du Pont
   Winterthur Museum
6. "Boston" tumbler
7. "Mifflin" goblet
8. "Guest" tumbler and cover
9. "Great Seal of the U.S." tumbler
10. "Repold/Amelung" goblet
11. "Mauerhoff" goblet

CAT. NO.

12. "Stenger" flask
13. "Trisler" goblets
14. "J. Amelung" goblet
15. "C.G.C." goblet
16. "König" goblet
17. "Marshall" goblet and cover
18. "Schley" goblet and cover
19.–21. Undecorated goblets
22. "G.R." wineglass (Corning example)
24. "A.G." tumbler
29. "GMR" tumbler
31. "C.G." sugar bowl and cover
34. Sugar bowl and cover
35. Sugar bowl and cover
37. Cream jug
38. "M.T." bowl
42. Candlestick

TABLE 3
ANALYSES OF EXCAVATED FRAGMENTS*

	337	339	349	562	563	565	568	572
K_2O	9.92	8.09	8.66	15.94	15.51	9.32	13.66	13.68
CaO	5.35	5.12	5.18	8.97	9.09	4.72	8.24	7.15
TiO_2	0	.018	.021	.036	.021	.051	.033	.013
V_2O_5	0	0	.00009	.0002	.00007	.0002	.00017	.00003
Cr_2O_3	0	0	0	0	0	0	0	0
MnO	.11	.19	.29	.22	.26	.31	.51	.61
Fe_2O_3	.18	.014	.46	.11	.21	.11	.21	.22
CoO	0	0	.38	0	.023	0	.00041	.002
NiO	0	0	0	0	0	0	0	0
CuO	0	0	0	0	0	0	0	.001
ZnO	0	0	0	0	.0036	0	.0005	.007
Ga_2O_3	0	0	0	.0004	.0008	0	0	.001
Rb_2O	.0071	.010	.010	.0071	.022	.012	.023	.011
SrO	.008	.013	.0052	.013	.026	.011	.035	.011
Y_2O_3	.0041	.0006	.00067	.0012	.0012	0	.0022	.012
ZrO_2	.020	.020	0	.021	.0095	.0053	.012	.026
Ag_2O	0	0	0	0	0	0	0	.0003
SnO_2	.00017	0	0	0	0	0	0	.00056
PbO	.17	.060	.059	.61	.55	0	.0041	.56
As_2O_3	.00033	.0070	.81	.43	.28	0	.0026	.036
Sb_2O_5	.052	.052	.034	.0018	.041	.003	0	.012
BaO	.0091	.036	.034	.018	.013	.033	.044	.041
La_2O_3	0	0	0	0	0	0	.0042	.0046
Bi_2O_3	0	0	.0005	0	.0004	0	0	.0006

*—Sample descriptions appear in Section III.

NOTES

1. Victor F. Hanson, "Quantitative Elemental Analysis of Art Objects by Energy-Dispersive X-Ray Fluorescence Spectrometry," *Applied Spectroscopy*, 27, No. 5, 1973, pp. 309–334.

2. The following lists the reference glasses. All were prepared by Dr. A. A. Erickson of Corning Glass Works and his co-workers.

   a) Nos. 611, 612, 614, and 616 distributed by the National Bureau of Standards.

   b) Reference glasses A, B, and D of a series prepared for The Corning Museum of Glass for interlaboratory comparison analyses.

   c) Three glasses prepared for The Corning Museum of Glass, which contain only the major ingredients in the reference glasses A, B, and D and not the trace elements.

   d) Glasses SPE, TVX, and TVY prepared for The Corning Museum of Glass simulating the compositions anticipated for the Amelung glasses.

3. In keeping with glassmaking convention, all compositions were recorded in weight percentages of the oxides. For readers unfamiliar with chemical symbols, the formulas below represent the oxides of the corresponding chemical elements.

K_2O	potassium	Y_2O_3	yttrium
CaO	calcium	ZrO_2	zirconium
TiO_2	titanium	PbO	lead
MnO	manganese	As_2O_5	arsenic
Fe_2O_3	iron	Sb_2O_5	antimony
Rb_2O	rubidium	BaO	barium
SrO	strontium		

4. Some remarks on the functions of the various ingredients and their levels of concentration appear in Section III. Also included there are comparisons between the analyses of the documented objects and the excavated fragments.

III. CHEMICAL ANALYSES AND OTHER LABORATORY STUDIES OF GLASS FRAGMENTS EXCAVATED AT THE SITE OF THE NEW BREMEN GLASSMANUFACTORY

ROBERT H. BRILL

THE OBJECTIVE OF THIS STUDY was to determine what chemical compositions or peculiarities might characterize the glass excavated at the site of John Frederick Amelung's New Bremen Glassmanufactory.[1] From among the thousands of fragments excavated, thirty were selected for chemical analysis. The sampling was not intended to be representative, in a proportional sense, of the entire body of glass uncovered. Instead, there was a strong bias in the sampling towards colorless glasses, which evidently were used for fine quality production. About half of the specimens analyzed (fourteen fragments) are of this colorless glass. These were chosen in the hope of establishing compositional connections with museum objects attributed to Amelung. The remainder consists of a small assortment of colored glasses (purples and blues) and several specimens thought to represent production of more ordinary wares or window glass. A list of sample descriptions is appended at the end of this text.

The sampling contains specimens recognizable as vessel fragments, some cullet, and waste glass, such as drippings and knock-offs. One can rarely be absolutely certain that particular glass vessel fragments or even pieces of cullet must necessarily have been made at a factory site because they were excavated there. Some scrap glass and cullet could always have been brought into a factory. However, we feel quite confident that the colorless specimens and cullet analyzed here really were made at this factory. Moreover, the indications are that the specimens of more ordinary glasses also were, because, as will be demonstrated below, their compositions closely match those of knock-offs and drippings. Only two specimens are really suspect of having outside origins. The dates of the specimens analyzed are assumed to fall somewhere within the factory's operating period, that is, 1785 through 1795, although they are associated with the building which is believed to have burned in 1790 and not been rebuilt afterwards.

Quantitative analyses by atomic absorption were carried out for the following elements, expressed throughout as weight percentages of the oxides:[2] potassium (K_2O), calcium (CaO), sodium (Na_2O), magnesium (MgO), aluminum (Al_2O_3), iron (Fe_2O_3), and manganese (MnO). Phosphorus (P_2O_5) was determined colorimetrically. All of the other elements at minor and trace levels were analyzed by semi-quantitative emission spectroscopy. Duplicate determinations starting with new samples were run for any questionable values. Silica (SiO_2) was

229

estimated by difference from 100 percent.

Several special reference glasses were prepared for these analyses and for the object analyses carried out at Winterthur. These included "synthetic Amelung glasses" which contained major, minor, and trace elements at levels corresponding to those obtained in preliminary studies. Analyses of the synthetic Amelung glasses yielded excellent agreement with the theoretical compositions calculated from the known batch compositions.[3] Therefore, the analytical procedures used are closely calibrated for the analyses of both the Amelung fragments and the objects.[4]

The data are summarized in Table 1 and compiled in Tables 2–5. The specimens are grouped according to two main categories which emerged from the results and are arranged within those categories according to color.

The first important observation made was that all but one of the specimens are potash:lime:silica glasses (K_2O:CaO:SiO_2). Whereas lead (PbO) was frequently found at trace or low minor levels, a fact of some significance, it was a major component in only one specimen, no. 4283. This fragment, a stem base with faceted cutting, is a true lead glass, containing 34.5 percent PbO. The question arises as to whether it was actually manufactured at the factory or if it is an intrusion or glass brought in for cullet. It appears that the majority of glass made at this factory, if not all of it, was of non-lead formulations.

The second important observation is that although all the glasses are potash:lime formulations (excluding the one lead glass), two distinctly different categories emerge from the data. One is a low-lime formulation, and the other a high-lime formulation. The low-lime group has an average CaO content of 9.05 percent. It contains eighteen glasses ranging from 7.08 to 10.8 percent CaO. The high-lime group has an average CaO content of 19.6 percent. It contains five glasses ranging from 18.6 to 20.6 percent CaO. The separation between the groups is well-defined, and there is no overlapping.

The data for the other chemical elements reenforce the separation. The same specimens which cluster together in the low-lime group also cluster together in their percentages of other chemical elements. Similarly, the specimens in the high-lime group remain clustered in the other chemical elements. In all, ten different chemical elements serve to discriminate between the two

chemical types. The discriminating oxides are: CaO, K_2O, Na_2O, MgO, Al_2O_3, Fe_2O_3, SrO, BaO, PbO, and Sb_2O_5. There are two partially-discriminating elements, P_2O_5 and TiO_2, while MnO and B_2O_3 are nondiscriminating. Repeat analyses will be required to establish whether or not Li_2O and Rb_2O, are discriminating.

The sharp separation into two groups proves to have a rational basis in that all the glasses in the low-lime group are either colorless, purple, or blue. Clearly, this composition reflects the basic formulation used for manufacturing the "fine glass" production of the factory. All of the specimens in the high-lime group are green, aqua, or amber—the colors characteristic of more ordinary production. The chemical groups are tight and the separation is complete, there being no crossovers between the two groups.

There are six glasses which have been designated intermediate or uncertain as shown in Table 5. There are various ways of interpreting their analyses. Two of them (nos. 346 and 573) could possibly be glasses made by melting together a mixture of glasses of the low-lime and high-lime groups. The others could be badly off-composition examples of the low-lime and high-lime groups. Alternatively, some of these six might be intrusions on the site—especially the bottle fragments—or could be scrap glass brought in for remelting as batch cullet. Among these, only no. 350, an irregularly-shaped piece of waste glass, was certainly melted at the site. Its unusual color, probably the result of devitrification, is consistent with its identification as an off-composition waste glass. The others appear to be fragments of vessel or window glass. It is probably wiser not to press too far in interpreting these analyses now, but to await the results of follow-up analyses of additional specimens.

It is noteworthy that the purple and blue glasses fall in the same category as the colorless glasses. The vessels made from the colored glasses must have been regarded as being of the same level of quality as the colorless vessels, because for practical purposes, as far as the colors would have been concerned, the addition of the same colorants to the high-lime formulation would have yielded an identical appearance to the eye.

The color chemistry of the purple and blue glasses is familiar. The three blue glasses are colored by cobalt oxide (CoO). The two pale blue glasses (nos. 363 and 1821) have about 0.03 percent CoO and no. 349, a much darker blue color, contains about 0.4 percent CoO. Certain other trace elements seem to be higher in the blue glasses than in their colorless companions within the low-lime group. These elements could have been introduced, probably unintentionally, with the ingredient which contained the cobalt. They are bismuth (Bi_2O_5), copper (CuO), lead (PbO), probably arsenic (As_2O_5), probably iron (Fe_2O_e), and possibly nickel (NiO). On several other occasions arsenic has been found to accompany cobalt in early glasses.[5] This is because arsenic often occurs in association with cobalt in natural minerals, such as cobaltite, CoAsS. The blue glasses made at the Amelung factory were probably colored by the addition of cobalt imported in the form of zaffre or smalt.

The purple glasses (nos. 347, 348, 362, and 568) are all colored, as is to be expected, with manganese (MnO) at a level of approximately 2–3 percent. The ingredient used to introduce the manganese also brought in barium (BaO), lead (PbO), nickel (NiO), copper (CuO), vanadium (V_2O_5), some aluminum (Al_2O_3), and possibly bismuth (Bi_2O_3), zinc (ZnO), and tin (SnO_2).

The presence of manganese in all of the fragments from the site, the low-lime, the high-lime, and even the uncertain group, ties the glasses together somewhat. At the concentrations found (a mean value of 0.40 percent), it is reasonable to assume that the manganese was an intentional additive meant to act as a decolorizer. Its function was to offset the greenish color introduced by iron impurities. Because manganese was so commonly used for this purpose, it is not likely to prove useful for distinguishing Amelung glass from other glasses of the period.

A rather vexing question grows out of the fact that some of the discriminating elements in this study occur at levels which are difficult to interpret. The same is true of some of the "Amelung features" in Mr. Hanson's object analyses. For example, lead concentrations in the range of a few tenths of a percent do not seem sufficient to confer any advantageous properties to the glasses. Similarly, the level of the antimony in some of the glasses is somewhat low for performing its usual functions as a decolorizer or as a fining agent. Because the glasses are believed to contain manganese as a decolorizer, presumably the antimony was intended as a fining agent, that is, an ingredient used to remove "seed" or small bubbles from glass. Antimony is probably not very effective as a fining agent at

concentrations less than about 0.05 percent. In this connection, the Amelung glasses do not seem to be particularly well-fined, even by eighteenth-century standards. The presence of arsenic (As_2O_5) may also be explained by its use as a fining agent, particularly in the colorless glasses, where it would not have been associated with any colorant.

The trace levels of the copper and zinc and the occasional traces of vanadium might be explained in either of two ways. All three could be associated with the manganese, or the vanadium might have come in through the corrosion of a crucible, since it is a common impurity in clays.[6] On the other hand, that plant ashes used for preparing the potash ingredient must have been purified by leaching, and the alkali could have picked up copper and zinc from brass pots or other utensils used in that process. If the alkali had been prepared in lead-sheathed vats, that might also explain the presence of lead in the low-lime glasses. The alkali would have had to contain about one percent of lead to account for the 0.23 percent average PbO content of the glasses. It is possible that some lead was introduced accidentally through the use of high-lead cullet. (Recall, for example, the piece of high-lead glass, no. 4283, which was analyzed.) One would expect, however, that if scrap cullet was the source of the lead, that the lead contents would be more variable.

In any event, the most important point is that the lead and antimony *are* present, regardless of how they got there, and may someday serve to differentiate the glass made at this factory from glasses made elsewhere. Whether or not that hope materializes depends upon the outcome of analyses of glasses from other sources.

There are two bodies of analytical data for American glasses at The Corning Museum, excluding miscellaneous analyses of single objects. One relates mainly to pressed glasses, but these objects are mostly lead glasses and differ too much in date for direct comparison with the Amelung fragments. (It might be noted in passing, however, that even those which are not lead glasses are quite different from the Amelung compositions.) Of more immediate interest here is a group of twelve glasses from the Wistar factory. Among this suite of samples, containing bottle fragments, cullet, and trailings, there are two somewhat different compositions. The Wistar glasses can be distinguished from both Amelung compositions (the low-lime and high-lime groups) by four elements: calcium, sodium, lead, and antimony. There are other elements, too, which may be discriminating.

The Wistar glasses contain lead, but the concentration is only of the order of 0.00X percent, markedly lower than in the fine Amelung glasses. Antimony was not detected. Actually, the Wistar analyses of bottle fragments are quite close to the composition of the stray sample no. 346 from the Amelung site. Although the agreement is not perfect, the composition of that vessel fragment seems as close to the Wistar glass as it does to its Amelung companions, lending support to the supposition that this piece is an intrusion.

The explanation of why there were two formulations in use at the factory can be seen from either of two viewpoints, both involving aesthetic, technological, and economic factors. Seen from the viewpoint of what is known about glass compositions today, the low-lime compositions would be taken as the norm, and the high-lime compositions seen as unusual. The high-lime content made the glass appreciably harder, so that it would have stood up better under heavy usage and might have been more resistant to breakage, both of which are clearly advantageous properties for utilitarian wares. This was confirmed by the results of simple scratch tests on some of the analyzed glasses. These tests showed that the five glasses with the high-lime composition have a hardness somewhere between 6.5 and 7 on the Mohs hardness scale, while the glasses in the low-lime group have a hardness of about 5.5 to 6.[7] A further advantage to the glassmaker was an economic one, for the high-lime composition would have resulted from the use of a low-grade, impure potash as alkali. More expensive, purified potash would have been needed for the colorless and softer low-lime composition of the fine glass.

Seen from a contemporaneous viewpoint, however, the situation takes a different twist. The period of this factory's operation began just at the time that Lavoisier's revolutionary discoveries which set the foundation for our modern concepts of chemistry were gaining acceptance. In fact, in the very month when Amelung was advertising his glass in the *Maryland Journal and Baltimore Advertiser* (February 11, 1985), Lavoisier was demonstrating crucial experiments of The Chemical Revolution before a group of eminent scientists assembled in Paris for the occasion.

It is clear that the glassmakers of the time would not have had the same understanding as we do of the compositions of their glasses. Instead, they would have taken a purely empirical approach, thinking in terms of the properties of the glasses which would result from their choices of starting materials. What we call the high-lime group of glasses were really the norm of the day, and the low-lime glasses, which required the expensive, purified materials, were the specialty glasses. But the formulation which led to the colorless glass had another equally important technological advantage. The fact that the glass was appreciably softer meant that it also could be cut and engraved more easily—not as easily as high-lead glasses, but certainly it was an improvement over the hard high-lime glasses. This practice should not be thought of as being an innovation by Amelung or as being unique to the Amelung factory. It had probably prevailed for some two centuries previously in the glasshouses of Europe and England.

Some approximate calculations have been made starting with the composite compositions given in Table 6 for the Amelung glasses of the low-lime and high-lime groups. By making assumptions as to probable compositions of probable raw materials; it was estimated that the basic recipes used for preparing the batches could have been as follows:

	Best quality colorless glass for fine wares
Sand	100 lb.
Pearl ash	40 lb.
Lime	20 lb.
Decolorizing cullet	1 lb.
Fining agent (?)	2 oz.

	Green glass for common wares and window glass
Sand	100 lb.
Low-grade Potash	40 lb.
Lime	20 lb.
Decolorizing cullet	1 lb.

The significance of these estimates is that both grades of glass could have been made by following the same whole-number weight-proportion recipes with different grades of raw materials. In each case, some quantity of crushed cullet would also have been added to facilitate melting. The numbers calculated are admittedly conjectural and are presented here mainly as an illustration of the way in which archaeological chemists like to explore their data.

Although the physical-properties studies

have not been completed, there are some pre-liminary findings which aid in visualizing the working qualities of the two types of Amelung glass. Viscosity determinations have shown that both the low-lime and the high-lime glasses have similar, and very steep, viscosity-temperature curves.[8] In order to have gathered either glass it would have had to have been brought to a temperature of 1150-1200°C (log viscosity ~3). The glasses would have gathered like a modern soda-lime glass, but would have begun to set up very quickly as they cooled,

giving the glassblower a relatively short working time in which to finish his blowing, shearing, and other shaping operations before having to reheat the glass. Present-day glass-blowers would not like working with these glasses at all. The coefficients of expansion are not very different from modern soda-lime glasses, with the ordinary Amelung formulation being somewhat better on this count than the formulation used for the fine wares. Some of the estimated properties, based upon averages of four glasses of each type, are:

	Softening Point	Annealing Point	Strain Point	Coefficient of Expansion $(x10^7/^0C)$
High-lime glasses	800°C	610°	565°	91
Low-lime glasses	820°	640°	600°	77

Eight of the excavated fragments reported here were also included among the nineteen fragments analyzed by Dr. Hanson.[9] All eight of these glasses are of the low-lime type. They are nos. 337, 339, 349, 562, 563, 565, 568, and 572. In all, twenty-one elements were sought in common by the two laboratories. These include two major components (calcium and potassium) and one minor component (manganese). The remainder, even if they are intentional additives such as antimony and cobalt, are at trace levels.

A comparison of the analyzed values for K_2O and CaO shows that the agreement on four glasses (nos. 562, 563, 568, and 572) is satisfactory, but that the x-ray flourescence data for the other four glasses (nos. 337, 339, 349, and 565) are systematically lower than the atomic absorption-analyses.[10] The x-ray values are consistently about 60 percent of the atomic-absorption values. For the most part, the agreement on the trace elements is acceptable. In other instances, however, the agreement is poor, even taking into account that the two methods are only semi-quantitative at trace levels. Thus, the agreement between the two sets of data is not as good as one would like to have, but that can be improved in the future, and the two procedures should be brought into better cross-calibration as further comparative studies are made. Nonetheless, the analyses are generally in agreement in a qualitative sense, and each is self-consistent. For example, the agreement on lead, one of the important elements, is good quantitatively, and that on antimony is good qualitatively. This matter has an important bearing on any at-

tempts to compare the atomic-absorption/emission spectroscopic data for the excavated fragments (which have the advantage of containing information on the light elements) with the x-ray fluorescence data on the Amelung objects. With these reservations in mind, such a comparison has been attempted.

Table 6 contains data which allow a comparison between the documented Amelung objects analyzed by x-ray fluorescence at the Winterthur Museum and the excavated fragments analyzed by The Corning Museum using a combination of atomic absorption and emission spectroscopy. The data are composite compositions consisting of mean values for each element. The means were computed from ten objects in the case of the documented Amelung pieces.[11] and nineteen glasses in the case of the excavated fragments.

Adjustments were made in the fragment analyses to offset the effect of colorants or colorant-associated elements. Thus, the glasses of these groups are comparable on the basis of colorless glasses containing impurity trace elements. The lead and antimony values have been split so as to reflect the fact that both bodies of data contained these elements at two different levels. To have reported a single mean value would have been misleading.

Of the twelve elements reported for x-ray fluorescence, ten agree either well or acceptably with the compositions of the low-lime fragments. Only titanium and arsenic do not agree. The author is inclined to see the match as being quite persuasive towards the inference that the documented Amelung objects were made in the same factory which yielded the fragments—or at least in a closely-related factory. But the evidence is not conclusive. The discrepancies in the arsenic and titanium analyses might be attributable to experimental errors, or in the case of the arsenic, an intentional additive, it may have been used for only certain short periods.

The close match between the split means of the lead in the objects with those for the fragments is intriguing, recalling that the split may separate the objects made before 1790 from those made afterwards.[12] If it had turned out that the New Bremen factory fragments were all of the higher-lead content (the "early level"), then a straightforward interpretation would have been possible. It could have been concluded that the higher-lead glasses were made there, that the factory did not reopen after the 1790 fire, and that the lower-lead glasses came from another (later) Amelung factory. But that possibility is not borne out by the evidence, because both levels of lead are found among the New Bremen fragments. This problem becomes quite complicated if one attempts to sort out all the possibilities, but the author has come to a tentative conclusion that two of the hypotheses involved are mutually exclusive (unless one assumes that the change in composition occurred at about the time of the fire by coincidence). These hypotheses are (1) that the split in lead separates the pre-1790 glasses from the post-1790 glasses and (2) that the excavated factory did not reopen after the 1790 fire. However, the data are really too few at present to accept either one of these important hypotheses at the expense of rejecting the other. Therefore, the question should be held in reserve.

A minor flaw in the logic of comparison lies in the fact that the x-ray fluorescence data are lacking in light-element information. On the basis of the restricted number of elements included in Table 6, one might well find compositions matching the fragments—marginally so, at least—among the objects known not to be Amelung glass. Without detracting from the prowess of the x-ray fluorescence method in any way, it is now recognized that data on such elements as sodium, magnesium, aluminum, phosphorus, and lithium are very useful for characterizing glasses. The situation is similar to that arising in the study of compositions of medieval stained glasses, where major- and minor-element contents are more useful than trace elements in characterizing glasses from different factories or periods. In addition, neither method of analysis included determinations of sulfate or chloride, each of which is believed to be helpful for characterizing glasses in the potash:lime:silica system.

Perhaps the best way to describe the author's present feelings is to say that we now look forward to obtaining activation analyses of the pontil glass samples which may confirm the inference that the documented objects came from the excavated factory. In the meantime we shall continue the analyses of excavated materials (including additional glass specimens) and complete our research on the physical properties and fluorescence behavior of Amelung glasses. Having gained encouragement from the results of this study, we shall also pursue more vigorously the analysis and laboratory examination of other American glasses.

ACKNOWLEDGEMENTS
The author of this section gratefully acknowledges the assistance and encouragement of the following persons in various stages of this work: Ivor Noël Hume, Kenneth M. Wilson, Paul N. Perrot, John F. Wosinski, Robert H. Bell, Dwight P. Lanmon, Victor F. Hanson, Charles F. Hummel, and George J. Reilly. The Mss. Judy Seal and Linda Randall assisted in the handling of the data.

SAMPLE DESCRIPTIONS

The primary entries are Analytical Sample Numbers of the Scientific Research Department of The Corning Museum of Glass. "AS" numbers refer to excavation field numbers, and Figure references are those in Mr. Noël Hume's section of the *Journal*.

The term *colorless* refers here to glasses which appear to have been decolorized. In some cases the colors vary somewhat from being "water-white" and show a smoky or faint purplish tinge. In the author's judgment, however, they were intended to be colorless. The purple color is synonymous with amethyst.

LOW-LIME GROUP
Colorless Glasses

337	Disk-shaped fragment. AS 67; after 1785, before 1790.
339	Knop (?). AS 94; after 1785, before 1790.
344	Rim fragment, internal shattering. AS 107; after 1785, before 1790.
570	Goblet stem. AS 153B; ca. 1790. Fig. 39, No. 15.
571	Hollow stopper. AS 125C; ca. 1790. Fig. 39, No. 22.
572	Handle (?) fragment. AS 135; topsoil, no dating. Fig. 40, No. 23.
4281	Solid stopper. AS 163A; topsoil, no dating. Fig. 39, No. 23.
4282	Handle with pincered decoration. AS 125B; ca. 1790. Fig. 39, No. 28.
562	Drippings. AS 142 (1963); topsoil, no dating.
563	Knock-off. AS 94 (1963); after 1785, before 1790.
565	Knock-off (?). AS 153B (1963); ca. 1790.

Purple Glasses

347	Thin fragment. AS 94; after 1785, before 1790.
348	Rim fragment. AS 94; after 1785, before 1790.
362	Blown fragment. AS 25; topsoil, no dating
568	Piece of cullet. AS 104 (1962); topsoil, no dating.

Blue Glasses

349	Heavy-walled fragment, blue streaks. AS 113; disturbed, no dating.
363	Fragment. Structure 1A, at mouth of furnace; unstratified.
1821	Fragment. Structure 1A, at mouth of furnace; unstratified.

HIGH-LIME GROUP
Green or Aqua Glasses

342	Window-glass (?) fragment. Unstratified.
356	Knock-off. AS 1; topsoil, no dating.
361	Piece of cullet. AS 35, Structure 1A; probably disturbed, no dating.
365	Thin-walled, flat fragment. AS 33, Trench 1, east segment, burnt layer; possibly as late as 1795.

Amber Glasses

345	Thin-walled fragment. AS 105; probably disturbed, no dating.

HIGH-LEAD GROUP
Colorless Glasses

4283	Stem base. AS 185; topsoil, no dating. Fig. 39, No. 12.

INTERMEDIATE OR UNCERTAIN
Colorless Glasses

366	Blown fragment. AS 25, west of Unit 1A; unstratified, no dating.

Green or Aqua Glasses

573	Molded fragment. AS 179; topsoil, no dating. Fig. 40, No. 27.
4284	Tumbler base, molded pattern. AS 127; topsoil, no dating. Fig. 40, No. 14.

Olive Glasses

343	Bottle (?) fragment. AS 71; up to ca. 1795.

Amber Glasses

346	Flat window-glass or vessel fragment. AS 120; up to ca. 1795.

Grayish-Opaque Glasses

350	Piece of cullet or waste glass. Color may be due to devitrification. AS 105; probably disturbed, no dating.

TABLE 1 · ANALYSES OF EXCAVATED FRAGMENTS

LOW-LIME GROUP* ("FINE GLASS")	HIGH-LIME GROUP* ("COMMON GLASS")	HIGH-LEAD GROUP (MAJOR PbO)
Colorless — 11 specimens Purple — 4 specimens Blue — 3 specimens	Greenish — 4 specimens Amber — 1 specimen	Colorless — 1 specimen

INTERMEDIATE (MIXTURES OF ABOVE?)
Amber — 1 specimen Aqua   — 1 specimen

UNCERTAIN (OFF-COMPOSITION LOW-LIME?)	UNCERTAIN (OFF-COMPOSITION HIGH-LIME?)
Colorless — 2 specimens	Olive — 1 specimen Whitish opaque — 1 specimen

*Categories based upon concentration groupings of ten discriminating elements:
CaO, K_2O, Na_2O, MgO, Al_2O_3, Fe_2O_3, SrO, BaO, PbO, Sb_2O_5.

P_2O_5 and TiO_2 are partially discriminating. Li_2O and Rb_2O may be discriminating.

TABLE 2 · LOW-LIME GROUP (Colorless)

		337	339	344	570	571	572	4281	4282	562	563	565
SiO_2	d	$\simeq$72.7	$\simeq$75.8	$\simeq$72.2	$\simeq$71.5	$\simeq$73.5	$\simeq$75.0	$\simeq$73.5	$\simeq$74.1	$\simeq$68.1	$\simeq$71.9	$\simeq$75.1
K_2O	a	17.9	15.0	17.8	17.3	16.0	13.6	15.2	15.2	17.7	16.1	16.0
CaO	a	7.99	8.29	8.70	9.24	9.01	9.01	9.69	8.87	10.5	9.82	7.08
Na_2O	a	0.3	0.1	0.5	0.25	0.33	0.31	0.28	0.47	0.28	0.28	0.37
MgO	a	0.12	0.068	0.10	0.069	0.059	0.073	0.076	0.062	0.094	0.074	0.078
Al_2O_3	a	0.2	0.2	0.2	0.34	0.31	0.44	0.38	0.35	0.58	0.40	0.49
Fe_2O_3	a	0.05	0.05	0.10	0.15	0.11	0.18	0.13	0.10	0.18	0.11	0.16
TiO_2		0.02	0.02	0.02	0.08	0.05	0.08	0.10	0.08	0.08	0.06	0.06
Sb_2O_5		0.008	0.008	0.01	0.05	0.02	0.15	0.01	0.15	nf	0.02	nf
MnO	a	0.29	0.27	0.25	0.67	0.39	0.55	0.44	0.30	0.45	0.21	0.46
CuO		0.001	0.001	0.003	0.003	0.001	0.004	0.003	0.003	0.003	0.002	0.004
CoO		nf	nf	nf	nf	nf	nf	nf	nf	nf	nf	nf
SnO_2		nf	nf	nf	nf	nf	nf	nf	nf	0.001	nf	nf
PbO	a	0.25	0.10	0.10	0.15	0.005	0.46	0.05	0.16	0.67	0.38	0.002
BaO		0.01	0.02	0.03	0.09	0.03	0.03	0.02	0.01	0.03	0.01	0.04
SrO		0.01	0.02	0.02	0.02	0.01	0.01	0.01	0.01	0.02	0.01	0.01
Li_2O		0.04	0.03	nf	0.001	<0.001	<0.001	0.003	0.003	0.008	0.004	nf
Rb_2O		—	—	—	0.03	0.02	0.01	0.02	0.05	0.02	0.01	0.02
B_2O_3		0.03	0.02	0.02	0.02	0.02	0.02	0.05	0.05	0.02	0.02	0.02
V_2O_5		0.005	0.003	nf	0.005	nf	nf	0.005	nf	nf	nf	nf
NiO		nf	nf	nf	nf	nf	nf	nf	nf	nf	nf	nf
ZrO_2		—	—	—	0.01	0.01	0.01	0.01	0.01	0.01	0.01	0.01
Bi_2O_3		nf	nf	nf	nf	nf	nf	nf	nf	nf	nf	nf
P_2O_5	c	<1	<1	<1	0.050	0.092	0.060	0.078	0.054	0.51	0.31	0.12
As_2O_5		—	—	—	nf	0.06	0.06	nf	nf	0.70	0.23	nf

NOTES:
a = by atomic absorption, unless reported to only one significant figure
c = by colorimetry
d = SiO_2 estimated by difference
    All other values by emission spectroscopy.
— = not sought or analysis uncertain

Sought but not found: Cr_2O_3, Ag_2O. All samples appear to contain a trace of ZnO above level of blank.

All analyses my Dr. Robert H. Bell and co-workers of Lucius Pitkin, Inc., New York City, December 1971 and February 1976. There are some discrepancies in trace elements between the 1971 and the 1976 analyses.

TABLE 3 · LOW-LIME GROUP (Colored)   HIGH LEAD

		Purple 347	Purple 348	Purple 362	Purple 568	Blue 349	Blue 363	Blue 1821		Colorless 4283
SiO_2	d	≃69.9	≃71.5	≃68.2	≃69.6	≃72.1	≃72.7	≃72.0		≃57.3
K_2O	a	15.8	15.4	15.7	15.2	15.5	15.3	15.8		7.48
CaO	a	9.86	7.90	10.8	9.34	8.52	9.72	10.2		0.33
Na_2O	a	0.3	0.2	0.3	0.34	0.35	0.3	0.4		0.09
MgO	a	0.10	0.10	0.17	0.42	0.090	0.096	0.15		0.014
Al_2O_3	a	0.5	0.7	0.4	0.83	0.43	0.5	0.3		0.24
Fe_2O_3	a	0.1	0.3	0.1	0.34	0.51	0.3	0.1		0.055
TiO_2		0.02	0.02	0.01	0.06	0.05	0.05	0.05		0.05
Sb_2O_5		0.05	0.005	0.05	nf	0.04	0.10	0.05		0.01
MnO	a	≃2	≃3	≃3	3.19	0.62	0.33	0.38		0.10
CuO		0.01	0.009	0.009	0.008	0.01	0.005	0.009		0.02
CoO		nf	nf	nf	nf	≃0.4	≃0.03	≃0.03		nf
SnO_2		0.01	0.01	—	<0.001	nf	—	—		nf
Ag_2O										0.08
PbO		1.0	0.5	0.8	0.06	0.04	0.5	0.4		a 34.2
BaO		0.35	0.33	0.35	0.35	0.05	0.05	0.10		nf
SrO		0.02	0.01	0.02	0.03	0.01	0.01	0.02		nf
Li_2O		nf	0.01	nf	0.004	0.005	nf	—		nf
Rb_2O		—	—	—	0.04	0.02	—	—		nf
B_2O_3		0.03	0.03	0.03	0.02	0.02	0.03	0.01		0.05
V_2O_5		0.005	nf	0.02	0.02	nf	nf	nf		nf
NiO		0.01	0.01	—	0.008	0.06	—	—		nf
ZrO_2		—	—	—	0.01	0.01	—	—		—
Bi_2O_3		nf	nf	nf	0.001	0.042	0.004	0.003		nf
P_2O_5		<1	<1	<1	0.12	0.40	<1	<1		0.030
As_2O_5		—	—	—	nf	0.76	—	—		0.02

TABLE 4 · HIGH-LIME GROUP

		Green 342	Amber 345	Green 356	Green 361	Green 365
SiO_2	d	$\simeq 69.1$	$\simeq 65.9$	$\simeq 67.1$	$\simeq 65.8$	$\simeq 68.8$
K_2O	a	5.80	7.24	5.34	4.70	5.52
CaO	a	18.6	18.7	20.6	20.6	19.3
Na_2O	a	0.94	1.02	1.06	2.84	1.52
MgO	a	1.22	1.74	1.24	1.14	1.27
Al_2O_3	a	1.72	2.59	1.90	1.90	1.17
Fe_2O_3	a	0.7	0.8	0.7	0.72	0.6
TiO_2		0.20	0.20	0.25	0.60	0.13
Sb_2O_5		nf	nf	nf	nf	nf
MnO	a	0.29	0.41	0.33	0.62	0.29
CuO		0.001	0.002	0.002	0.004	0.002
CoO		nf	nf	nf	nf	nf
SnO_2		nf	nf	0.06	0.003	nf
PbO	a	nf	nf	nf	0.002	0.02
BaO		0.25	0.30	0.30	0.25	0.20
SrO		0.10	0.08	0.15	0.07	0.10
Li_2O		nf	0.01	nf	0.008	nf
Rb_2O		—	—	—	nf	—
B_2O_3		0.03	0.02	0.04	0.02	0.03
V_2O_5		0.005	0.005	0.005	0.005	0.005
NiO		nf	nf	nf	0.005	nf
ZrO_2		0.01	—	$\sim$ —	0.01	—
Bi_2O_3		nf	nf	nf	nf	nf
P_2O_5	c	$\simeq 1$	$\simeq 1$	$\simeq 1$	0.68	$\simeq 1$
As_2O_5		—	—	—	nf	—

TABLE 5 · INTERMEDIATE AND UNCERTAIN

		Mixture?		Low-lime Group?		High-lime Group?	
		Aqua 573	Amber 346	Colorless 366	Colorless 4284	Olive 343	Opaque 350
SiO₂	d	≃67.5	≃66.6	≃68.7	≃64.2	≃62.7	≃61.2
K₂O	a	12.1	12.3	17.5	16.3	3.11	3.97
CaO	a	14.9	15.3	11.2	13.1	21.4	21.6
Na₂O	a	2.26	0.70	0.91	0.42	1.06	0.10
MgO	a	0.63	0.79	0.52	0.14	3.64	2.60
Al₂O₃	a	1.15	1.51	0.58	0.81	3.53	6.30
Fe₂O₃	a	0.50	0.5	0.18	0.22	1.5	1.2
TiO₂		0.25	0.12	0.10	0.13	0.25	0.65
Sb₂O₅		nf	nf	nf	nf	nf	nf
MnO	a	0.28	0.82	0.12	0.89	0.57	0.41
CuO		0.004	0.004	0.003	0.005	0.008	<0.001
CoO		nf	nf	nf	nf	nf	nf
SnO₂		nf	nf	0.001	nf	0.06	nf
PbO	a	0.001	0.02	nf	2.49	0.12	nf
BaO		0.08	0.23	—	0.03	0.25	0.33
SrO		0.05	0.05	0.01	0.02	0.20	0.13
Li₂O		0.001	nf	0.005	0.002	0.01	0.01
Rb₂O		0.01	—	0.02	0.01	—	—
B₂O₃		0.02	0.03	0.02	0.02	0.07	0.02
V₂O₅		0.005	0.005	nf	nf	0.005	0.008
NiO		nf	nf	nf	nf	nf	nf
ZrO₂		0.01	—	0.01	0.01	0.03	0.01
Bi₂O₃		nf	nf	nf	nf	nf	nf
P₂O₅	c	0.23	1	0.13	0.37	≃1.5	≃1.5
As₂O₅		nf	—	nf	0.87	—	—

TABLE 6 · COMPARISON OF MEAN COMPOSITIONS

		Winterthur (XRF) Documented Amelung Objects (10 glasses)		CMG (AA & Spect.) Fragments, Low-Lime Group (14 glasses)†	CMG (AA & Spect.) Fragments, High-Lime Group (5 glasses)
SiO_2	d	72.5		72.9	67.3
K_2O		16.5	**	16.0	5.72
CaO		9.95	*	9.05	19.6
Na_2O				0.32	1.48
MgO				0.086	1.32
Al_2O_3				0.37	1.86
Fe_2O_3		0.19	*	0.12	0.70
TiO_2		0.016	(?)	0.06	0.28
Sb_2O_5		0.16	*	0.01 or 0.09	nf
MnO		0.46	**	0.40	0.39
CuO				0.003	0.002
CoO				nf	nf
SnO_2				nf	nf or 0.06
PbO		0.01 or 0.35	**	0.02 or 0.32	nf or 0.01
BaO		0.046	*	0.030	0.26
SrO		0.017	**	0.014	0.10
Li_2O				0.007	0.004
Rb_2O		0.012	*	0.022	nf
B_2O_3				0.025	0.03
Y_2O_3		0.005			
V_2O_5				0.001	0.005
NiO				nf	nf
ZrO_2		0.009	**	0.01	0.01
Bi_2O_3				nf	nf
P_2O_5				0.18	0.7
As_2O_5		0.009	(?)	0.20	nf
SUM		100.0		100.1	99.8

NOTES:
  ** Indicates good agreement.
   * Indicates acceptable agreement.
  (?) Indicates poor agreement.
   † Excludes colorants and colorant-associated elements.
   d All SiO₂ values estimated by differences.

NOTES

1. The factory will be referred to here simply as "the Amelung factory" without intending to imply either that it was the only "Amelung factory" or that it was always under the control of John Frederick Amelung.

2. For readers unfamiliar with chemical symbols, the formulas below represent the oxides of the corresponding chemical elements.

SiO_2	silicon	PbO	lead
K_2O	potassium	BaO	barium
CaO	calcium	SrO	strontium
Na_2O	sodium	As_2O_5	arsenic
MgO	magnesium	Li_2O	lithium
Al_2O_3	aluminum	Rb_2O	rubidium
Fe_2O_3	iron	B_2O_3	boron
TiO_2	titanium	V_2O_3	vanadium
Sb_2O_5	antimony	NiO	nickel
MnO	manganese	ZrO_2	zirconium
CuO	copper	Bi_2O_3	bismuth
CoO	cobalt	P_2O_5	phosphorus
SnO_2	tin		

3. The reference glasses used for all analyses reported here are listed below. All the glasses were prepared by Dr. August A. Erickson of Corning Glass Works and his co-workers.

a) Nos. 611, 612, 614, and 616 distributed by the National Bureau of Standards.

b) Reference glasses A, B, and D of a series prepared for The Corning Museum of Glass for interlaboratory comparison analyses.

c) Three glasses prepared for The Corning Museum of Glass, which contain only the major ingredients in the reference glasses A, B, and D and not the trace elements.

d) Glasses SPE, TVX, and TVY prepared for the Corning Museum of Glass simulating the compositions anticipated for the Amelung glasses.

4. The only discrepancy was in one glass, where the Y_2O_3 by conventional x-ray fluorescence yielded a value of 0.06 percent instead of the theoretical 0.10 percent.

5. Unpublished analyses of The Corning Museum of Glass.

6. In this connection there is an interesting quote in W. Rosenhain, *Glass Manufacture*, New York: D. Van Nostrand Company, 1912, p. 189." . . . vanadium occurs in small proportions in a number of fireclays, including some of those of the Stourbridge district, and glass melted in pots containing this element is liable to have its colour spoilt by taking up the vanadium from the clay."

7. The absolute values of the hardness values estimated may be in error, because of the nature of the tests, but the difference of approximately one unit (on the Mohs scale) between the two groups of glasses is about right.

8. The measurements reported here were made by Mr. Loren Morse and Mr. Eugene Fontana, both of Corning Glass Works. For a discussion of viscosity-temperature relationships see: R. H. Brill, "A Note on the Scientist's Definition of Glass," *Journal of Glass Studies*, IV, 1962, pp. 127–138.

9. See Table 3 in the preceding section.

10. This might be a result of geometry, because the samples in some cases are small and have curved or irregular surfaces.

11. Analyses of parts of some objects were omitted, because they seemed suspiciously low in the reported K_2O and CaO values, possibly because of problems of geometry.

12. See Table 1, Section II.

SAMPLE DESCRIPTIONS

The primary entries are Analytical Sample Numbers of the Scientific Research Department of The Corning Museum of Glass. "AS" numbers refer to excavation field numbers, and Figure references are those in Mr. Noël Hume's section of the *Journal*.

The term *colorless* refers here to glasses which appear to have been decolorized. In some cases the colors vary somewhat from being "water-white" and show a smoky or faint purplish tinge. In the author's judgment, however, they were intended to be colorless. The purple color is synonymous with amethyst.

LOW-LIME GROUP

Colorless Glasses

337 Disk-shaped fragment. AS 67; after 1785, before 1790.

339 Knop (?). AS 94; after 1785, before 1790.

344 Rim fragment, internal shattering. AS 107; after 1785, before 1790.

570 Goblet stem. AS 153B; ca. 1790. Fig. 39, No. 15.

571 Hollow stopper. AS 125C; ca. 1790. Fig. 39, No. 22.

572 Handle (?) fragment. AS 135; topsoil, no dating. Fig. 40, No. 23.

4281 Solid stopper. AS 163A; topsoil, no dating. Fig. 39, No. 23.

4282 Handle with pincered decoration. AS 125B; ca. 1790. Fig. 39, No. 28.

562 Drippings. AS 142 (1963); topsoil, no dating.

563 Knock-off. AS 94 (1963); after 1785, before 1790.

565 Knock-off (?). AS 153B (1963); ca. 1790.

Purple Glasses

347 Thin fragment. AS 94; after 1785, before 1790.

348 Rim fragment. AS 94; after 1785, before 1790.

362 Blown fragment. AS 25; topsoil, no dating

568 Piece of cullet. AS 104 (1962); topsoil, no dating.

Blue Glasses

349 Heavy-walled fragment, blue streaks. AS 113; disturbed, no dating.

363 Fragment. Structure 1A, at mouth of furnace; unstratified

1821 Fragment. Structure 1A, at mouth of furnace; unstratified.

HIGH-LIME GROUP

Green or Aqua Glasses

342 Window-glass (?) fragment. Unstratified.

356 Knock-off. AS 1; topsoil, no dating.

361 Piece of cullet. AS 35, Structure 1A; probably disturbed, no dating.

365 Thin-walled, flat fragment. AS 33, Trench 1, east segment, burnt layer; possibly as late as 1795.

Amber Glasses

345 Thin-walled fragment. AS 105; probably disturbed, no dating.

HIGH-LEAD GROUP

Colorless Glasses

4283 Stem base. AS 185; topsoil, no dating. Fig. 39, No. 12.

INTERMEDIATE OR UNCERTAIN

Colorless Glasses

366 Blown fragment. AS 25, west of Unit 1A; unstratified, no dating.

Green or Aqua Glasses

573 Molded fragment. AS 179; topsoil, no dating. Fig. 40, No. 27.

4284 Tumbler base, molded pattern. AS 127; topsoil, no dating. Fig. 40, No. 14.

Olive Glasses

343 Bottle (?) fragment. AS 71; up to ca. 1795.

Amber Glasses

346 Flat window-glass or vessel fragment. AS 120; up to ca. 1795.

Grayish-Opaque Glasses

350 Piece of cullet or waste glass. Color may be due to devitrification. AS 105; probably disturbed, no dating.